Ante-Bellum Alabama

Town and Country

D1566276

The Library of Alabama Classics,
reprint editions of works important
to the history, literature, and culture of
Alabama, is dedicated to the memory of

Rucker Agee,

whose pioneering work in the fields
of Alabama history and historical geography
continues to be the standard of
scholarly achievement.

ANTE-BELLUM ALABAMA
TOWN AND COUNTRY

Weymouth T. Jordan

With an Introduction by
Kenneth R. Johnson

The University of Alabama Press
Tuscaloosa and London

Library of Congress Cataloging-in-Publication Data

Jordan, Weymouth T. (Weymouth Tyree)
   Ante-bellum Alabama.

   (Library of Alabama classics)
   Reprint. Originally published: Tallahassee,
Fla.: Florida State University, c1957.
   Bibliography: p.
   Includes index.
   1. Alabama—History—1819–1950. I. Title.
II. Series.
F326.J66   1987   976   86-16137
ISBN 0-8173-0333-2 (pbk.: alk. paper)

CONTENTS

INTRODUCTION by Kenneth R. Johnson   vii

PREFACE   xvii

I   METROPOLIS BY THE SEA   1

II   A BLACK BELT TOWN   22

III   A BLACK BELT PLANTER FAMILY   41

IV   A FAMILY DAYBOOK   62

V   NEGRO "PECULIARITIES"   84

VI   THE CRUSADE FOR AGRICULTURAL REFORM   106

VII   THE INDUSTRIAL GOSPEL   140

BIBLIOGRAPHY   161

INDEX   167

INTRODUCTION

Dr. Weymouth T. Jordan, a native of North Carolina and graduate of the University of North Carolina, joined the history faculty at Judson College in 1938. He thought of himself as an American and Southern historian, but he was sensitive to the fact that good regional and national histories are built upon sound scholarship in local history. Soon a steady stream of scholarly articles, professional papers, and stimulating book reviews were flowing from his pen. In 1949 he published *Hugh Davis and His Alabama Plantation*, his first book-length work. In 1957 various strands of scholarly activity were brought together in the publication of *Ante-Bellum Alabama: Town and Country*. Most of the articles in this work had been presented earlier in the form of papers before professional groups or had been published in scholarly journals. Meanwhile, in 1943, Jordan joined the faculty at Auburn University; and in 1949 he moved to Florida State University.

Professor Jordan's scholarly interest reflected the times in Alabama. During the general time period that his research for this work was in progress, other works related to the ante-bellum period were published. In 1934 A. B. Moore published his *History of Alabama*. Shortly thereafter, in 1939, Charles S. Davis brought out *The Cotton Kingdom in Alabama*. In 1949 Charles G. Summersell published *Mobile: History of a Seaport Town*, and the following year James B. Sellers completed *Slavery in Alabama*. The broad interest in Alabama history took on definite structure in 1947 when the Alabama Historical Association was organized with a large membership among professional and lay historians. The success of the Association's quarterly journal, *The Alabama Review*, clearly demonstrated a widespread fascination for the history of the state.

Ante-Bellum Alabama: Town and Country emerged as a part of this scholarly environment. Through an examination of selected topics, Jordan hoped to produce a work that would give greater depth than the surveys could provide. Also, without offering major new interpretations, this work would provide new perspectives and possibly new directions for research and study in Alabama history. This was especially true of the essays on the movement for agricultural reform and industrialization. Also, the essays on the rise of Mobile and the town of Marion tended to presage the rise of the field of urban history. Taken as a whole, the essay topics constitute a sampling of the social and economic development of the cotton-growing sections of ante-bellum Alabama, especially the Black Belt region.

Like other historians, Professor Jordan ties the rise of Mobile to the growth of South Alabama. In looking at the past, one is made aware that the present is always quietly preparing the way for the future. Long before the French thought of establishing Mobile, the Black Belt was forming, and the rivers of Alabama were cutting their way toward Mobile Bay. The decision in 1702 to locate the settlement on the Gulf at the mouth of the Mobile River demonstrates a keen understanding of the way commerce was carried on and the importance of geography in history. From Mobile, explorers and traders—and later, planters and merchants—could use the rivers as highways to the interior. Seagoing ships could make their way from the Port of Mobile to all parts of the world. Thus, from the moment of its founding, Mobile had the potential of becoming a prominent commercial center. However, through the colonial administrations of the French, English, and Spanish from 1702 to 1813, business consisted mainly of exporting and importing products associated with the Indian trade. Progress was slow.

Between 1813 and 1819 a series of events launched Mobile on a period of growth that made it by 1860 the second largest city on the Gulf Coast and the primary commercial center in ante-bellum Alabama. During the War of 1812, West Florida, including Mobile and the surrounding area, became a part of the United States. Shortly thereafter, the United States government signed treaties with the Creek, Cherokee, Chickasaw, and Choctaw Indians, whereby the Indians gave up over two-thirds of the land in Alabama. Land-hungry settlers poured into Alabama. By 1860 the population of the state stood at 964,201, including 526,271 whites and 437,770 blacks. The population increase and economic growth of Mobile paralleled the growth of the state.

While all parts of Alabama experienced population growth, the Black Belt region of South Alabama made the most noticeable advances. As settlers cleared the land, subsistence farming became the dominant way of life. A well-built log house, a crib full of corn, and a smokehouse full of meat became the symbols of success and security. Subsistence farming remained the dominant form of agriculture in the ante-bellum period. But those settlers with wealth, luck, and good management skills rapidly turned to commercial agriculture. For this group, corn gave way to cotton as the main crop. Cotton production became the most popular avenue to wealth and prosperity. It was the primary influence that made Mobile a "metropolis by the sea." The growth of most other major economic activities—steamboating, railroading, banking, and the rise of towns—was closely tied to cotton. Planters not only dominated economic life in Alabama, but they shaped the cultural, social, and political life of the state as well.

While settlers were carving farms and plantations out of the frontier wilderness, the process of town building was under way. Following well-established practices in western civilization and the theories of Alexander von Humboldt, most frontier town builders accepted the beliefs that certain geographical spots were natural sites for the building of towns. These natural sites were generally along the major rivers, at crossroads, and at large springs. While most towns were founded by profit-seeking land speculators, some were founded to meet community needs and located for human convenience. The town of Marion was typical. Perry County was created by the Alabama Territorial Legislature in 1819. When a seat for the county government was needed and popular demand for a centrally located county seat made itself apparent, a site known as "Muckle's Ridge" was chosen. The town was "laid off" by the county sheriff and individual lots were sold. Soon thereafter, public buildings were constructed, businesses established, and private homes built. Gradually, churches, schools, and other institutions began to appear. While many frontier towns never really got beyond the planning stages, others gradually became the social, cultural, and commercial centers for the surrounding local area.

Many accounts of Southern history portray Southerners as being closed-minded, unreceptive to new ideas, and uninterested in new techniques of agriculture and industrial production. In two essays Professor Jordan presented evidence rebutting these views. Unquestionably, the farming methods of the planters and yeomen farmers were crude. To increase cotton production, planters usually expanded their acreage and acquired more slaves. The yeoman farmer was more likely simply to sell out and move to new land. There was no widespread effort made to preserve or increase the fertility of the soil or employ more effective techniques. By the 1840's the wasteful and inefficient farm methods were becoming a matter of increasing concern. Gradually private individuals began experimenting with new farm techniques. Also, they sought to popularize the need for agricultural reform. These private efforts in time took on the character of an agricultural reform movement that eventually touched the lives of most Alabamians. Articles about agriculture began to be common material in newspapers. The number of farm journals increased dramatically. Local and agricultural societies were organized, often with large memberships. The county and regional fairs with their agricultural exhibits, competitions, and educational activities did much to popularize the need for agricultural reform.

Although ante-bellum Alabama was overwhelmingly agricultural, industrial manufacturing was an integral part of the state's economic life from the earliest days of settlement. Every town and village had several types of handicraft industry. Most were small shops and served only small local clientele. The shortage of investment capital, the lack of trained labor and experienced managers, and the great wealth resulting from cotton production all slowed progress toward industrialization. Despite these obstacles and a general lack of public sympathy and support, large-scale manufacturing gradually emerged in Alabama as an infant industrial system. A small group of dedicated manufacturers led the movement. Motivated not primarily by the hope of personal advancement, these industrial leaders argued that further development of Alabama's extensive resources would give the state and Southland greater self-sufficiency and less dependence on the factories of New England. Industrialization was not offered as an alternative to agriculture, especially cotton production; it was suggested as a corollary that would bring greater wealth, prosperity, and economic independence to more Alabamians and the entire South.

Scholars may disagree over the short-term success of the movements for agricultural reform and industrialization, but the evidence presented by Professor Jordan certainly does not describe a closed-minded, tradition-bound society. Examples of that same openness can be found in other essays.

While no single theme holds these seven essays together as a unit, two almost stand alone insofar as content is concerned. Cotton dominated the planter's economic life; his domestic life was guided to a great extent by the family daybook. The daybook may be best described as a collection of "household hints" for people who had to depend on their own knowledge for the solution of everyday problems. The typical daybook contained information about how to preserve and prepare food, treat common illnesses, care for clothing and household articles, control pests, and deal with numerous other problems of life. The entries in the daybook were collected from a wide variety of sources. Reported solutions to common problems made good copy for newspapers and magazines. Oral accounts were eagerly heard with a view for future use. Finding solutions to the problems of life was a constant challenge.

The presence of a large black minority and the practice of slavery aroused even greater concern. Black people and the institution of slavery were significant parts of ante-bellum Alabama history. Professor Jordan did not treat the larger subject but chose to concentrate on the shaping of white attitudes toward black Alabamians. The overwhelming majority of blacks in Alabama were slaves; they lived mainly in the Black Belt and were engaged in the production of cotton on large plantations. Most planters accepted slavery as a fact of life. It was a condition established by custom and by law. It was maintained by racial fears and what was thought to be economic necessity. Even the most insensitive slaveowner was conscious of the conflict between American ideals and the practice of slavery. A strong, persuasive justification for slavery was a felt need.

The field of science came to the support of proslave thought. Physicians like Dr. Josiah Nott of Mobile took the lead in trying to prove that blacks were a separate species of animal, not fully human and therefore inherently different and inferior to members of the white race. Ministers, newspaper editors, teachers, and others with influence gave support to this doctrine. Through books, periodicals, newspapers, lectures, sermons, and by other means, the separate-species doctrine and the related belief in black inferiority became an integral part of the proslave thought. But this kind of thinking never rested easy in the Southern mind. The claim that Negroes were a species separate from members of the white race ran counter to the accepted Biblical view of the unity of the races of man. In the face of this conflict with traditional religious views, the separate-species doctrine never achieved widespread acceptance, but the related belief in black inferiority became a pervasive part of white racial thought.

Dr. Jordan was a professional historian. This work earned the praise of his colleagues. Ernest M. Lander, Jr., of Clemson University, who reviewed *Ante-Bellum Alabama: Town and Country* for the *Mississippi Valley Historical Review*, stated that the volume was skillfully written, well documented, and that the author's interpretation was sound. Henry T. Shanks of Birmingham-Southern College assured the reader of the *Journal of Southern History* that the work was based on a careful search of original sources and that materials had been handled judiciously. While these complimentary words from fellow historians added stature to the work, they only partially satisfied the objectives of the author.

Professor Jordan knew that history—the study of the past—was not for the professional historian but for a wider audience. It was his hope that *Ante-Bellum Alabama: Town and Country* would give some pleasure to the general reader as well as the historian. Despite a very limited distribution of this work in its original form, it whetted the intellectual interest of those who sought to understand Alabama before the Civil War. Now it should be no less valuable to a new generation of scholars and to a larger and more sophisticated general audience.

University of North Alabama   KENNETH R. JOHNSON

Alabama Counties 1860

Hubert Blue
University of North Alabama
Department of Geography

To my Alabama cousins,
Edith and Zebulon Judd

PREFACE

This little book relates to ante-bellum Alabama's social and economic developments. It deals with a city, a town, a planter family, rural social life, certain attitudes of white people toward Negroes, and Alabama's early crusade in behalf of agriculture and manufacturing. Its purpose is to present certain case studies with the hope that by bringing them together they will furnish an insight into some of the important facets of Alabama's late ante-bellum history. It is written for the scholar and the general reader.

In town and country, pre-Civil War Alabama's leading interest was agriculture. Alabama's chief crop was cotton; most of her people were agriculturists; her towns and cities came into existence for the express purposes of furnishing supplies, credit and other services to farmers, in order to process and distribute farm commodities, and to manufacture articles for farm use. Rural-agricultural influences dominated the American scene; and in this respect Alabama was typical of her region as well as of most of the United States. An urbanized-industrial America was for the most part a thing of the future, although not of a too far-distant future.

Research for this book was begun in the year 1938, and in one form or another, in addresses to various historical societies and in historical journals, some of the materials have been presented to listeners and readers since 1940. In their present form, the Chapters are the result of much additional research and writing. I have not hesitated to interpret my materials. It is my hope that the book will bring some pleasure to a wider audience than the one to which my addresses and papers were originally addressed.

Many historians, archivists, librarians, historically-conscious Southerners, and others have aided me in gathering my materials. Persons who have been particularly helpful are the following: the entire staff of the Alabama Department of Archives and History, especially Mrs. Mary Livingston Aiken and Miss Frances Hails; staffs of other historical depositories from Washington to Texas; staffs of the Libraries of Vanderbilt University, Judson College,

Alabama Polytechnic Institute, Iowa State University, and Florida
State University; the late Everett E. Edwards of the Bureau
of Agricultural Economics, United States Department of Agriculture; Malcolm C. McMillan of Alabama Polytechnic Institute; W.
Stanley Hoole and James B. McMillan of the University of Alabama;
and James A. Preu of Florida State University. Special encouragement has been rendered, as always, by my wife, Louise E. Jordan,
and by three former professors, Hugh T. Lefler of the University of
North Carolina, William C. Binkley of Tulane University, and the
late Frank L. Owsley of the University of Alabama, all of whom, in
their individual fields of activity, have no equals as far as I am
concerned.

Grants-in-aid have been received from the Social Science Research Council, the General Education Board, and the Research
Council of Florida State University. I should like to thank each of
these organizations for its assistance. I am also deeply grateful to
the John Simon Guggenheim Memorial Foundation for a fellowship
which has freed me from my regular duties and allowed me the
time needed to complete my writing.

Weymouth T. Jordan

Tallahassee, Florida

July, 1957

Ante-Bellum Alabama

Town and Country

I

METROPOLIS BY THE SEA

Among the many factors affecting the rise of Mobile to a position of importance as an agricultural market place in the pre-Civil War period, the most significant were port facilities, accessible and navigable rivers, cotton production, and the population of the region in which it was located[1] . For these reasons perhaps more than any others "The city of Mobile has [had] the longest continuous existence of any settlement on the Gulf coast."[2] In an era when water was the chief means of transportation in the South the port attracted wide attention. Alabama, its significant hinterland, possessed more navigable river miles than any other state in the nation. And most of the rivers converged on Mobile. The city's economic significance and prosperity also resulted from a booming and increasing production of cotton in Alabama and adjoining states, for it was the place where most of Alabama's cotton was sold before 1861. Moreover, then as now, farmers and planters needed extensive supplies in order to conduct their operations, and in Mobile they found their supplies in large quantities, usually obtainable on credit. In these as well as other respects Mobile served their needs. However, the city's population grew slowly before 1820; but from that date to 1860 the number of inhabitants increased from about 1,500 to nearly 30,000. At the outbreak of the Civil War it was the only city in Alabama containing as many as 10,000 people. Other important towns in 1860 were Montgomery, 8,843; Tuscaloosa, 3,989; Huntsville, 3,634; and Selma, 3,177; but Mobile, with 29,259 people, overshadowed all other urban areas. Alabama's population of 964,201 looked to Mobile as its metropolis by the sea.[3]

Mobile's rise to a place of economic eminence extended over many years. Established as a French outpost in 1702 at a place

---

[1]Portions of this chapter were printed as "Ante-Bellum Mobile: Alabama's Agricultural Emporium," *Alabama Review*, I, 180-202 (1948), and are presented here with the permission of the editors of the *Review*, W. Stanley Hoole and James B. McMillan.

[2]Thomas McAdory Owen, "Alabama Archives," in *Annual Report of the American Historical Association for the Year 1904* (Washington, 1905), 537.

[3]*Eighth Census of the United States, 1860, Population* (Washington, 1864), 9; *Hunt's Merchants' Magazine*, XL, 181 (1859), XLVII, 372 (1862).

known as Twenty-seven Mile Bluff, the settlement is said to have attained in its first year a population of 139, consisting of 9 officers, 24 sailors, 2 couriers, 14 workmen, 64 Canadians, and 26 soldiers.[4] It was moved to its present site in 1711 and the next year became the seat of government of the Louisiana Province. That important position was maintained until 1720. Before the middle of the eighteenth century Mobile was in this and other ways superseded by New Orleans as the most important locality in the Gulf area. The future Alabama metropolis remained the chief trading center of the Muskogee Indians of its region, however, and its population increased to a respectable 300 or slightly more during this period.[5] While under British control, from 1763 to 1783, Mobile was laid out in town plan. It annually shipped skins and furs valued at 12 to £15,000 to London,[6] and a report was submitted to the Crown, in 1772, predicting that the Alabama River valley "in Process of time must Indubitably become a fine Settlement not Inferior by itself to any Province now known."[7] Such a development might indeed have taken place shortly if the American Revolution had not come, for West Florida was, after all, the first British colony within the present boundaries of the United States west of the line of the Appalachian Mountains and possessed many attractions for settlers.

In 1785, during the period of Spanish rule, Mobile had 746 inhabitants, and three years later it claimed nearly 1,500.[8] A traveler in the area in 1791 predicted even greater growth, prophesying "from its Locality [it] must 'ere long surpass Pensacola, in Population, Trade and Buildings." He added that the Coosa, Tallapoosa, Tombigbee and Mobile River valleys were being settled "by Corn, Hemph and Tobacco-Makers, who will have a nearer and better Navigation to *Mobille* [sic] than to Pensacola—add to this the Peltry-Trade, which will trebly exceed that of Tensocala [sic], . . . being nearer to the Hunting-Grounds from whence they may have Water-

---

[4]*DeBow's Review*, I, 525 (1846).

[5]*Ibid.*, XXVIII, 306 (1860); Mary Powell Crane, *The Life of James R. Powell, and Early History of Alabama and Birmingham* (Brooklyn, 1930), 27; John Massey, *Reminiscences* (Nashville, 1916), 86-87.

[6]*DeBow's Review*, II, 418 (1846).

[7]C. N. Howard, "Some Economic Aspects of British West Florida, 1763-1768," *Journal of Southern History*, VI, 203 (1940).

[8]*DeBow's Review*, XVI, 397 (1854); *Hunt's Merchants' Magazine*, XL, 181 (1859).

Carriage, except at one or two places, where a slight portage will be necessary."[9] However, these predictions did not immediately materialize, for Mobile was later described as being in 1804 "a city of West Florida, formerly of considerable splendor, but now in a state of decline."[10]

West Florida, after its many trials and vicissitudes, finally became United States territory during the administration of President James Madison. Events, as far as Mobile was concerned, immediately speeded up considerably and noticeably: the town, consisting of less than 300 people, "came into American hands in 1813;"[11] West Florida petitioned the United States Congress to be placed under the jurisdiction of the Territory of Mississippi, which had been created in 1798; that request was granted; and the Mississippi Territorial Legislature, in January, 1814, incorporated the so-called "President and Commissioners of the Town of Mobile."[12] At about the same time there arrived in the Mobile area "an enterprising gentleman" named T. L. Hallett. "Besides merchandize for an extensive business" he brought along "several frames of houses with workmen ready to erect them." Hallett "first went to Blakely," a nearby town on the east bank of the Tensas River, "but so extravagant were the views of the lot owners, that he was induced to come to Mobile, where he settled, and became a very influential, active, and enterprising merchant." Hallett is credited with having given "prepondence to Mobile" over Blakely and should probably be considered as the town's outstanding citizen during its early formative years under United States control. In 1846, according to one traveler's description of Blakely, "Its beautiful hills, crowned by gigantic live oaks, refreshed by perennial springs of delicious water, are left to the enjoyment of the solitary keeper of a public house, who can solace himself with the occasional visits of the traveler."[13] On the other hand, in Mobile the assessed value of real estate amounted to $198,000 as early as 1814.[14]

[9]John Pope, A Tour through the Southern and Western Territories of the United States of North-America (New York, 1888 reprint of the 1792 edition), 46-47.
[10]DeBow's Review, II, 418 (1846).
[11]Niles' Weekly Register, XXII, 96 (April 6, 1822).
[12]DeBow's Review, XXVIII, 309 (1860).
[13]Ibid., XXVIII, 308 (1860).
[14]R. H. Thompson, "Suffrage in Mississippi," in Publications of the Missis-

Presumably, Mobile continued its rapid development between 1814 and 1817. In the June 7, 1817, issue of the highly respected *Niles' Weekly Register* (Baltimore) was printed the following glowing account of the town's progress as a port: "*Mobile* promises soon to become a place of much trade. The imports, coastwise, were valued at a million dollars for the last year—1700 bales of cotton were shipped there in the last six months, and a like quantity remained to be shipped."[15] Colonel Nicholas Parmentier, a member of Alabama's well-known Vine and Olive Colony, wrote to a friend in July, 1817:

> Until lately there was no quay at Mobile to moor vessels to. One is now constructing, which is to be built out far enough to have nine feet of water at its eastern extremity at low tide. It will when completed be very long. The city is situated on a sandy beach perfectly clear. The streets are from 60 to 100 feet wide. The houses are almost all of wood, one story high, with some few two stories. They are raised from two to four feet above the ground on piles of large dimensions. There are from 80 to 100 houses, and they continue to build very fast. The population is estimated at from 1000 to 1500, of every description.[16]

During Alabama's short Territorial period Mobile cotton exports rose from 7,000 bales in 1818 to 10,000 in 1819. A total of 209 ships entered the port in 1817, the number increased to 280 the next year, and imports for 1818 amounted to $3,000,000.[17] One contemporary newspaper stated that "the port of Mobile is crowded with vessels—among them one from Liverpool. The house-room of the town has been insufficient to accommodate the great influx of strangers."[18] The same publication also claimed that the town had a population of 1,127 in December, 1818. This figure is open to question, however, because about a year later, on December 19, 1819, when the town was incorporated by the new Alabama State

sippi Historical Society, I, 29 (1898). See also Peter J. Hamilton, *Colonial Mobile* (Boston, 1897); Thomas P. Abernethy, *The Formative Period in Alabama, 1815-1828* (Montgomery, 1922), 33-36; Albert B. Moore, *History of Alabama* (Tuscaloosa, 1934), 40, 46, 51, 52, 62; and Charles G. Summersell, *Mobile: History of a Seaport Town* (Tuscaloosa, 1949).

[15]*Niles' Weekly Register*, XII, 240 (June 7, 1817).

[16]Gaius Whitfield, Jr., "The French Grant in Alabama, A History of the Founding of Demopolis," *Transactions of the Alabama Historical Society, 1899-1903*, IV, 328 (1904).

[17]*Niles' Weekly Register*, XVI, 240 (May 29, 1819), XXII, 240 (June 8, 1822).

[18]*Ibid.*, XIII, 343 (January 17, 1818).

Legislature, it is credited with a population of only 809. It had about 1,500 inhabitants in the year 1820.[19]

From these rather unpretentious beginnings Mobile gradually took on importance as a port during the decade of the 1820's. Flatboats had been worked on the rivers of Alabama for a number of years, with trips to Montgomery from Mobile requiring as much as three months. Both travel time and facilities were improved greatly in 1819, when a steamboat began service between Mobile and Demopolis; and steamboats were put to much wider use within the next two years.[20] According to an account appearing a number of years later in the Mobile Register, "In 1821, there were two steamboats plying from Mobile on the Alabama, Tombigbee, and Warrior Rivers, the Harriet of forty-three tons, and engines of fifty horse power; and the Cotton Plant of eighty tons, and thirty horse power engines—both engines of the low pressure plan. But these, with the flatboats [on the rivers], were sufficient for a trade of ten thousand bales of cotton, and a little tar, pitch, and turpentine, beeswax, hides and tallow."[21] In the year ending September 30, 1821, a total of 232 vessels entered the Mobile port, of which 192 were coasters and 42 were from foreign ports.[22] Mobile was on the threshold of becoming a Gulf port of first-rate importance.

These boats and others handled more business the next year. Cotton, lumber, staves and peltries were exported to such places as Cuba, Gibraltar and New York; and the value of these 1822 cargoes, mostly produced in Alabama, was placed at approximately $2,250,000.[23] A Mobile Directory reported that in 1822 "there were in the corporate limits 240 dwelling houses, 110 stores and warehouses, one Catholic and one Protestant Church, two seminaries,

[19]Ibid., XXII, 96 (April 6, 1822); Safford Berney, Handbook of Alabama (Mobile, 1878), 73; DeBow's Review, XVI, 397 (1854); Hunt's Merchants' Magazine, XL, 181 (1859).

[20]Mell A. Frazer, "Early History of Steamboats in Alabama," in Alabama Polytechnic Institute Historical Studies (Auburn, 1907); Hamilton, Colonial Mobile, 447-448, 471-472; B. F. Riley, Makers and Romance of Alabama History (n. p., n. d.), 589.

[21]Mobile Register, quoted in Hunt's Merchants' Magazine, XL, 180 (1859). See also Mobile Directory and Commercial Supplement, for 1855-1856 (Mobile, 1855), 11-13.

[22]Niles' Weekly Register, XXI, 367 (February 2, 1822).

[23]Ibid., XXIV, 21 (March 15, 1823).

two printing offices, [a] Post Office, Customhouse, a Bank, three Hotels, . . . with a winter population of about twenty-seven hundred."[24] At about the same time *Niles' Weekly Register* advertised, "Mobile is becoming a place of great importance, and it is possible, may soon be one of the most populous of our southern cities."[25] This year (1822) was also significant because it saw the construction of the first cotton press in Mobile.[26]

Between 1820 and 1830 Alabama, referred to by one writer of the period as "the wonder of the south," witnessed a population increase from 127,901 to 309,527.[27] This represented a ten-year growth of 141.6%, or one that was larger than that of any other American states except Illinois (185.4%) and Michigan (250.1%).[28] Mobile naturally profited immensely from this influx of settlers to the state. It continued as the market-place of South Alabama, that is, for the counties of Shelby, Tuscaloosa and Fayette and the counties south of them. Territory to the east of Shelby was still Indian country. North Alabama, consisting of twelve counties as late as 1830,[29] conducted most of its business with Tennessee and New Orleans because its outlet was through the Tennessee and Mississippi Rivers.[30] The remaining twenty-four counties were considered by the United States Census Bureau as South Alabama since their outlet was through the Alabama River system. All of these latter counties, with the possible exception of Pike and Henry,[31] which at the time were associated with the Chattahoochee River area and

---

[24]*Mobile Directory and Commercial Supplement, for 1855-1856*, p. 22.

[25]*Niles' Weekly Register*, XXII, 96 (April 6, 1822).

[26]*Mobile Directory and Commercial Supplement, for 1855-1856*, pp. 23-24.

[27]*Eighth Census of the United States, 1860, Population*, 602-604; *Hunt's Merchants' Magazine*, XXVI, 130 (1852); *Niles' Weekly Register*, XXVII, 259-260 (December 25, 1824).

[28]*Niles' Weekly Register*, LV, 152 (November 3, 1838).

[29]These North Alabama counties were Madison, Jefferson, Walker, Marion, Morgan, Lawrence, St. Clair, Franklin, Lauderdale, Blount, and Jackson. *Ibid.*, XLIII, 35 (September 15, 1832).

[30]For example, *ibid.*, XXX, 241 (June 3, 1826), states: "South Alabama is thought to have produced 75,000 bales of cotton, and North Alabama 50,000 in the last season [1825-1826]. The first is chiefly exported from Mobile, the latter from New Orleans."

[31]The South Alabama counties in 1830 were Mobile, Baldwin, Monroe, Dallas, Pickens, Bibb, Montgomery, Clark, Shelby, Butler, Henry, Marengo, Pike, Green, Perry, Conecuh, Autauga, Wilcox, Fayette, Dale, Covington, Washington, Lowndes, and Tuscaloosa. *Ibid.*, XLIII, 35 (September 15, 1832).

Pensacola,[32] looked to Mobile as their seat of commercial activity. From September 1, 1819, to August 30, 1829, South Alabama produced more than half a million bales of cotton for shipment to the Mobile and world markets. Yearly production during the decade averaged about 55,000 bales, and the largest annual output, almost 90,000 bales, was made in 1827.[33] At the close of the decade Mobile was outranked as a cotton port only by New Orleans, Savannah and Charleston. In tonnage of ships it ranked sixth in the South, after New Orleans, Charleston, Norfolk, Wilmington, and Savannah, in that order.[34] Also of interest to Mobilians in the period was the arrival of a Pittsburgh barge, described as a "horse trough," stacked high with flour and bacon "from the back of Virginia." Of more lasting importance was the establishment of "a regular line of packets, ships of the first class, and of about 300 tons," to run monthly between Mobile and New York.[35]

Three travelers who passed through Mobile during the 1820's have left some noteworthy impressions of the town. One New York businessman's report, as described in *Niles' Weekly Register*, was that eight steamboats were operating on the Alabama and Tombigbee Rivers in 1823.[36] The well-known and stolid Duke of Saxe-Weimar Eisenach, in January, 1826, praised the people for their erection of several brick houses and other buildings of the same kind of material. But he feigned astonishment at finding a

---

[32]*Ibid.*, XXXIV, 121 (April 19, 1828), reports "that 50,000 bales of cotton will this year [1827-1828], be brought to the bay of Appalachoicola [*sic*] from the country bordering on the Chattahoochie [*sic*], Flint, and Appalachicola[*sic*] rivers. . . ."

[33]The annual cotton production of South Alabama shipped to Mobile, with each year's season closing on August 31, was: 1820, 16,000 bales; 1821, 25,390; 1822, 45,423; 1823, 49,061; 1824, 44,924; 1825, 58,283; 1826, 74,379; 1827, 89,779; 1828, 71,155; and 1829, 80,329. *DeBow's Review,* IX, 654-660 (1850); *Hunt's Merchants' Magazine,* XXIII, 659 (1850); *Mobile Journal of Commerce Letter-Sheet Price-Current,* September 1, 1851; *Mobile Shipping and Commercial List,* October 2, 1837; *Niles' National Register,* LXIII, 68 (October 1, 1842); Justus Wyman, "A Geographical Sketch of the Alabama Territory," *Transactions of the Alabama Historical Society, 1898-1899,* III, 107-127 (1899).

[34]*Niles' Weekly Register,* XXXIV, 399-400 (August 16, 1828), XXXVI, 146 (May 2, 1829).

[35]*Ibid.*, XXIV, 1 (March 8, 1823), XXIX, 147 (November 5, 1825). See also Robert Greenhalgh Albion, *The Rise of New York Port, 1815-1860* (New York, 1939), 46, 103-112, for discussions of Mobile's growth as a port.

[36]*Niles' Weekly Register,* XXIV, 294-295 (July 12, 1823).

number of gambling houses, kept by Frenchmen, paying a yearly tax of $1,000 each to city authorities for a license. He remarked, too, that he had been told that "respectable merchants were in the habit of going there to have an eye on their clerks, and also to observe what mechanics, or other small tradesmen, played [there, in order to] stop giving credit to such as haunted the resorts of these gentry. . . . "[37] No matter how naive the Duke might have been, he could have observed that among others frequenting the places were up-country planters who undoubtedly often managed to indulge in such activities while on their business trips to Mobile. Moreover, it is not too much to assume that merchants and planters conducted an appreciable share of their more sedate business over the gaming tables. The third traveler to be mentioned is the choleric and crusty Britisher, Captain Basil Hall, who, while in Mobile, was as usual mostly concerned with his personal comforts. He arrived in the city shortly after a devastating fire had destroyed about two-thirds of the city's business property. Hall later complained, "On the 7th of April [1828], we reached what remained of Mobile, for the town had been almost entirely burnt down not quite six months before. . . . One of the few buildings which had escaped the fire, was a large hotel, and this, as might be supposed, was overcrowded from top to bottom, so that we had to squeeze into a most uncomfortable corner."[38]

The fire mentioned by Captain Hall was indeed a dreadful occurrence, one report being as follows: "We have a list of the houses destroyed by the late fire [on October 21, 1827] at Mobile—they amount to one hundred and sixty-nine, exclusive of back buildings or out-houses, and much damage was done to the wharves. About 7-8th of the buildings destroyed were wood - hence the extent of the calamity. In many instances, entire sets of books of the merchants were destroyed [and] of course, large quantities of goods and furniture."[39] But from this chaos the city proceeded almost immediately into one of its greatest boom periods before the Civil

---

[37]Karl Bernhard, *Travels through North America, during the Years 1825 and 1826*, 2 vols. (Philadelphia, 1828), 50-51.

[38]Basil Hall, *Travels in North America in the Years 1827 and 1828*, 3 vols. (Edinburgh, 1829), III, 315, 331.

[39]*Niles' Weekly Register*, XXXIII, 196 (November 24, 1827). See also *ibid.*, XXXIII, 182 (November 17, 1827).

War. In 1830 it had a population of slightly more than 3,000 and ten years later 12,000 or more. Of all the cities of the United States having 10,000 people and over in the year 1840, Mobile's increase during the 1830's was proportionately the greatest. Editorializing in 1833 the Mobile *Register* proclaimed, "Six years ago, this city of Mobile was reduced to ashes, by a dreadful conflagration—it has since risen in all the vigor and beauty of a phoenix."[40]

Such unusual developments resulted, as always, from unusual causes. In the first place the Creek, Cherokee, Choctaw, and Chickasaw Indians (estimated at about 19,200 in Alabama in 1829) were deprived of their Alabama lands during this period.[41] About one-third of present-day Alabama was thereby opened to white settlers and by 1840 the state's population shot up to nearly 600,000, almost doubling in the ten-year period.[42] Furthermore, cotton output in the state more than tripled during the 1830's, mainly as a result of an extraordinary increase in the Black Belt and South Alabama and in other portions of the newly settled Indian lands. South Alabama, which from this period must be designated merely as those regions trading directly with Mobile, pushed its cotton production from slightly over 100,000 bales in 1830 to more than 300,000 in 1838. This spectacular increase resulted primarily from the introduction of a new type of blightproof cotton and improved methods of drilling for water in the Black Belt area.[43] Altogether, the amazing total of nearly 1,850,000 bales, each weighing approximately 500 pounds, was shipped to Mobile from between 1830 to 1839.[44] In the first half of the decade cotton prices rose steadily

---

[40]Mobile *Register*, quoted in *ibid.*, XLV, 165 (November 9, 1833). See also *Hunt's Merchants' Magazine*, X, 461-464 (1844). Mobile's population in 1830 was 3,194. *Ibid.*, XXXIII, 193 (1855); *DeBow's Review*, XXVII, 135 (1859).

[41]This estimate of Alabama's Indian population in 1829 was made by the United States Department of War. *Niles' Weekly Register*, XXXVI, 132 (April 25, 1829).

[42]*Eighth Census of the United States, 1860, Population*, 602-604; *Fifteenth Census of the United States: Population* (Washington, 1931), I, 66.

[43]See Chapters II and III, below.

[44]Annual cotton production in South Alabama during the 1830's was 1830, 102,684 bales; 1831, 113,075; 1832, 125,605; 1833, 129,366; 1834, 149,513; 1835, 197,847; 1836, 237,590; 1837, 232,685; 1838, 309,807; 1839, 251,742. *DeBow's Review*, IX, 654-660 (1850); *Hunt's Merchants' Magazine*, XXXV, 626 (1856); *Mobile Journal of Commerce Letter-Sheet Price-Current*, Sep-

from about 9¢ to 14¢ per pound. But with a greater output in Alabama and the South, coupled with the effects of the nation-wide panic of 1837, prices declined to 7¢ in 1839.[45]

Nevertheless there was much progress and wealth to be noticed in Mobile during the decade. For example, the city's branch of the Second United States Bank ranked fifth in the South in 1831 (after New Orleans, Charleston, Nashville, Louisville) in the amount of notes discounted on personal securities.[46] The next year it was third in the total amounts of business conducted in the South and ninth in the United States.[47] In August, 1837, the Mobile office had more money on deposit than any other branch in the whole country: $1,020,856.[48] At the time of the 1827 fire the city had maintained only two fire companies. Six additional ones were organized during the 1830's, adding both to the citizens' feeling of security and protection, as well as to their social life.[49] Cockle-shells were used to pave some of the city's business and residential streets.[50] In 1836 Mobile became the second city of the South to make arrangements for a gas lighting system, and the next year saw the system inaugurated.[51] There was also enthusiastic support of an active local theater. But, as always, there were some critics. Even in regard to the theater, an observer later complained that the performers had become guilty of what he called "sneak stage kisses." A stage kiss, he maintained, should be heard as well as seen, and he thought that such kisses should be "real old-fashioned smacks as loud as

tember 1, 1851; Mobile *Register*, September 5, 1842; *Mobile Shipping and Commercial List*, October 2, 1837.

[45]Charles S. Davis, *The Cotton Kingdom in Alabama* (Montgomery, 1939), 188.

[46]The sums discounted in these five southern cities in 1831 were as follows: New Orleans, $6,454,730; Charleston, $3,054,014; Nashville, $2,602,213; Louisville, $2,516,075; and Mobile, $1,503,678. *Niles' Weekly Register*, XLII, 150 (April 21, 1832).

[47]Cities outranking Mobile in business conducted were Portland, Boston, New York, Philadelphia, Baltimore, Washington, Savannah, and New Orleans. *Ibid.*, XLIV, 220 (June 1, 1833).

[48]*Ibid.*, LIII, 35 (September 16, 1837).

[49]The first two fire companies were established in 1818; in addition to the six that were organized during the 1830's, another one was set up in the year 1843. *Directory of the City of Mobile, 1858-1859* (Mobile, n. d.), Appendix, 47.

[50]*Niles' Weekly Register*, LXV, 132 (October 26, 1833).

[51]*Ibid.*, LI, 144 (October 29, 1836), LII, 272 (June 24, 1837).

bursting bladders."[52] And Thomas Hamilton, a British traveler, made the following cutting conclusion about Mobile after a short visit to the city in April, 1831: "Mobile is a place of trade, and of nothing else. The quays were crowded with shipping, and in amounts of exports it is inferior only to New Orleans. The wealth of Mobile merchants must accumulate rapidly, for they certainly do not dissipate it in any expenditure. There are no smart houses or equipages, nor indeed any demonstration of opulence, except huge warehouses and a crowded harbour. Of amusements of any kind I heard nothing."[53]

Another outsider observed in 1836 that 45 steamboats were "employed in the Mobile trade," and he personally counted 50 sailing vessels in the harbor. He reported, too, that "300 stores and dwelling houses have been erected. No less than 4,000 seamen were employed in the trade of Mobile last season [1835]."[54] Shortly thereafter, a third visitor was amazed at the local scramble for business sites: "A block of brick stores recently [was] erected near the wharf, the dimensions of which . . . [were] about 25 feet front by about 80 feet deep, 3 stories high, without any cellar, . . . [and were renting] for $7,000 a year; [that is,] the lower story . . . [rented] for $4,000, and the upper two stories for $3,000. The price of them . . . [was] held at about $30,000 each."[55] The editor of the Mobile *Transcript* had earlier claimed that, although "many of the stores will vie with the best structures of a similar kind in the northern cities . . . the truth is, every thing is too much on the extravagant order."[56] Many activities and articles were indeed "on the extravagant order" throughout the United States, and soon the panic of 1837 hit Mobile along with the rest of the country.

Because of the panic and the drastic drop in cotton prices, the

52 Sub Rosa [Paul Ravesies], *Scenes and Settlers of Alabama* (Mobile, 1885), 25.

53Thomas Hamilton, *Men and Manners in America*, 2 vols. (Edinburgh, 1833), II, 240. See also *Niles' Weekly Register*, XLVIII, 374 (January 31, 1835), LXI, 100 (October 16, 1841), for references to Mobile as the second ranking cotton port, after New Orleans, in the United States.

54See Hosea Holcombe, *History of the Rise and Progress of the Baptists in Alabama* (Philadelphia, 1840), 299-300.

55Springfield *Journal*, quoted in *Niles' Weekly Register*, LII, 48 (March 18, 1837).

56Mobile *Transcript*, quoted in *Niles' Weekly Register*, XLIX, 242 (December 12, 1835).

latter part of the 1830's was not a happy time for Mobile business-men and their up-country clientele. In 1836 the city was conduct-ing so much business that its warehouses were inadequate to house cotton and other produce. Indeed, this lack of storage space re-sulted in an estimated loss of $200,000 in damages.[57] The next spring there was gloom of another sort. The Mobile *Mercantile Advertiser* of April 21, 1837, lamented, "Business is in the same flat condition that it has been for weeks past. Every thing is dull in the way of trade. The lawyers and sheriffs are the only busy men in town. Money continues to withdraw itself from the mer-chants and traders and other men's hands, except those in the banks, and a few misers besides. Two or three more of the very few . . . remaining important [commission merchant and factorage] houses in our city, have gone since our last. There are but few more to go."[58]

Public meetings were held to seek means of alleviating con-ditions. At one gathering a moratorium on all debts was suggested. Participants of another local session opposed cancellation of any contract and requested the state to issue twenty-year bonds at 6% interest in order to help increase circulation of mediums of exchange. Another palliative requested, and later actually accomplished, was the issuance of bank "post notes, . . . receivable in payment of debts, ..."[59] Some relief was forthcoming, as one authority has written, when post notes, warehouse certificates or cotton loans, bank notes, and other substitutes for currency were issued by the thousands.[60] Other local efforts made to beat the depression were the promotion of more interest in direct trade with European markets and establishment of closer trade relations with Central America. As if the panic had not brought enough difficulties, Mobile experienced a series of six horrible fires late in 1839 which destroyed about 500 buildings and other property valued at $1,600,000.[61]

---

[57]Mobile *Commercial Register and Patriot,* March 5, 1836.
[58]Mobile *Mercantile Advertiser,* quoted in *Niles' Weekly Register,* LII, 146 (May 6, 1837).
[59]*Niles' Weekly Register,* LII, 146 (May 6, 1837). See also *ibid.,* LII, 115 (April 22, 1837).
[60]Moore, *History of Alabama,* 223-227.
[61]*Niles' Weekly Register,* LIV, 416 (August 25, 1838), LVII, 146, 192 (November 2, 16, 1839). See also Thomas P. Govan, "An Ante-Bellum Attempt

Cotton prices continued their downward trend in the first half of the 1840's, finally hitting an average of 5¼¢ per pound in 1845. Some individual sales were of course even lower. In that year prices stabilized somewhat and climbed slowly, reaching 10¢ per pound in 1849. Partially because of such fluctuations, farmers and planters of the state turned more to crop diversification. Throughout the decade there was an increasing interest in home production of tobacco, oranges, sugar cane, grain crops, silk, rice and other commodities. In value of livestock Alabama was outranked only by Virginia among the southern states at the end of the decade. But as always the state failed to produce enough corn for its own consumption.[62] Some progress was made in this respect, however, as a result of new interests in the "live-at-home" program. As described in 1848 by the Mobile *Alabama Planter*, for many years "everything was merged in cotton [in Alabama]; the log cabin was sufficient shelter, education was disregarded, nobody had time to beautify estates with gardens or fruit-trees. It is now the reverse. In Cahawba, Coosa, Talladega, Jones' Vallies, etc., the cotton product decreases, while wheat, rye, oats, corn, and stock increases. Wheat and flour are now shipped from some of these counties."[63] Such activities of course meant more business for the city.

Another type of diversification and activity in Mobile and Alabama took the form of a pronounced industrial gospel. So-called "manufactures" seem to have been organized in every region of the state during the 1840's and some, of course, were continued from previous years. The state possessed many zealous advocates of manufacturing, poised and ready to lead Alabama to financial and economic salvation if it would only follow their entreaties. Mobilians took a leading role in this movement, their chief interest being the desire to produce finished articles that could be sold to up-country clients. As early as 1835 there was in the city a cotton-

---

to Regulate the Price and Supply of Cotton," *North Carolina Historical Review*, XVII, 302-312 (1940), and Lewis C. Gray, *History of Agriculture in the Southern United States to 1860*, 2 vols. (Washington, 1933), II, 1027.

[62]*DeBow's Review*, I, 488 (1846), XII, 685 (1852), XIX, 468 (1855), XXV, 351 (1858); *Niles' Weekly Register*, LXII, 280-281 (July 2, 1842), LXVIII, 180 (May 24, 1845), LXXIV, 343 (November 29, 1848), LXXV, 64, 80 (January 24, 31, 1849).

[63]*Alabama Planter*, quoted in *DeBow's Review*, VI, 229, (1848). See also Moore, *History of Alabama*, 121.

seed oil manufactury whose product was said "to be decidedly superior to the best sperm oil."[64] In the 1840's an iron and brass foundry was in operation, and the "Mobile City Mills" were turning out "good merchantable flour . . . produced from Southern grain," some from Alabama.[65] A cotton factory was running 3,000 spindles. By 1850 the state was operating more than 1,000 factories of all kinds, with much of their output being distributed through the business houses of Mobile.[66] As interesting as these beginnings in industry might have been, however, cotton was still the chief source of wealth of the state, and its sale remained Mobile's most important business activity.

According to one contemporary account, Mobile's concern with cotton led to the neglect of certain other interests. A visitor in May, 1840, was of the following opinion:

. . . Mobile might be made a delightful place in Winter and a pleasant one in Summer, but unfortunately like too many of the Southern Towns & Cities but little attention is paid it by the authorities. Hence it is dirty and about the wharves very filthy and stinking. Added to this so many of the inhabitants leave there in the Summer [because of lack of business and fear of fever epidemics], that their erratic life forbids them making many improvements or paying much attention to these little inconveniences & Comforts without which any life & especially a city one is unpleasant — . . . .[67]

That these charges were at least partially true is borne out by the fact that the Alabama state legislature passed an act the next year prohibiting masters of vessels from dumping various kinds of ballast and waste in the harbor. Pilots were authorized to report infractions to the harbor-master and violators were to be fined $2,000 and imprisoned up to three months.[68]

In the 1840's South Alabama produced over 4,000,000 bales of cotton. The biggest year was 1849, the smallest was 1841; but even in the latter year the value of cotton exports alone exceeded $10,000,000.[69] At the beginning of the decade Alabama was out-

---

[64]*Niles' National Register*, XLVIII, 186 (May 16, 1835).

[65]*Ibid.*, LXXV, 344 (May 30, 1849). See also *DeBow's Review*, VI, 295 (1848).

[66]*Ibid.*, IX, 214 (1850); *Hunt's Merchants' Magazine*, XLV, 144 (1861).

[67]William H. Willis, "A Southern Traveler's Diary in 1840," in *Publications of the Southern History Association*, VIII, 136-137 (1904).

[68]*Hunt's Merchants' Magazine*, V, 184 (1841).

[69]South Alabama cotton output during the 1840's was: 1840, 445,725 bales; 1841, 317,642; 1842, 318,315; 1843, 482,631; 1844, 468,126; 1845, 517,550; 1846, 421,669; 1847, 322,516; 1848, 438,324; 1849, 517,846. *DeBow's*

ranked by Mississippi as a cotton state. Ten years later Alabama was the leader, and Mobile therefore handled an even greater trade.[70] Also passing through the city to the interior, as was the case throughout the ante-bellum period, were such agricultural supplies as bagging, rope, iron, bacon coffee, corn, flour, hay, lard, lime, molasses, oats, potatoes, pork, rice, salt, sugar, medicines, whiskey, and others. Whereas cotton was sold by factors, the above articles were purchased by farmers and planters through the offices of commission merchants. As a result of all this activity Mobile's population almost doubled during the 1840's, rising from approximately 12,000 in 1840 to more than 20,000 in 1850. The state's population moved above 750,000 in the same period. Both in the city and state, however, despite greater economic activity, the rate of increase in population was declining. By 1850 the state was old and settled enough for about one-third of its people to have been born within its limits. On the other hand, Mobile's citizens continued to come from widely scattered places. Over 4,000 of them were foreigners, mainly Irish, and more than 5,000 had moved to the city from states other than Alabama, especially from New York, South Carolina, Georgia, Virginia and Massachusetts, in that order.[71]

During the 1840's and 1850's Mobile was described variously by foreign travelers as "a tolerably large and handsome town," a "commercial emporium," and the "metropolis of Alabama."[72] One visitor considered the city "neither very agreeable nor very pic-

Review, XII, 166 (1852), XXII, 488 (1857), XXVIII, 666 (1860); *Hunt's Merchants' Magazine*, XXXV, 626 (1856); *Mobile Journal of Commerce Letter-Sheet Price-Current*, September 1, 1851; Mobile *Register*, September 5, 1842.

[70]*Eighth Census of the United States, 1860, Agriculture* (Washington, 1864), xciv; *Niles' National Register*, LX, 148 (May 8, 1841).

[71]*DeBow's Review*, II, 419 (1846), XVII, 325 (1854), XIX, 262-263 (1855), XXIX, 210 (1860); *Hunt's Merchants' Magazine*, XXXII, 39 (1855); *Eighth Census of the United States, 1860, Population*, 602-604; *Fifteenth Census of the United States: Population;* I, 66. See also Herbert Weaver, "Foreigners in Ante-Bellum Towns of the Lower South," *Journal of Southern History*, XIII, 62-73 (1947).

[72]Philip Henry Gosse, *Letters from Alabama* (London, 1859), 26; Alexander Mackay, *The Western World; or, Travels in the United States in 1846-47*, 2 vols. (Philadelphia, 1849), II, 74; S. Augustus Mitchell, *A General View of the United States . . . at Different Periods, as Well as in the Year 1840* (Philadelphia, 1846), 65; Lady Emmeline Stuart Wortley, *Travels in the United States, etc. during 1849 and 1850* (New York, 1851), 131, 132.

turesque . . . streets being almost incessantly clodded with mud, and the luxury of a clean pavement . . . yet but a blessing in contemplation."[73] A more charitable observation was as follows: "The position of Mobile is favourable to health, and advantageous for commerce. It lies at the head of an open bay . . . close upon the sea. . . . The town runs along the edge of the water from north to south, and recedes backward from east to west, covering in the whole an area of about a mile in length by three-quarters of a mile in breadth . . . the main street . . . , called Government-street, is as handsome an avenue as is to be seen in the country. . . ."[74] The streets were long and broad, "admirably paved" with oyster shells. Other impressions of Mobile were equally interesting. One traveler concluded, "Mobile has nothing gracious about it but her name. We are in haste to reach New Orleans and we left [Mobile] that very night [after arrival]."[75] However, another visitor was keenly interested in watching little steamers take on cargoes from ships for transshipment across Mobile Bay to the city. He also stated: "When one arrives from Louisiana into Alabama, it seems he can breathe better due to the simple elevation of the soil on which it [Mobile] is built. . . . The climate of the southern part of Alabama is much more healthy than that of Louisiana."[76] Two anchorages were employed in the Mobile trade, one near the city, the other down the bay and out of sight of the city. It was a strange experience for the traveler to pass what he thought of as a large port, with as many as sixty vessels at anchor, then suddenly to come upon another anchorage containing an equal number of vessels.[77]

Travelers were as impressed with river transportation on the Alabama River as with any other aspect of their trips through the state. A Frenchman, for example, described the River in this fashion: "The Alabama, in certain spots, is fairly narrow, with here

---

[73]Gosse, *Letters from Alabama*, 26.

[74]James Silk Buckingham, *The Slave States in America*, 2 vols. (London, 1841), I, 281-282.

[75]Vicomte de Florimond Jacques Basterot, *De Quebec a Lima: journal d'un voyage dans les deux Ameriques en 1858 et en 1859* (Paris, 1860), 257. See also Mackay, *The Western World*, II, 74.

[76]Charles Olliffe, *Scenes Americaines: Dix-huit Mois dans le Nouveau Monde* (Paris, 1853), 52.

[77]Mackay, *The Western World*, II, 76.

and there delightful little islands that look like bouquets of foliage placed there by a nymph to keep them from withering; others are just sandy shoals. . . . In other parts, on the contrary it [the Alabama] is so wide that it seems one has the feeling of being lost in one of those deserts of the ocean, seeing only the majesty of God."[78] Perhaps of equal interest was an Englishman's description of a river steamer on which he traveled: "The engine was a high pressure one; and gave out a burst of steam from a tall chimney, at every rotation of the wheels, the sound being like the hard breathing of some huge mastadon labouring under the asthma; while the two chimneys vomiting forth volumes of black smoke, with the third breathing forth at momentary intervals its blasts of white curling steam."[79] Another account was as follows: "The steamer is a long slender vessel, having a vast saloon running through its centre, divided into two compartments—that nearest the bow for the gentlemen, also used for dining, and that nearest the stern, being the remotest from the engine, for the ladies, who remain apart throughout the voyage, unless at meals, ..."[80] Such vessels as these, with their shallow drafts, made possible the transportation of produce and goods to and from Mobile, enabling it to become the agricultural focus of Alabama. Transported to market were such articles as grain, flour, meats, lumber, liquors, tobacco, cotton, and corn; and every possible sort of household item and luxury found their way up the rivers to consumers. Stops were frequent, 200 being a normal number on the river route between Mobile and Montgomery. The trip between the two cities required two days.[81]

With its 30,000 or so inhabitants in the year 1860, Mobile was the twenty-seventh in size among the cities of the United States.[82] The state, with almost 1,000,000 people, had, according to one

[78]Louis Xavier Eyma [Adolphe Ricard], Les Deux Ameriques: histoires, moeurs et voyages (Paris, 1853), 214-215.

[79]Buckingham, The Slave States of America, I, 262-263.

[80]Reverend G. Lewis, Impressions of America and the American Churches: from Journal of the Reverend G. Lewis (Edinburgh, 1845), 162.

[81]Ibid., 165; Buckingham, The Slave States of America, I, 260; Mackay, The Western World, II, 66; Louis Fitzgerald Tasistro, Random Shots and Southern Breezes, 2 vols. (New York, 1842), I, 79.

[82]United States Census, 1860, Mortality and Miscellaneous Statistics (Washington, 1866), xviii.

writer, "like young Hercules in his cradle . . . done wonders in her infancy."[83] The last decade before 1860 differed little from preceding ones, except that there was more economic activity and business. Cotton was plentiful, with South Alabama making more than 5,000,000 bales during the 1850's, and prices ranged between 8¢ and 10¢ per pound.[84] In the 1850-1851 season, for example, ships from Mobile were transporting cargoes to Great Britain and France, as well as Amsterdam, Rotterdam, Antwerp, Hamburg, Bremen, St. Petersburg, Stockholm, Ghent, Gibraltar, Barcelona, Havana, Genoa, and Trieste. Important American ports receiving Mobile goods were New York, Boston, Providence, Baltimore, and New Orleans. In the five fiscal years ending June, 1860, over 2,000 vessels, representing more than 1,000,000 tons of shipping, cleared Mobile harbor.[85]

As early as 1849-1850, the following articles, as well as cotton, were being exported from Mobile: tallow, iron, shingles, laths, lime, tar, hides, spirits of turpentine, crude turpentine, pitch, rosin, rope cuttings, rice, bricks, horns, leather, bones, sugar, corn, ash logs, pine masts, deck planks, beams, square pieces of timber, oars, empty tierces, hand-spikes, empty barrels, staves, and cedar logs.[86] Even in 1857, the least active year in this period, exports were valued at more than $20,000,000. Accordingly, the 1850's comprise one of the most prosperous periods in the entire ante-bellum era for Alabama agriculturists and for Mobile. The value of taxable

---

[83]*DeBow's Review*, XVIII, 21 (1855).

[84]Cotton production in South Alabama during the 1850's was: 1850, 350,-297 bales; 1851, 451,697; 1852, 549,777; 1853, 546,514; 1854, 538,110; 1855, 454,595; 1856, 659,738; 1857, 503,177; 1858, 522,843; 1859, 704,406. The 1860 crop amounted to 843,012 bales, the 1860-1861 crop to 549,441 bales. Cotton bales pressed at Mobile seem consistently to have averaged 500 bales. Davis, *The Cotton Kingdom in Alabama*, 188; Berney, *Handbook of Alabama*, 82; *DeBow's Review*, XVIII, 507 (1855), XXIII, 488 (1857), XXV, 568 (1858), XXIX, 666 (1860); *Hunt's Merchants' Magazine*, XXXV, 91, 626 (1856).

[85]These clearances were: 934 vessels, 312,973 tons in 1855-1856; 238 vessels, 156,110 tons in 1856-1857; 443 vessels, 330,948 tons in 1857-1858; 542 vessels, 292,321 tons in 1858-1859; and 343 vessels, 255,387 tons in 1859-1860. *DeBow's Review*, XXV, 473 (1858), XXVIII, 221 (1860); *Hunt's Merchants' Magazine*, XXXV, 612 (1856), XXXVIII, 708 (1858), XLV, 182 (1861); *Mobile Journal of Commerce Letter-Sheet Price-Current*, September 1, 1851.

[86]*DeBow's Review*, IX, 654-660 (1850).

property (lands, money at interest, money in corporate companies, and sales merchandise) in Alabama in 1858 was $177,714,150. In Mobile in the same year, real estate was assessed at $13,402,635 and merchandise on hand at $3,123,705.[87] Although Alabama was officially surpassed in value of exports by Louisiana and New York, one of its citizens, Clement C. Clay, claimed first place for his state. New Orleans' exports in 1857 amounted to $91,433,306, New York City's to $74,538,238, and Mobile's to $20,575,987, but Clay contended with some reason that "when we consider the sources whence those States derive a large portion of their exports, it would not be arrogant or extravagant to claim for Alabama precedence over them as an exporter."[88]

Clay was by no means the only local booster in the 1850's. Some descriptions of Mobile must of course be adjudged mere exaggeration, but others seem to be at least partially authentic. One unidentified promoter in 1851 was of the opinion "that the facilities for storing and compressing cotton . . . are, beyond dispute, better than those of any cotton receiving port in the Union, in proportion to the amount received. There are in Mobile," he said, "*forty-two* Fireproof Brick Warehouses, which are capable of receiving, and storing, at least 310,000 bales of cotton— . . . . These warehouses cover forty acres of ground— . . . ."[89] Local presses were also reputed to have been capable of compressing over a million bales of cotton in six months, and ship captains were said to admit that Mobile compressing surpassed that of all other market centers. The city also operated forty-eight wharves, which in some cases could be reached by a channel with a depth of twenty-two feet of water.[90]

Another boastful Alabamian, writing in 1855, asserted, "To those who have long been accustomed to look upon the Crescent City [New Orleans] as the Queen of southern commerce, it will be incredible that Mobile has shipping facilities far superior and is much the best port on the Gulf."[91] Moreover, a writer in *Hunt's*

---

[87]*Hunt's Merchants' Magazine*, XL, 185 (1859), LXII, 218 (1860).

[88]*DeBow's Review*, XIX, 726 (1855), XXIV, 553 (1858); *Hunt's Merchants' Magazine*, XL, 179 (1859).

[89]*Hunt's Merchants' Magazine*, XXIV, 266 (1851).

[90]*Ibid.*

[91]*DeBow's Review*, XVIII, 159 (1855). For a comparison of rates of

Merchants' Magazine, in 1859, maintained that "The situation of Mobile is one of the most beautiful among the many attractive sites of American cities . . . [and] at the mouth of . . . [Mobile] bay is Dauphin Island, on either side of which is a strait. That on the west admits vessels drawing only five feet, but that on the east admits a draught of twenty-two feet."[92] Less complimentary was the description made by the well-known traveler, Frederick Law Olmstead, in the same year: "The great business of the town is the transfer of cotton, from the producer to the manufacturer, from the wagon and the steamboat to the sea-going ship. Like the other cotton-ports, Mobile labors under the disadvantage of a shallow harbor. At the wharves, there are only a few small craft and steamboats. All large sea-going vessels lie some thirty miles below, and their freights are transhipped in lighters."[93]

But on the basis of accomplishments as an agricultural market there was good reason to be proud of Mobile. In cotton alone South Alabama shipped the amazing total of 13,355,588 bales to Mobile between 1817 and 1861. Agricultural supplies in an enormous amount passed through the city to upstate consumers. In 1859 cotton and supplies were bought and sold by more than 150 factors and commission merchants. In the same year the city supported 3 local banks and 16 insurance companies. Steamboats were making more than 700 official landings or stops along the Alabama, Tombigbee, and Warrior rivers. Six pilot boats and 23 pilots were working the waters in and near the city. Three lighthouses were in operation,[94] and between 1826 and 1857 the federal government appropriated more than $200,000 to improve the harbor.[95] The Mobile and Ohio Railroad, projected by Mobile

---

exchange and handling charges and prices of cotton in Mobile and New Orleans, see *ibid.,* XVIII, 477-485 (1855).

[92]*Hunt's Merchants' Magazine,* XL, 179 (1859).

[93]Frederick Law Olmstead, *Journey in the Seaboard Slave States, with Remarks on Their Economy* (New York, 1859), 567.

[94]*Directory of the City of Mobile, 1858-1859, passim.*

[95]These appropriations of the federal government were: $10,000 in 1826, $20,000 in 1829, $10,000 in 1834, $17,997 in 1835, $50,000 in 1837, $50,000 in 1838, $50,000 in 1852, and $20,833 in 1857. William E. Martin, "Internal Improvements in Alabama," in *Johns Hopkins University Studies in Historical and Political Science,* XX, 173 (Baltimore, 1902). In 1861 Mobile harbor was described as follows: "On the bar of the deepest channel the water lies twenty feet in depth" near Sand Island. At this time there was also a pass sixteen feet deep between Petit Bois and Horn Island; and Mississippi Sound, west-

business leaders, was in operation,[96] and the Mobile and Ohio Telegraph Company was incorporated in 1859. At various times during the 1850's consuls representing 16 foreign governments were stationed in the city.[97]

To those Alabamians dependent upon the river systems closely associated with Mobile during the pre-Civil War period, the city might well have been the center of the economic universe.[98] Its chief interest was cotton; and as one traveler so quaintly described the situation in the late 1850's: "Mobile is a pleasant cotton city of some thirty thousand inhabitants—where people live in cotton houses and ride in cotton carriages. They buy cotton, sell cotton, think cotton, eat cotton, drink cotton, and dream cotton. They marry cotton wives [and husbands], and unto them are born cotton children. In enumerating the charms of a fair widow, they begin by saying she makes so many bales of cotton. It is the great staple, the sum and substance of Alabama. It has made Mobile and all its citizens."[99] To some extent, this remark about Mobile applied to the city and to the rest of Alabama, but, as will be seen, to conclude that the people of ante-bellum Alabama gave all of their attention to the production and sale of cotton is a gross misconception.

---

ward from Mobile, was six feet in depth. *Hunt's Merchants' Magazine*, XLV, 22 (1861).

[96]*Ibid.*, XLIII, 632 (1860), reports that the Mobile and Ohio Railroad shipped 107,450 bales of cotton to Mobile in 1857-1858, 137,430 bales in 1858-1859, and 233,890 bales in 1859-1860. For information on this railroad, see Grace Lewis Miller, "The Mobile and Ohio Railroad in Ante-Bellum Times," *Alabama Historical Quarterly*, VII, 37-59 (1945); *Poor's Manual of the Railroads of the United States* (New York, 1868-1924), *1877-1878*, pp. 214-215; and John F. Stover, "Southern Ambitions of the Illinois Central Railroad," *Journal of Southern History*, XX, 499-510 (1954).

[97]The consuls at Mobile represented Great Britain, France, Spain, Netherlands, Hamburg, Belgium, Portugal, Russia, Mexico, Sardinia, Austria, Tuscany, Sweden, Norway, Holland, and Switzerland. *Mobile Directory and Commercial Supplement, for 1855-1856*, p. 121; *Directory of the City of Mobile, 1858-1859*, p. 45; *Daughrill's & Walker's General Directory for the City and County of Mobile for 1856* (Mobile, 1856), 21.

[98]One problem faced by ante-bellum Mobile that was never solved was its recurrent fever epidemics, which occurred usually during summers and greatly retarded business in the city. Among the more devastating epidemics were those of 1819, 1825, 1829, 1837, 1839, 1843, and 1857. *DeBow's Review*, XI, 526-530 (1851); Massey, *Reminiscences*, 87.

[99]Hiram Fuller, *Belle Britain on Tour, at Newport and Here and There* (New York, 1858), 112.

II

A BLACK BELT TOWN

In many respects the settlement and early growth of the town of Marion, Perry County, serves as a typical example of the rise to importance of such establishments in the Alabama black belt.[1] Relatively speaking, it was founded quite late in the region's history. Candidly speaking, it has not maintained the significant position that it attained in the period before 1861. It deserves attention, nevertheless, because of its location and because it was representative of many similar localities in the general area of the state in which it is situated.

Like most other comparable towns in central Alabama, Marion owed its settlement to the many economic and social readjustments made necessary in the country by the War of 1812. Of special significance, too, was the famous Treaty of Fort Jackson of 1815, which opened up to whites much of the territory that soon became part of Alabama. In 1813, the Tennessee River bend and lower Tombigbee, the important settled areas in eastern Mississippi Territory, had a population of about 13,000. Then, the War of 1812 and the Treaty of Fort Jackson brought settlers to Jackson, Lauderdale, Limestone, and other counties. As a result, by 1816 the population figure for all of Alabama (eastern Mississippi) increased to more than 25,000. Large agricultural establishments were set up in Madison County; others appeared in the lower Tombigbee region; and settlers began arriving in Alabama from all directions. By March 3, 1817, the white population passed the 33,000 mark, and, after several unsuccessful attempts, was able to induce Congress to establish the Territory of Alabama. The important settled areas also increased in number. Besides the older, established regions, the upper Tombigbee and the Mobile River Valley attracted many people. By the summer of 1817, South Alabama (at the time con-

---

[1]Much of the material in this chapter first appeared under the title of "Early Ante-Bellum Marion, Alabama: A Black Belt Town," in the *Alabama Historical Quarterly*, V, 12-31 (1943). It is reprinted with the permission of Mrs. Marie Bankhead Owen, former editor of the *Quarterly*.

sisting of Mobile, Baldwin, Washington, and Clarke Counties) claimed twenty of the thirty-five thousand people in the Territory. As already mentioned, Alabama's total population reached more than 70,000 when statehood was attained in 1819. The federal census of the year 1820 showed that the state's total population had jumped spectacularly to 127,000.[2] Alabama was one of the states that gained in an amazing fashion from the migration movements which occurred in the United States during the years immediately following the War of 1812.

Meanwhile, some land later to be included in Perry County was gradually being taken up. In 1816, when the first permanent settlers from South Carolina and Tennessee arrived there, they found all the characteristics of a frontier region. Indeed, for more than a decade after 1816 the area had little to offer in the way of cultural advancement. Few roads traversed the region and population increased slowly. Little formal education or religion was evident for several years; and in 1816, despite the provisions of the Treaty of Fort Jackson, the land in the area was still partially held by Creek Indians. When settlers first arrived they found a large Creek establishment at a place known as Cahaba Old Town, located at the point where Old Town Creek flows into the Cahaba River, about seven miles northeast of the present location of the town of Marion. White men entered the area by the end of 1816, however, and in December of that year a settler named Anderson West, who was perhaps the first permanent settler in the region today included in Perry County, built a log cabin near Old Town. About the same time establishments were also made near a place that became known as Perry Ridge, located a few miles south of Old Town. The earliest white settlers there probably were William Ford and his sons, John and Enos, who had moved from Georgia. Within a year after their arrival, Perry Ridge had attracted enough people to become the most important settlement in the area.[3]

---

[2]Abernethy, *The Formative Period in Alabama*, 9-12, 17, 24-33; Davis, *The Cotton Kingdom in Alabama*, 11-14; John W. Monette, *History of the Discovery and Settlement of the Valley of the Mississippi*, 2 vols. (New York, 1846), II, 380, 383, 392, 446-447; Thomas M. Owen, *History of Alabama and Dictionary of Alabama Biography*, 4 vols. (Chicago, 1921), I, 14, 86; Albert James Pickett, *The History of Alabama* (Sheffield, Alabama, 1896), 461.

[3]Marion *Standard*, February 26, March 26, April 2, 1909. Captain W. L. Fagin was an early settler in Perry County. About the year 1886, Captain

During 1817 there occurred three events of particular importance in the development of the region. One was the construction by the Ford family of a saw mill and a grist mill near Perry Ridge, these mills being the first definite signs of white civilization in the area. A second noteworthy event was the arrival in the Old Town vicinity of two enterprising men by the names of Thomas M. Oliver and John Durden. Their special significance arises from the fact that immediately after their arrival they constructed a cotton gin, which, according to one source of information, was "the first cotton gin between the Warrior and Cahaba rivers."[4] This assertion is perhaps open to question but the construction of the gin at such an early date is important since it is evidence that cotton was already being grown, or that plans were on foot for its early cultivation. It seems beyond all doubt that the plant was cultivated the next year, for, according to local tradition, in 1818 cotton bloomed as late as December 23 in Perry County. It is thus assumed that either 1817 or 1818 marked the beginning of a definite interest by the people of the area in the production of the white staple, an interest that gradually came to monopolize the interests and activities and thoughts of the Perry County inhabitants and to influence their entire history.[5]

The third noteworthy event of 1817 in the early developments in Perry County was the arrival there, in November, of a man named Michael McElroy, a man whose name was first changed to Muckleroy by his friends and relatives and then to Mickle Muckle. Traditionally he is known as Mickle Muckle; and it was he who first settled within the boundaries of the present town of Marion, the seat of Perry County. Some time in 1817 he arrived in the region with his father-in-law, Nathan Reid, who became the founder of a family soon to be prominent in both the social and economic life of the county. Also accompanying Reid was another son-in-law, Warner Young. Reid settled about eight miles west of the present site of Marion, Young took up land somewhat closer, and Muckle cleared about one acre of land at the exact location of the present-

---

Fagin's reminiscences about Marion and Perry County were published in a local newspaper. In 1909 these reminiscences were reprinted in the Marion *Standard*.

[4]Marion *Standard*, April 2, 1909.
[5]*Ibid.*, February 12, 1909.

day Perry County courthouse square, located in the center of
Marion. The Muckle clearing soon acquired the title of "Muckle's
Ridge," bearing that designation until May, 1822, when it was
changed to Marion.[6]

Although the Territory of Alabama was established in 1817
and the population of the Territory as a whole increased rapidly,
only slight progress was made before 1819 in the vicinities of Perry
Ridge, Old Town, and "Muckle's Ridge." The year 1818 was a
hard one for the settlers because of the failure of their corn crops.
As much as three dollars per bushel was offered for corn, but there
was none to be had, and it was necessary to travel as far as the
settlements in lower Tennessee to obtain supplies of food. This
unfortunate condition retarded the growth of the region, but nevertheless a few minor changes in the status of the area were apparent
during the Territorial period. In 1817, hardly before he had settled,
Mickle Muckle, the sole inhabitant of his "Ridge," became dissatisfied because of "overpopulation" and sold his clearing to Anderson
West. The latter added a few acres to the clearing, but for almost
two years took Muckle's place as the only inhabitant of the "Ridge."[7]
Moreover, as late as the spring of 1819 the place was still little
more than a wilderness. According to an early settler of the area,
West's residence "at this time, had nothing more to entitle it to
peculiar attention, than any other private neighborhoods."[8] Perry
Ridge, on the other hand, continued to attract settlers, and the
importance of that place was both recognized and further enhanced
during the Territorial period when a "rude log building" was constructed there for use as a courthouse.

When Alabama's first Legislature was called at Huntsville, in
1819, one of its first acts was the establishment of Perry County.
Immediately there were signs of governmental activity in the county,
and local officials were soon appointed. Anderson West, still occu-
pying "Muckle's Ridge," became County Sheriff. A judge of Circuit
Court and a County Court clerk were selected.[9] On April 17, 1820,

---

[6]*Ibid.*, February 26, 1909.
[7]*Ibid.*, February 12, 26, 1909. See also S. A. Townes, *The History of
Marion, Sketches of Life, etc. in Perry County, Alabama* (Marion, 1844), 9.
[8]Marion *Standard*, February 12, 1909.
[9]*Ibid.*, February 12, April 9, 1909.

Elisha F. King, a Georgian who with his relatives later comprised one of the state's wealthiest and leading cotton producing families, was appointed County Treasurer.[10] An Orphan's Court, so-called, of five members, was selected to direct the government of the county. Its important function, however, during its first years of existence was the supervision and construction of county roads, and it is noteworthy that for several years nearly all of the entries made in the records of the Court concerned roads and nothing else. Perry Ridge remained the seat of government for about two years. During that time two public ferries were authorized for use in crossing the Cahaba River. A mill dam was constructed near "Muckle's Ridge." Rates to be charged by ferries and public taverns and the retail price of liquors were other matters with which the Orphan's Court concerned itself. On October 7, 1821, the Court met in special session and at that time issued its first permit to a minister in the county when it was ordered "that William West be ordained to Preach the Gospel and Solemnize the Rites of Matrimony he having presented Credentials for the Same."[11]

One of Perry County's earliest problems was the selection of a county seat which would be satisfactory to a majority of its settlers. Perry Ridge was the first seat of government, but after the original boundaries of the county were laid off it became evident that the place was inconveniently located for many of the farmers in the county. As in the case of the early settlers of Alabama and their agitation for a split of the Mississippi Territory because the seat of government was too distant for them, people in the outlying portions of Perry County became dissatisfied with the location of their county seat. Demand for a more centrally located county seat was both natural and to be expected in frontier areas; and in answer to the request, the State Legislature, on November 21, 1821, authorized the election of seven commissioners to select a permanent seat of government for the county. On February 4, 1822, the commissioners were elected and a month later met to make their decision. The commissioners, all of importance in the

---

[10]Perry County, Alabama, Orphan's Court Register, A, 2. These and all other county records referred to in this chapter are on deposit in the Office of the Probate Court, Perry County Court House, Marion.

[11]Perry County, Alabama, Orphan's Court Minutes, July, 1821-June, 1832, p. 18. See also Perry County, Alabama, Orphan's Court Register, A, 3, 8-12, 56.

later development of Perry County, were Joseph Evans, George Weissinger, J. K. C. Pool, John Welch, Reuben Lockett, James Shackelford, and William Ford.[12]

Four prospective sites were suggested when the commissioners came together. One of the commissioners wished to retain Perry Ridge, while two others preferred a place known as Burroughs Springs because, as they expressed it "the spring was thought to contain decided medicinal virtues," and there "the boys could learn to swim, and the gentlemanly loafers would be near good fishing ground, ..." Another commissioner proposed Indian Old Town because a cotton gin was in operation there and a store had been opened which "sold whiskey by the half pint." He stated, moreover, that Indian Old Town was the most thickly populated settlement in the county. Joseph Evans was the only commissioner whose first preference was "Muckle's Ridge," and he gave as reasons for his choice the central location of the place and the "beauty and healthfulness of the situation." Probably also of significance was the fact that three mercantile concerns were in operation there by 1820. After bickering for a whole day over the matter, Evans was able to persuade the other commissioners that "Muckle's Ridge" should become the county seat.[13]

Lots which had been laid off by the sheriff were sold at public auction on May 22, 1822. A small group of people present at the auction paid from $150 to $280 for individual lots, and sales amounting to $1,558 were concluded. When the auction had been completed it was suggested by some person in the crowd that a new name ought to be selected for the "Ridge." After several suggestions were offered for consideration, it was decided by the crowd that the new name of the place should be Marion, in honor of Francis "Swamp-fox" Marion, of American Revolution fame. Thus the site received its present name. Although it still contained only one family, that of Anderson West, the county sheriff, a few signs of advance were not long in appearing. In June, 1822, the first church in Marion, the Siloam Baptist, was established, and a second family, that of a woman named Mrs. Ann Smith, moved to

[12]Ibid., A, 62, 67-68; Marion Standard, February 12, 1909; Townes, History of Marion, 11.

[13]Marion Standard, February 12, 1909; Townes, History of Marion, 16.

Marion, and opened its first tavern or "hotel." In the same year two other taverns were opened.[14]

Now that Marion had been made county seat, a courthouse was needed. In 1823 a "two story framed building, thirty six feet in length" was erected. It "was a peculiar looking building, having the appearance of a smoke house with windows," and sat on wooden blocks three feet high. A jail, "a double pen cabin of hewn logs, covered with boards," was also put together.[15] In 1823 a lawyer opened an office in Marion. Cotton was definitely replacing corn as the chief crop in parts of Perry County. A second private residence was erected in the county seat, and the three stores in the place, with goods for sale to the amount of approximately $2,000, continued to operate. Direct commercial contact between Marion and Mobile, the trade center of Alabama, was made, with goods being brought by pole boats up the Alabama River from Mobile to Cahaba, the state capital, thence being hauled overland to Marion.

The increasing population of Perry County is also illustrated by the number of licenses for the sale of drinks issued by the county government in 1823, when eleven such permits were issued to "retail Wines and Spirits by the Small measure" in the county. Several "houses of entertainment," that is, barrooms, were also opened. One of these so-called "dram shops," whose owner took for himself the interesting motto of "Dum Vivimus, Vivimus," was set up in Marion.[16] By February, 1824, enough interest existed among the people of the vicinity to extend the boundaries of the town. Town lots were once more offered at auction and $1,784.62 was realized from the sales. If the prices received for the individual lots on this occasion were about the same as the prices obtained in 1822, it may be assumed that the limits of the town were now approximately doubled.[17]

Some noteworthy cultural developments took place in the region

[14]Marion Standard, February 12, 19, March 5, 1909; Townes, History of Marion, 11-15.

[15]The courthouse built in 1823 was used until 1832, when a brick structure was erected. Marion Standard, March 26, 1909; Townes, History of Marion, 21.

[16]Marion Standard, February 19, March 12, 26, April 2, 1909; Perry County, Alabama, Orphan's Court Register, A, 43-44; Perry County, Alabama, Orphan's Court Minutes, July, 1821-June, 1832, p. 20.

[17]Ibid.

at this period. In October, 1824, a school was begun near Marion, and in the next year one was started in the town itself. The town school very naturally began in a small way, and during its first year the school's patrons consisted of five Marion families, three near the village, and one near old Perry Ridge. The procedure followed in instruction was of the customary type for such primitive enterprises. Books in use were the New Testament, the American Reader, Murray's Grammar, Smiley's Arithmetic, and Webster's Spelling Book. Spelling was the principal course, and only one study at a time was the rule. Not until the pupils had learned to spell proficiently were they allowed to advance to the use of even a slate and a copy book. Geography was an advanced course and was taught "round or flat," according to the wishes of the pupils' parents. Teachers had to be able to sing because in teaching geography "the master formed his school in line, and marching either inside or outside of the house, beating time with his switch, he sang the states, capitals, and rivers, to some tune improvised by himself." Multiplication tables were also taught in this manner.[18]

The teacher in early Marion had his "Articles" and his "Rules," the former of which had to be approved by his patrons, while the latter was established for the purpose of governing his pupils. The "Rules" were read each Monday morning, and in nearly every case an infraction of a rule resulted in a whipping. In retaliation for such strictness the pupils, not yet far removed from a frontier conception of fun making, usually contrived to duck their teacher in a creek or a pond at least twice a year. If the pupils failed to execute this ritual, their parents, the patrons of the school, "assembled some Friday evening to lend a helping hand." The pupils and patrons in and near Marion enjoyed this sporting event so much that they continued to indulge in it as late as 1840 and perhaps even later. One contemporary's account of the custom contains the following description: "In 1840, a teacher not far from Marion was ducked by the patrons of the school until nearly drowned. He was carried to a deep hole in a creek and pitched in, and as fast as he crawled out, was thrown in again." A statement from the same source explains partially the reason for such a prank. It was recorded that "the founders of these institutions ate hog

---

[18]Marion *Standard*, March 5, April 2, 1909.

potatoes and bull nettles; cleared and ditched land; built log cabins;
. . . made and drove wagons; owned jacks; moulded bricks; peddled
chickens and tin; and rode neck-tailed horses."[19]

Frontier characteristics such as these were difficult to change,
but some economic and social advances soon became evident in
the region around Marion. In 1825 a new and better jail house
was constructed. The first public roads to Marion were opened,
one entering the town from "Burroughs Ferry" on the Cahaba River,
the other from Indian Old Town, where it connected with a road
to Centerville; and in 1826 the sum of $671 was spent on roads and
other transportation improvements in Perry County. Two more
stores were opened in Marion, and more business naturally developed there as a result.[20] However, a housewarming held in Marion
in the early part of 1827 indicates that many social graces had to
be acquired before the region could claim it had reached a high
degree of social attainment. The occasion was the opening of the
first frame house in Marion, and possibly the first house of that
type to be erected in the county. Twenty-five people were present
for that affair. The housewarming opened with a "stag dance," in
which all the young men present cavorted about, with "not much
regard for steps—every man for himself." The procedure was followed because the young blades, so says a contemporary, "possessed
such an excess of agility, that a breakdown was needed to render
them sufficiently graceful to be partners for the ladies." After some
dancing the guests turned to the table where "Wine, whiskey,
brandy, and eggnog composed the drinkable, while the tables were
filled with every procurable luxury." Altogether five gallons of
eggnog were consumed. The guests danced until day break.[21]

By 1826 Marion's population, including Negroes, had increased
to only 144. But in the course of the year this number increased
appreciably, particularly because the capital of Alabama was moved
at this time from the nearby Dallas County town of Cahaba to
the town of Tuscaloosa. When the governmental offices left Cahaba
some of the residents there moved to Marion and to other com-

---

[19]*Ibid.*, April 23, 1909.
[20]*Ibid.*, March 19, April 23, 1909; Perry County, Alabama, Orphan's Court
Register, A, 102, 131.
[21]Marion *Standard*, March 12, 26, April 23, 1909.

munities in central Alabama. There was still nothing resembling a boom in Marion,[22] but during the next year several noteworthy changes occurred in the little black belt community. A cabinet shop and a tan yard were opened, and soon both developed thriving businesses among the farmers of the county; the town limits were again extended; and two additional ministers, one a Presbyterian from Kentucky, were licensed to preach. However, the little place could not yet claim any special significance, for as an early settler has written, "indeed until the year 1828 it had the appearance of a private gentleman's country residence." One cause of the town's slow growth was the uncertainty of its permanence as the county seat. Before the year 1828 the State Legislature, by a mere majority vote, could change sites of county government in the state whenever it desired. But in 1828 a law passed which provided that in the future neither the boundaries of a county nor the county seat could be changed except by a two-thirds vote of the State Legislature. The result of this law, as far as Marion was concerned, was to encourage settlement. There was a noticeable and immediate increase in the county seat's growth, and "stores and shops began to multiply, and the little village assumed all the bustle and importance of a thriving town."[23]

Within a few months another minister was licensed to preach in the county; a second physician moved to Marion and opened an office there; and in order to handle the increased traffic in the region the first road in Perry County with a width of thirty feet was constructed, whereas formerly the best roads had been only twenty feet in width. But despite these advances, and of others such as the arrival of two more ministers, of a tinsmith, and the construction of another saw mill, Marion was still not much to behold in the year 1830. Even the person who had earlier described it as having "the importance of a thriving town" pictured it in 1830 as merely a "delapidated [sic] Sleepy town, with dingy

---

[22]Ibid., March 19, 1909; Townes, History of Marion, 22; Anna M. Gayle Fry, Memories of Old Cahaba (Nashville, 1905), 14.

[23]Townes, History of Marion, 23. See also Marion Standard, March 19, April 9, 1909; Perry County, Alabama, Orphan's Court Minutes, July, 1821-June, 1832, pp. 103, 105; Perry County, Alabama, Record Book, February, 1820-October, 1840, p. 268.

houses."[24] No newspaper was yet published in Marion, although newspapers had been in print in Cahaba and Greensboro, nearby towns, as early as 1826 and 1827. Tree stumps had been only partially removed from the town streets, and the business group amounted to only three tavern keepers, one bar owner, three merchants, three physicians, four lawyers, one carpenter, one cabinet maker, one tailor, and one Negro blacksmith. At this period, nevertheless, perhaps in anticipation of early growth, the town limits were extended two more times. In March, 1830, town lots to the amount of $1,546 were purchased at public auction; and in October, 1831, lots valued at $581 were sold.[25]

Regardless of the progress made by the people living in and near Marion during the 1820's, their region was still backward in comparison with certain other parts of the state. Alabama had become an important agricultural state, but Marion was not yet of any particular importance economically or socially. Between 1820 and 1830, the state's population jumped from slightly more than 125,000 to about 300,000. Although the slaves in Alabama in 1830 made up thirty-eight per cent of the population, and were shortly to assume more importance in the black belt, they had not arrived in large numbers in Perry County before 1830. In that year they were still centered to a great extent in regions other than the black belt. According to the best authority, the reason for the absence of large numbers of Negroes in the black belt before the 1830's was the inability of planters to overcome the difficulties in cultivating the sticky soil of the region.[26] South Alabama, of which Perry County was later considered a part, had become the leading cotton producing section of the state, and the river valleys, converging on Mobile, had established themselves as the chief cotton growing areas of the state.[27] Mobile itself had already attracted

---

[24]Marion *Standard*, March 26, 1909. See also Perry County, Alabama, Orphan's Court Minutes, July, 1821-June, 1832, pp. 58, 88, 107; Perry County, Alabama, Record Book, February, 1820-October, 1840, pp. 1-152, 155.

[25]Marion *Standard*, April 9, 1909; Perry County, Alabama, Record Book, February, 1820-October, 1840, p. 268.

[26]Abernethy, *The Formative Period in Alabama*, 57-58.

[27]For a reference to the amount of cotton produced in South Alabama and shipped to Mobile during the 1820's, see footnote 33, Chapter One, above.

attention as a cotton market and port, and by 1830 had a population of 3,194.[28]

It was particularly during the 1830's that Marion and Perry County arrived at a place of importance. Interest in the construction of county roads continued, and by 1832 it was necessary to appoint a total of 53 overseers whose duty it was to keep roads in their districts in good repair. Of particular local importance was the adoption by county officials, in February, 1832, of plans for the construction of a new courthouse in Marion. The building was to be erected at a cost of $5,000, and was to be completed two years after the contract was let. In March a contractor and superintendent of construction were selected, and in May the sum of $900 was advanced by the county to the contractor in order that he might begin work. Before completion, however, the new building cost the county $9,356.[29] The expenditure of such a sum is evidence enough of the economic advance of the region, particularly when it is remembered that the original courthouse, built eleven years earlier, had been a framebuilding "having the appearance of a smoke house with windows." Another sign of increased activity was the establishment, in 1832, of a second tan yard in Marion.[30]

Two churches were organized in the village in 1832. In the previous year, subscriptions for the establishment of a Presbyterian church were collected, and on July 30, 1832, the church began its operations.[31] At about the same time the Perry County Court also ordered "that the Methodist Episcopal denomination of Christians be permitted to erect a Church on the South West Corner of the four acre lot Reserved in the town of Marion for Churches."[32] One important characteristic of the founders of these churches was that they were still not far removed from a typical frontier outlook, although many of them had settled down and become farmers. Their dress seems noteworthy. They are not supposed to have been

[28]See Chapter One, above, for a discussion of Mobile's growth.

[29]Perry County, Alabama, Record Book, February, 1820-October, 1840, pp. 240-247, 255, 259, 260, 280, 294, 295, 304, 320, 328, 341, 378.

[30]Perry County, Alabama, Orphan's Court Minutes, B, 71.

[31]The Marion Presbyterian Church increased its membership to 225 in the year 1843. Marion Standard, April 16, 1909.

[32]Perry County, Alabama, Record Book, February, 1820-October, 1840, p. 266.

much concerned about the style of their clothing; and at such social gatherings as church functions and funerals, their customary outfit consisted of brown jeans, jacket, and pants, all homemade. One account indicates that at a Baptist meeting in 1832, near Marion, there were only "three citizens who wore broad cloth, and one who owned a buggy."[33]

However, in the early 1830's there occurred some events which changed the life of the people in and near Marion, namely, the final realization that the soil of the adjacent black belt was extraordinarily adaptable for the cultivation of cotton, especially of an upland, blight-proof variety of the staple which was introduced into the region. By the year 1834, moreover, the planters of the black belt solved their water supply problem by boring wells, sometimes to a depth of 600 feet.[34] Farmers and planters in Perry County and other counties of central Alabama now learned that the sticky, messy black belt soil and the reputedly unhealthy area where it was located could be turned to their advantage.[35] Cotton production became their chief interest, and they played a major role in Alabama's rise to the position of the foremost cotton producing state in the South in 1850. Furthermore, with this absorbing interest and activity came many new customs, great wealth, a highly developed social order, many new social problems, all-out support of the institution of slavery, and finally, in an effort to maintain the social and economic system which resulted from cotton culture with slave labor, a willingness to enter the Civil War. It is the considered opinion of the great majority of historians that Southerners developed a way of life that was quite different from that of other Americans and that this way of life was based to some extent on the agricultural practices as typified by the black belt.

There is an interesting local tradition concerning the manner in which the farmers and planters of the Marion vicinity became

---

[33]Marion *Standard,* April 9, 1909.

[34]*Farmer's Register,* II, 630-631 (1835), contains a letter dated December 20, 1834, by its editor, Edmund Ruffin, describing the "Bored Wells of Alabama."

[35]See *ibid.,* II, 276 (1833), for a statement by "H" of Mobile, who wrote: "The fine rich Prairie soil [in Alabama] is calcareous manure itself. . . . The fact is, that the Prairies have proven to be the healthiest parts of the State— . . . [and] strongly corroborates your [Edmund Ruffin's] views regarding the healthy action of calcareous earths on putrescent matter, ..."

convinced that the black belt could be farmed. Not only had they previously been dubious of the fertility of the region, but because of the extremely muddy condition of the top soil following rainy weather they believed the region to be unhealthy and fever ridden. In addition, the low-hanging mists which are often noticeable over parts of the black belt were designated as "swamp gas" or "miasma" and were believed to cause fevers. In the early 1830's, in order to check on these beliefs, it is said that a number of farmers purchased a Negro slave, constructed a small hut in the black belt near Marion, put in a store of supplies for the Negro, gave him some tools, and left him to live or die. After some time when the owners rode out to the slave's hut and found him fat and healthy and working a patch of vegetables, they became convinced that the region was inhabitable. It is impossible to check precisely on the truthfulness of this story. However, immediately after it supposedly happened, numerous cotton plantations were opened in the area, and Marion at last indeed became a thriving trade center.

Evidence of the boom is the amount of black belt land taken up in the county. As it happens, there are only five territorial subdivisions of Perry County which are completely within the black belt.[36] They contain a total of 180 irregular sections, comprising 112,565½ acres, most of which was purchased after 1830, thus indicating that it was after this date that the people in Perry County showed enough interest in black belt soil to buy it. In 1819 only 5,497 and a fraction acres were bought. The state reserved five sections, about 3,000 acres, for educational purposes. From 1820 to 1829, inclusive, only 11,921 acres were purchased; whereas of the 112,565½ acres in the above mentioned five subdivisions, the amazing total of 91,394 acres was entered from 1830 through 1835. In 1830 alone the amount entered at the land office was 31,128 acres. Following the year 1835 the rest of the black belt soil was bought intermittently until 1852, when all of the land except the few acres still owned by the state was privately owned.[37]

---

[36]These subdivisions are: township 18, north, ranges 6, 7, 8, east; township 17, north, range 6, east; and township 16, north, range 6, east.

[37]Perry County, Alabama, Tract Book, 1-36, 97-108, 151-162. A total of 5,782 acres was bought in 1820; 630 in 1821; 958 in 1822; none in 1823; 771 in 1824; 80 in 1825; 478 in 1826; 478 in 1827; 849 in 1828; and 1,891 in 1829. Other entries amounted to: 11,304 acres in 1831; 14,711, 1832; 9,212, 1833;

Some of the results of the final appreciation of Perry County black belt soil in the early 1830's is described in a statement accredited to an unknown settler of the period: "I came to Perry County in 1832 with Anderson West, who was speculating in Negroes, and brought a drove with him at the time. Passing through the Creek Indians, we camped at Mt. Meigs, east of Montgomery. Farmers were picking cotton and clearing land, — axes were cutting until midnight, and an hour before day next morning. Camped near Marion Saturday night. Negroes were cutting timber all night until sunrise Sunday. Marion was thronged with people on Sunday, talking about cotton and 'niggers.' Every man we met, either wanted to buy a 'nigger' or 'take a drink.' "[38] George W. Featherstonhaugh, an Englishman traveling from Montgomery through western Georgia in January, 1835, wrote: "In the course of the day we met a great many families of planters emigrating to Alabama and Mississippi to take up cotton plantations, ... We passed at least 1,000 negro slaves all trudging on foot, ..." A few days later the Englishman added, "At one time of the day we certainly passed 1,200 people, black and white on foot."[39]

Great changes indeed took place in the economic and social life of Marion and the black belt from the 1830's to the Civil War.[40] As a whole, the state prospered immensely because of the cotton economy developing during those years; population increased enormously; Indians were removed from the state; important towns sprang up; and transportation facilities, mainly for the purpose of moving cotton and agricultural supplies, were augmented. Marion was among the towns to benefit particularly from the new interests, and after the year 1857 was a terminus of the Cahaba and Marion Railroad. Perry County was in the middle of the

---

13,379, 1834; 11,657, 1835; 1,151, 1836; 199, 1837; none in 1838 and 1839; 40, 1840; 40, 1841; none in 1842 and 1843; 40, 1844; 280, 1845; 39, 1846; 919, 1847; 161, 1848; 359, 1849; 80, 1850; none in 1851; and 80 in 1852. *Ibid.*

[38]Marion *Standard*, April 9, 1909. For other glowing accounts of Alabama soils and emigration to the state, see *Farmer's Register*, II, 327 (1834), and *Niles' Weekly Register*, XLVI, 117 (April 19, 1834).

[39]Walter Brownlow Posey, ed. "Alabama in the 1830's as Recorded by British Travellers," *Birmingham-Southern College Bulletin*, XXXI, 29-30 (Birmingham, 1938).

[40]See Clanton W. Williams, "Early Ante-Bellum Montgomery: A Black Belt Constituency," *Journal of Southern History*, VII, 495-525 (1941).

cotton country, and Marion became a local trade center for some of the largest planters in Alabama. Except for the nation-wide Panic of 1837 and for a period of low cotton prices in the middle 1840's,[41] good times continued until 1861. Marion became a place of extensive legal transactions resulting from an almost unending purchase and sale of land and slaves. The little town also was the site of numerous palatial homes of planters who chose to live there while operating their land holdings in the surrounding region. Some of these homes are still in use.

Some of the interests and activities of the people in and near Marion were of the kind which could have developed only in a region making impressive cultural advance. Crudeness in many respects was admittedly present, but as was usually the case in regions passing from a somewhat frontier outlook, a cultural conflict existed between those people little interested in enlightenment and those striving for a society fashioned after that of the more settled areas to the east. By 1834, however, Marion was the terminus of at least two stage coach lines. Many new bridges and other transportation contrivances were constructed in Perry County. Contact with towns located along the Alabama River system was well established, with most local commercial transactions being with Selma, in Dallas County, with Cahaba, and with Mobile. The Marion people had access to information of all sorts from the outside, and although the town itself had no local newspapers until 1839 its citizens subscribed to numerous newspapers and other publications printed elsewhere. Among the state newspapers being read in 1834 were the Cahaba *Alabama Republican,* the Selma *Free Press,* and the *States Rights Exposition* and the *Spirit of the Age* of Tuscaloosa. Many out-of-state publications, particularly farm journals, were in circulation. Temperance speakers, preachers, side-shows, caravans of animals, and musicians also added to the pleasures of the citizens.[42]

---

[41]Specific information on the economy of the Alabama black belt in the years before the Civil War may be found in Davis, *The Cotton Kingdom in Alabama*; Weymouth T. Jordan, *Hugh Davis and His Alabama Plantation* (Tuscaloosa, 1948); and James B. Sellars, *Slavery in Alabama* (Tuscaloosa, 1950).

[42]Perry County, Alabama, Orphan's Court Minutes, July, 1821-June, 1832, p. 279; *ibid.,* B, July, 1832-March, 1838, pp. 40, 72, 139; Perry County, Alabama, Record Book, 366; Perry County, Alabama, Commissioners' Court Minutes, A, January, 1841-July, 1851, p. 13.

Among the most interesting cultural accomplishments of early Marion was the establishment and maintenance of three schools of higher learning. Except for a few private establishments, no important schools existed in the town in 1832, but within ten years the people boasted of three colleges, two for women, one for men. The first to open its doors was the Marion Female Seminary, a Methodist school organized in 1836. Its founders were Andrew Barry Moore, afterwards governor of Alabama; John D. Phelan, a local lawyer and later a judge; Leonard A. Weissinger, a successful Marion merchant; Mark A. Wyatt, another merchant; and William Albert Jones, an outstanding planter of Perry and Dallas Counties. The school never had a large enrollment, but managed to continue to operate as late as the year 1918. The other school for women was the Judson Female Institute, which afterwards became a Baptist institution and in 1904 had its name changed to Judson College. It was founded in 1838, is one of the oldest woman's colleges in America, and still functions in Marion. The third school to be established was Howard College for men, which began in 1842 and continued to operate in Marion until 1887-1888, when it was moved to Birmingham, Alabama, where it is at present. Associated with the early Marion colleges were many of the leading families of Alabama, economically, socially, and politically.[43]

By 1842, with its three schools, Marion was one of the leading educational centers of the state. Judson Institute, for example, prospered during the pre-Civil War period, having 142 students in 1850 and 234 in 1859. These students received training from primary to college work. One *Catalogue* states, "For the Greek language and Higher Mathematics, the Course of Study in the Judson substitutes the Latin or the French Language, English literature, Belles Lettres, Aesthetics, Music, Hygiene, the Science of Domestic Economy, etc."[44] Referring to the Judson student, this same *Catalogue* continues: "her soul is imbued with love of the beautiful, the true and the pure; she becomes prepared to be a

---

[43]Townes, *History of Marion*, 15, 52, 60; Louise Manly, *History of Judson College* (Atlanta, 1899), 9; *Howard College Bulletin*, XCVIII, 22 (Birmingham, 1940); and William A. Jones Papers (in possession of Miss Emma Jones and Mrs. Mary J. Lowrey, Perry County, Alabama).

[44]*Catalogue of the Trustees, Instructors and Students of the Judson Female Institute* (Marion, 1855), 17.

WOMAN—a woman, fitted for the practical duties of life; fitted, wisely and beautifully to fill and adorn her own appropriate sphere in society."[45] There is no doubt that the presence of Judson and the other two colleges helped bring about a social advance as important as that which cotton culture brought in the field of economics. Teachers from various sections of the United States, and even from Europe, moved to Marion and took with them new ideas and conceptions. Many novel social customs were introduced, and the teachers and the schools were certainly partially responsible for speeding up the general cultural growth of the town and region. With three colleges in the neighborhood, Perry County residents could without difficulty attend numerous functions such as public receptions, speeches, and concerts. In this connection, a Marion matron in 1847 wrote to her husband, a local merchant who at the time was in New York City buying goods for his mercantile establishment: "The Judson concert came off on last Thursday evening and was very well attended as the Judson concerts always are. . . ."[46]

Meanwhile, many noticeable physical improvements occurred in Marion. By 1844 the town comprised one square mile and a population of 1,500. Numerous new business concerns had been organized, and in 1844 a resident described them as follows: "We have eight dry goods stores, which all together sell annually, say $180,000, according to the estimate of one of our intelligent merchants. Marion has also two groceries—not dram shops—two confectionaries; two drug stores, two shoe makers' shops, one tin ware manufactory, two saddlers shops, two livery stables, three blacksmiths' shops, four tailors' shops, two carriage makers, one gin factory, two cabinet work shops, two printing offices—the Marion Telegraph office . . . and the Herald office . . . and the Independent Order of Odd Fellows, have opened a lodge. . . ." Already the Masonic Order was in operation. Professional men in the town were listed as "9 Preachers, 6 Doctors of Medicine, M. D., 3 Botanic or Steam Doctors, 15 Lawyers, 2 Resident Surgeon Dentists, 1 Barber."[47]

---

[45]*Ibid.*, 17-18. See also A. Elizabeth Taylor, ed., "Regulations Governing Life at the Judson Female Institute during the Decade Preceding the Civil War," *Alabama Historical Quarterly*, III, 23-29 (1941).

[46]Mary A. Fowlkes to Samuel H. Fowlkes, March 1, 1847, in Samuel H. Fowlkes Papers (in possession of Edward Lee, Perry County, Alabama).

[47]Townes, *History of Marion*, 30, 33-34.

In 1837 the Baptists erected a particularly elaborate edifice costing $7,000, "one of the most elegant and tasty houses of worship in the State." Church memberships in Marion in 1844 were Baptist, 375; Presbyterian, 213; Methodist, 78, and Campbellites, 15. An Episcopal Church was also in operation; and in 1844 even the Latter Day Saints claimed a small membership in Marion.[48] A temperance society in town, in keeping with the general drive against drink in the South in the 1840's, had about 500 members, although two taverns were in operation. In an effort to curb drinking, however, the city authorities passed an ordinance establishing a tax of $1,000 on retailers of whiskey. Preliminary arrangements were made for the founding of a poor house in the county, but it was not until January, 1852, that county officials got around to the appointment of a committee to purchase land on which to construct a poor house building. By the year 1844, Whig and Democratic discussion groups were organized, and at their meetings were talking about the expediency of a national bank, the European Quadruple and Holy Alliances, "and other such small matters."[49]

Marion was indeed very much alive during the middle 1840's. It was the county seat; its merchants handled a portion of the business of planters and farmers of Perry County; it served as a distributing point for goods from Mobile and as a point from which cotton and other agricultural produce were shipped to Mobile; and it was a social and cultural center for the people of the county in which it was situated. Marion had become a typical black belt town of Alabama. In 1846, when Montgomery was named the permanent capital of the state, Marion was important enough to be considered as one of Montgomery's rivals for the honor. As concluded by one historian, "Certainly the removal of the capital to Montgomery [from Tuscaloosa] signified the emergence of the Black Belt as the dominant section in the economic and political affairs of Alabama."[50] And Marion was an integral part of the black belt.

---

[48]*Ibid.*, 26, 31-33. On deposit in the Office of Probate Court, Marion, Alabama, is a Mormon Bible, containing an affidavit under the date of "1844" which grants permission to the Latter Day Saints to practice their religion in Perry County.

[49]Townes, *History of Marion*, 26.

[50]Malcolm Cook McMillan, "The Selection of Montgomery as Alabama's Capital," *Alabama Review*, I, 90 (1948).

III

A BLACK BELT PLANTER FAMILY

Among the earliest settlers of Perry County was Elisha F. King who, like so many of his contemporaries, moved from Georgia in 1819 in order to take up cheap land which became available shortly after Alabama attained statehood.[1] He immediately began to enter land in the county and eventually was one of the largest holders of land and slaves in the state. In his rise from the position of an obscure settler to a place of financial and social prominence, he was typical of the more intrepid persons who aided so materially in developing Alabama into one of the leading cotton-producing states in the South.[2] Thus, an account of the methods by which he and his family obtained their property, the general procedures they followed in operating their plantations, and their business interests all furnish some insight to the economic activities of the large planter class of the Old South.

At the time King reached Perry County, the agricultural regions of Alabama recognized as the most desirable were the bend of the Tennessee River in North Alabama and the river valleys of South Alabama. These areas, as already mentioned, were the most densely populated in the state, and it was presumably for this reason that King decided to settle in central Alabama, where there was available a greater abundance of cheap land. In his purchases of land he demonstrated the usual insatiable desire for its possession which was characteristic of the enterprising men of his type who settled in the Lower South during the early years of the nineteenth century. Beginning with 1,028 acres originally entered in the year 1820, he left 7,995 acres to his heirs in the year 1852. During the 1830's he was particularly active in acquiring land, and in only

---

[1]This chapter appeared in its first printed version as "The Elisha F. King Family, Planters of the Alabama Black Belt," *Agricultural History*, XIX, 152-162 (1945), and appears here with the permission of Everett E. Edwards, late editor of *Agricultural History*.

[2]Elisha F. King was the son of Wooly King. Family Bible of Rhoda B. King Family(in possession of Mrs. Thad Davis, Sr., Marion, Alabama); Owen, *History of Alabama and Dictionary of Alabama Biography*, III, 980; Townes, *History of Marion*, 52, 60; Elisha F. King Papers (in possession of Miss Clara Barker, Marion, Alabama).

one year after the year 1820 did he fail either to maintain or increase his acreage.[3]

Grain crops were the staples of Alabama when King arrived there, with corn being the chief crop in Perry County. However, even before his arrival, some cotton was being produced in the area, for in 1817, as referred to previously, at least one cotton gin was in operation.[4] During the 1820's cotton gradually replaced corn as the chief staple in the pine lands of the county; and when, during the 1830's, cotton production became highly profitable in the black belt, planters and small farmers began a race for possession of the land, taking up, as has been seen, over 90,000 acres in the black belt of Perry County. Also, as already mentioned, Mobile became a leading cotton port in the 1830's. In October, 1835, for example, it was reported from the metropolis that the previous cotton season was one of much prosperity, a local trade publication stating: "The planters have had good crops and high prices. . . . The business of the city has kept equal pace with the resources of the interior. Our population has increased at least one fourth, and still is increasing, . . . [and] rents have nearly doubled. Although very early, there are abundant signs of a prosperous and active business . . . . The number of strangers is already great."[5]

But this was only a beginning of the cotton boom. Production in South Alabama continued up and up, rising from 102,684 bales in 1830 to 445,725 in 1840.[6] In May, 1840, when Mobile had a population of nearly 13,000, the place was described as "a city of Cotton. It is to be found in the quay, warehouses, sidewalks, everywhere. They have recd upwards of 400,000 bales there this season & will probably reach half a million. There is more on hand

[3]Perry County, Alabama, Tract Book, 48, 97, 119, 152, 153, 154, 173, 187; Perry County, Alabama, Deed Record, B, 35, 43, 135, 205, 206, 561, 562, 615, 645, 729, 800; *ibid.,* C, 76; *ibid.,* D, 182; *ibid.,* E, 19, 309, 547; *ibid.,* F, 423, 596; *ibid.,* H, 325, 441, 442, 477; *ibid.,* I, 4, 430; *ibid.,* K, 423, 554. King paid $39,275 for 5,404 of his acres. These and other county records cited in this chapter are on deposit in the Office of the Probate Court, Perry County Court House, Marion.

[4]Marion *Standard,* April 2, 1909.

[5]*Mobile Shipping and Commercial List,* October 3, 1835. See also Perry County, Alabama, Tract Book, 1-16, 97-109, 151-162.

[6]*Mobile Shipping and Commercial List,* October 3, 1835; *Mobile Register Shipping List and Prices-Current,* December 7, 1839; *Mobile Journal of Commerce Letter-Sheet Price-Current,* September 1, 1851.

now than any preceding year at this season. . . . Mobile has abt 15,000 inhabitants in Winter. . . ."[7] In the ten-year period, 1841 to 1851, South Alabama cotton output amounted to 4,571,061 bales, and Mobile, drawing its cotton trade from South Alabama and parts of Florida and Mississippi, exported 4,230,730 bales during that period.[8] In September, 1851, which happened to be just a few months before Elisha F. King's death, another glowing report came out of Mobile: "The number of buildings completed is greater than any preceding year, and still, so great is the demand for them, rents are advancing. Public buildings are now under contract in the city, the estimated cost of which is over half a million dollars. Nine new steamboats are also building for the Mobile trade the coming year. Much of this city activity is doubtless owing to the increase in the receipts of cotton at this port of over 100,000 bales [in 1851 over 1850], and to the uninterrupted health which has uniformily prevailed."[9]

While Alabama was so spectacularly increasing its cultivation of cotton and Mobile was attaining its eminent position as a port, Elisha F. King continued to buy more land and more slaves. But he was not a land speculator in the sense of buying land, holding it for a rise in value, and then selling it at a profit. He bought land to raise cotton and other produce, and throughout his residence in Alabama (1819-1852) he sold only 250 acres. He issued dozens of due bills and drafts in payment of land and of accounts incurred in the operation of his plantations, usually to be paid with expected profits from the sale of cotton not yet produced. Most of his accounts current were paid in this manner, for it was the system of credit by which he and his contemporaries operated.[10] During the 1830's and 1840's, he extended his credit by thousands of dollars, paying cash for only a very few slaves and acres of land. This business practice, based upon the unpredictable and fluctuating price of cotton not yet made, was a chief factor in the failure of some cotton planters, but in King's case it worked advantageously.

---

[7]Willis, "A Southern Traveler's Diary in 1840," *loc. cit.*, 136-137.

[8]See footnote 6, above, and *DeBow's Review*, XII, 166 (1852), XXII, 488 (1857), XXVIII, 666 (1860).

[9]*Mobile Journal of Commerce Letter-Sheet Price-Current*, September 1, 1851.

[10]See, for example, Jordan, *Hugh Davis and His Alabama Plantation*, 77-78, 79, 114, 119, 120, 137, 141, 145, 166-168.

At his death, in addition to nearly 8,000 acres of farm land, he owned 186 slaves and a large number of town lots in Marion, Alabama. His property, other than farm lands and slaves, was valued at $106,202.[11]

At least as early as 1846, King was operating four plantations. His "home place" consisted of about 2,500 acres; another plantation, known as the "Rich place," was also under his management; a so-called "lower place" was conducted by his son, Edwin W.;[12] and the fourth plantation, on which 35 slaves and 10 hired hands usually worked, was located near Centerville, in Bibb County, Alabama. Overseers were hired to manage the work of the slaves at the various places, and at least once a week either Elisha F. or his son rode to the plantation not under their immediate direction in order to check on operations. Both father and son lived on the home place, near the little settlement of Hamburg, about ten miles from Marion, and from there distributed to their other plantations such supplies as foodstuffs, clothing, farm implements, and many other necessities. Slaves resided at the several plantations to conduct the necessary work, but whenever a labor shortage developed at one of the plantations or it was imperative to get out a crop without delay, they were shifted temporarily to take up the slack wherever it existed.[13] In nearly every sense of the word, Elisha F. King was a "big businessman," with problems of capital investment, credit, labor management, production, and distribution of produce.

In obtaining slaves, King followed the same procedure as in the acquisition of land. He extended his credit in almost every purchase. A single example of this practice seems sufficient to indicate a typically southern method in purchasing slaves. In April, 1840, he bought 27 Negroes from the Marion firm of King, Upson

---

[11]Elisha F. King Papers; Perry County, Alabama, Inventory of Estates, E, 553-558; Perry County, Alabama, Will Book, 278-282.

[12]Edwin W. King was born on November 28, 1813, in Georgia. For a time he was a student at the Georgia Athens College, Athens, after which he aided his father in operating the family plantations and other business enterprises. Family Bible of Rhoda B. King Family; Edwin W. King to Elisha F. King, May 4, 1829, in Elisha F. King Papers; and Edwin W. King Diary, May 23, 24, 1846 (in possession of Mrs. Leta B. Hart, Marion). The King Diary contains entries covering particularly the period from May, 1846, to May, 1860.

[13]Edwin W. King Diary, passim; Edwin W. King Papers (in possession of Miss Clara Barker, Marion).

and Company and signed ten notes in payment for the hands.[14] Each note provided that he "pay Edwin W. King or bearer twenty two thousand four hundred and Eighty three pounds merchantable gind and baled Cotton delivered in the port of Mobile for value recd this 16th April 1840." The notes were due on March 1 of each year from 1841 through 1845.[15] All slaves were of course not purchased with cotton, and King had extensive relations with neighboring planters and with slave traders who annually journeyed to the black belt. In his slave purchases, as in obtaining land on credit, King was very fortunate. According to his will, made in 1852, he bequeathed jointly 109 Negroes to his widow and son, 42 to one granddaughter, and 35 to another. Later in the year these slaves were valued at $113,703.[16]

Serving as agents for King and other planters in their purchases of land and slaves, as well as in nearly all financial transactions, were cotton factors, with headquarters at Mobile. The first available record of a money transaction between King and a factor was typical of one phase of his and other planters' relations with their agents. In September, 1828, he needed $2,700 for the purchase of some land, and he requested that his factor advance him the money. His agent, H. G. Holt of Mobile, immediately replied, "You can draw on us at sixty or ninety days sight" through the United States Bank at Mobile.[17] Holt continued to handle King's affairs until 1830, at which time the planter turned to a firm operated by James Taylor. Either in 1832 or the following year, his business was given to the firm of Alexander Pope and Sons, one of the largest cotton factorage houses in Alabama.[18] In 1836 his agent was the company of Lea and Langdon, the chief members of which had moved to Mobile from Perry County. During 1838 and 1839 his

---

[14]At this time, Edwin W. King was a member of King, Upson and Company, money for his investment in the Company's stock having been furnished, September, 1837, by his father. The firm was dissolved on April 29, 1840, at which time its accounts, to the amount of $55,539, were purchased by Napoleon Lockett, a Marion merchant. Elisha F. King Papers; Edwin W. King Papers; Perry County, Alabama, Deed Record, E, 364-371.

[15]These slaves were valued at the sum of $11,500. Elisha F. King Papers.

[16]Perry County, Alabama, Will Book, 278-282; Perry County, Alabama, Inventory of Estates, E, 553-558.

[17]H. G. Holt to Elisha F. King, September 8, 1828, in Elisha F. King Papers.

[18]Davis, *The Cotton Kingdom in Alabama*, 150.

factor was John R. Goree, to whom he gave his business because he wished to patronize a former neighbor and a kinsman. Goree had lived in Perry County and was King's grandson-in-law. In 1840, for some reason, King began selling his cotton and buying his supplies through the Mobile firm of Stringfellow and Hanna, the members of which also were from Perry County. During the later forties and until 1852, King's cotton sales and other business affairs were transacted by the firm of McDowell and Withers, one of the most active factorage houses in Mobile. Throughout the 1850's this firm handled the business of some of the largest planters in Perry County and, indeed, it seems to have become the most popular firm among the planters of the county.[19]

Black belt planters, including King, often complained of the changing conditions of the Mobile market. In answer to this dissatisfaction, which sometimes was intense, the factors of the city, on one occasion, tried to appease their clients' feelings as follows:

With regard to the Mobile market, we have to remark, that it is one of the most fluctuating in the United States; necessarily so from its peculiar situation. Our market is more or less acted upon by every change in the markets of New York, New Orleans and Havana, in such articles as are here made use of; and the surplus quantity of an article today may reduce its price—and its scarcity tomorrow advance it. Hence it often occurs that by the time a price current is published and received in the interior, many changes have occurred in the market—or the Planter may send his friends here with an order for goods, which from a sudden change in the market, is filled at prices above his expectation, which subjects his friends to undue censure. To obviate this, we would suggest to our friends the propriety of always limiting in price; or if they are to consider the order an unlimited one, to express it as such.[20]

Some Alabama planters took this advice, while others turned to factors and commission merchants in Savannah and in New Orleans, but most of them returned sooner or later to Mobile as the source of goods and credit. Many of the planters near Marion, Alabama, also traded with the country merchants in that little town. The common practice of the large mercantile houses in Mobile, such as McDowell, Withers and Company, was to send buyers to New York

---

[19]Among the clientele of McDowell and Withers in Perry County were such planters, all of them very successful, as Elisha F., Edwin D., and Edwin W. King, Hugh Davis, and William A., Thomas T., and Thaddeus Jones. Elisha F. King Papers, William A. Jones Papers; Hugh Davis Papers (in possession of Mrs. L. I. Davis, Perry County).

[20]*Commercial Report & Mobile Price-Current,* October 9, 1834, in William A. Jones Papers.

City,[21] and here, as in numerous ways, the Mobile houses had only the advantage of greater credit and business facilities over merchants of a little trade center such as Marion. For example, Samuel H. Fowlkes, a Marion merchant and local planter, is known to have gone to New York City in 1847 and each winter thereafter through the year 1856. While in New York he bought merchandise for his own store and supplies for his own plantation and for his friends. In his store in Marion, local planters could and did find many of the plantation supplies which were so necessary for the successful operation of their enterprises. One of the special features of the activities of a local merchant such as Fowlkes was the personal touch which he gave to his customers' wishes.[22]

Through his agents, mainly in Mobile, King bought such articles as cotton bagging, rope, twine, iron, tin, axes, tools, medicines, shoes, candles, nails, household furniture, dry goods, flour and other staples, books, and liquors. Information on prices of plantation supplies being of major importance to a planter, this was forwarded to him weekly through the columns of a *Price-Current*, published in Mobile. At least once a year, ordinarily in January or February, King made a leisurely business trip to Mobile to check over his accounts with his factors and to buy plantation supplies and other articles. While there he also usually managed to take in the sights, and was often accompanied by members of his family. Each year, too, he was visited at least three or four times by a representative of his factor.[23] It was in these days, as well as by talking over business problems and market conditions with his friends and neighbors, that he and other planters managed to keep abreast of prices of both plantation produce and supplies.[24] His business pace was a leisurely one; nonetheless, his business practices were quite effective.

King's factors made payments of his accounts current with firms in Mobile and elsewhere with which he conducted business.

---

[21]McDowell, Withers and Company to Edwin W. King, June 21, 1858, in Edwin W. King Papers.

[22]Samuel H. Fowlkes to Mary A. Fowlkes, February 23, 1847, February 22, 1854, February 26, 1856, February 22, 1866, in Samuel H. Fowlkes Papers.

[23]Elisha F. King Papers.

[24]See, for example, Wendell H. Stephenson, "Ante-Bellum New Orleans As an Agricultural Focus," *Agricultural History*, XV, 161-174 (1941).

For example, on November 1, 1843, he gave three due bills to each of thirteen merchants and other creditors. A due bill was made payable to each individual on March 1, 1845, 1846, and 1847. The total amount for the bills was $7,486. Later, in 1849, he gave to his creditors twenty-one such bills amounting to $9,993, all due on March 1, 1850. The bills were accepted by his factors when presented for payment, debited against King's account and later were deducted from the proceeds of his cotton when it was sold in Mobile. In most cases throughout his career the same factor who handled his due bills and paid for his supplies also sold his cotton.[25] When the factor advanced money for payment of due bills or drafts, King paid interest; if he left any money with the factor, the money drew interest in his behalf; and in either case the rate amounted to 2.5 percent. In most years, King managed to maintain a very favorable balance with his factor.[26]

The most important function of the Alabama factor was the sale of cotton shipped to him by the planters of the interior. Mobile was the natural outlet for the staple, and most sales in the state were concluded there. On occasion, however, especially during the 1830's, some Alabama planters sent cotton elsewhere, some even experimenting with shipping direct to England for sale. The firm of Alexander Pope and Sons was probably more active in this phase of the cotton trade than any other in Mobile. A letter of February 1, 1834, from this company to King shows that he was among those who attempted to increase profits by direct shipments to foreign markets:

We hand you the Weights of your Seventy Bales of Cotton and those of the 40 Bales belonging to Mr. E. W. King. They were Shipped on board the Plantina for Liverpool on the 1st instant and the following is the outline of our directions which you can direct us to alter in time if you do not approve of them. They were that the Cotton should be held on to, or the Sales delayed untill the dealers in the article in Liverpool should be fully informed as to the extent of the crop of the United States for the present Season or untill the 1st of August next unless they could previously sell so as to nett the owners here 14 or 15 Cents. . . .[27]

---

[25]Elisha F. King Papers, *passim.*

[26]*Ibid.* Other exceedingly successful Perry County planters of the pre-Civil War period, whose careers may be checked by an examination of the materials employed in the writing of this Chapter, were John T. Barron, L. Q. C. DeYampart, J. K. C. Pool, Sherod Sanders, and Daniel O. White.

[27]Elisha F. King Papers.

No record is available of the outcome of this venture. Likewise, it is not known if King ever shipped any cotton directly to Europe for sale after this experiment in 1834. There is also no evidence in his papers to show that, although the charges of factors were high, direct sale by planters returned more profit than through agents.[28]

Throughout his career, except in 1834 and possibly in 1835, King shipped his cotton by wagon or flatboat to the town of Cahaba, on the Alabama River, thence by water to Mobile, where the cotton was sold. After the shipments were received, all charges due for bill of lading, freight, weighing, drayage, wharfage, storage, mending, and river and fire insurance were debited against King by his factor. When the sale was completed, the factor submitted an account of the charges, the number of bales and pounds sold, price per pound and total price received, and deducted charges due as well as 2.5 percent commission, and reported the net proceeds credited to King's account. This information was forwarded on separate reports of individual sales, and on March 1 of each year, which was the end of the cotton season, an annual statement of sales was submitted. Interest at 2.5 percent was charged on all moneys expended by the factor in payments of King's accounts, and the balance due was noted.[29]

Some reports of King's cotton sales are not available, but complete sales reports of 1,438 bales handled by Mobile factors in fifteen of the years between 1829 and 1852 have been located. The 1,438 bales, weighing 660,833 pounds, brought gross receipts of $57,923, or an average of 8.07 cents per pound. Factors' commissions amounted to $1,448, all charges were $3,504, net proceeds were $54,418. Sales of an additional 1,060 bales in the same period, for which poundage, gross receipts, and charges are unknown, brought net proceeds of $45,869. These sales, of 2,498 bales completed in less than half of King's career as a planter, resulted in total net proceeds of $100,287. If the entire number of bales averaged the same weight, which was the intent of most planters,

---

[28]For an account of the efforts of southern cotton planters to control the sale of their crops during the 1850's, see Weymouth T. Jordan, "Cotton Planters' Conventions in the Old South," *Journal of Southern History,* XIX, 321-345 (1953).

[29]Elisha F. King Papers.

it may be assumed that King received approximately 8.86 cents per pound for his cotton. Such a price enabled him to raise cotton at a profit,[30] and was the chief basis of the wealth that he acquired. That he was indeed a successful businessman and a citizen is shown by an obituary notice about him that appeared in a Mobile publication in 1852: "Captain E. F. King, one of the oldest, most prominent and respectable citizens of Perry county, died at his residence, a few miles from Marion, on Tuesday last, the 11th inst. [May, 1852]. Capt. King had represented Perry several years in the State Legislature, at an early period of its history. — He moved to Perry among, almost the first settlers, and by his industry and sagacity amassed an ample fortune, while his many estimable traits of character secured for him, in an eminent degree, the respect and esteem of his fellow citizens. The death of such a man is a public calamity."[31]

In 1852 when Edwin W. King assumed management of his father's estate he became one of the wealthiest men in Alabama. Although Elisha F. King had had three children, only Edwin W. was alive in 1852. Edwin's important share of the estate, which he managed on behalf of his mother and himself until August, 1860, consisted of the home place and 109 slaves. He also operated the Rich place and the Bibb County plantation. The lower place, containing 1,934 acres, remained under his direction because it had been left to his daughter, Sarah Elizabeth, under his trust. Moreover, until another daughter, Margaret Clarissa, married in 1856, he also managed a place of 1,666 acres which she had inherited from Elisha F. King.[32] Despite all the work entailed in

---

[30]The figures included here have been compiled from hundreds of separate bills of sale which King received from his factors. *Ibid.* For the conclusion that a planter could hope to make profits if he received 8 cents per pound for his cotton, see Davis, *The Cotton Kingdom in Alabama*, 180, and Thomas P. Govan, "Was Plantation Slavery Profitable?" *Journal of Southern History*, VIII, 513-535 (1942).

[31]*Alabama Planter*, VI, 194 (1852). See also Family Bible of Rhoda B. King Family.

[32]Edwin W. King married Rhoda B. Langdon on July 25, 1833, she being a member of a prominent Marion family; and to them by the year 1852 were born five children. Edwin W.'s mother, the former Margaret Moore of Georgia, helped in managing the family plantations throughout the 1850's and until her death. Edwin W.'s daughter, Margaret Clarissa, was married, January 23, 1856, to William P. Holman, a physician who moved to Alabama from Missis-

running these plantations, Edwin W. King was almost as successful as his father.

By the year 1855 Edwin W. was the second largest slave owner in Perry County, being surpassed only by another local nabob named L. Q. C. De Yampart, who owned 245 Negroes. In three years, 1852 to 1855, King increased his number of slaves from 109 to 152.[33] Since he had inherited enough land, however, he added only 715 acres to his holdings. One of his land purchases is of special interest for the light it throws on the credit system that prevailed during his life. In 1859 he bought 560 acres of land from one W. L. Sanders, making the following entry in his diary: "I gave him [W. L. Sanders] a draft due 1 Jany next for Ten Thousand dollars & one for 4320$ due Jan 1861—I borrowed 5$ [from] Catlin [a Marion merchant] & paid Jno McCall 3.88"[34] Such a transaction was not at all strange for a man of King's position in his time and place. And it is worthy of note that in the same year he made the above transaction, 1859, he opened two new plantations, the so-called Mosely and Sanders places; thus, for more than a year, or until his death in 1860, King operated six plantations. Like many of his contemporary planters in the Alabama blackbelt, he was a very wealthy man, but on more than one occasion, he borrowed small sums of from three to ten dollars to pay certain debts.[35]

In other respects as well as agriculture, the younger King was

---

sippi. Reference should be made, also, to the fact that Elisha F. King's will provided that each of Edwin W.'s three young sons were to be paid the sum of $30,000 when they reached the age of twenty-one. Perry County, Alabama, Will Book, 278-282; Family Bible of Rhoda B. King Family; Edwin W. King Diary; William P. Holman Diary (in possession of Miss Clara Barker, Marion).

[33]Perry County, Alabama, Unpublished Census Returns, 1855 (Office of Probate Court, Perry County Court House, Marion). In 1855, eleven planters in Perry County owned more than 100 slaves; while 5 owned between 90 and 100; 11 between 80 and 90; 11 between 70 and 80; 15 between 60 and 70; 21 between 50 and 60; 35 between 40 and 50; 45 between 30 and 40; and 65 between 20 and 30. Altogether, 913 slave owners held 14,339 slaves. *Ibid.* In 1860, Perry County was one of the seven largest cotton-producing counties in Alabama. Davis, *The Cotton Kingdom in Alabama*, 199.

[34]Edwin W. King Diary, November 16, 1859. See also *ibid.*, December 1, 1856, November 16, 1859.

[35]*Ibid., passim.* Three daughters were born to Edwin W. and Rhoda B. King in the years from 1852 to 1860. Edwin W.'s will provided that his estate be held together for ten years after his death and then sold if so desired by

an active businessman. Until February, 1857, he owned the King House, a popular hotel in Marion,[36] and shortly before his death he subscribed $5,000, or 50 shares, in a bank in the same town.[37] His most extensive financial venture outside of his activities as a planter and slave owner, however, had to do with a railroad constructed between Marion and Cahaba. As early as February, 1848, there were 99 shareholders in the railroad company. Each share was valued at $100, and altogether $68,600 in stock was subscribed. The two largest stockholders at the time were Elisha F. King and his brother Edwin D., each with 50 shares.[38] It was, in fact, the Kings more than any others who made possible the construction of the railroad. Unfortunately for them, however, they were connected with the company at a time when it was burdened with construction costs, and they and the other stockholders lost money. On November 20, 1852, Edwin W. King, recorded in his diary that he had "subscribed four thousand dollars to the Railroad." For the next few years he was very active in the affairs of the enterprise, and his diary contains numerous notations of his attendance at meetings in Marion of the railroad's board of directors. In September, 1853, he, Edwin D. King, and Thomas T. Jones, all of Perry County, "Took the contract to grade the road." Each supplied 20 slaves and completed the work on October 22, 1856.[39] Shortly afterward, Edwin W. and four other directors endorsed the railroad's note of $7,000 for the purchase of iron to lay the tracks near Marion. This work was soon finished, and the road was in operation by July, 1857.[40]

---

his children and their mother. Each of his heirs was to receive at least $30,000, that is, the same amount that Elisha F. King had willed to his grand-daughters. Edwin W. King made no provision in his will for his five elder children because they had been provided for in the will of Elisha F. King. Family Bible of Rhoda B. King Family; Perry County, Alabama, Will Book, III, 105-107.

[36]The hotel was sold for $6,669. Edwin W. King Diary, February 19, 1857.

[37]*Ibid.*, April 9, 1860.

[38]List of Stock Holders in Cahawba & Marion Rail Road Company, February, 1848, Hugh Davis Papers. These Papers of Hugh Davis, who was attorney for the railroad, also contain an Official Report of John Lockhart, Treasurer of the Cahawba & Marion Railroad.

[39]Edwin W. King Diary, September 24, 1853, October 22, 1856.

[40]The other directors who signed the note of $7,000 were Thomas T. Jones, F. A. Bates, J. T. Barron, and Edwin D. King, the latter an uncle of Edwin W. King and an exceptionally wealthy man. *The Catalogue of the Trustees, Instructors and Students of the Judson Female Institute* (Marion, 1857), 25, and

The railroad was immediately popular because it furnished a convenient connection between the eastern part of Perry County and the Alabama River at Cahaba, from where cotton could be shipped by steamboat to Mobile. The Marion and Cahaba road also connected with another railroad that ran to Selma, Alabama, the latter of which joined the eastern region of the state's black belt with northeastern Alabama and the eastern part of the United States by the Alabama & Tennessee River Railroad.[41] As might be expected, planters of western Perry County and of adjacent Hale County soon began agitating for an extension of the little railroad into their vicinities and, as early as July, 1857, a public statement was made that a railroad would soon be constructed westward from Marion. Finally, during the fall of 1859, directors voted to extend the road to Greensboro in Hale County. In October, 1859, Edwin W. King "subscribed 500$ to extend R. R.;" other supporters came forward with money; the name of the road was soon changed to the Marion, Cahaba & Greensboro Railroad;[42] and work was begun on the extension, but it was not completed by the time of the outbreak of the Civil War.

Although the younger King was involved in numerous business enterprises, his chief interest always remained the management and operation of his plantations. He lived at his home place, having an overseer there and at each of his other plantations; and as was customary, he signed contracts with his overseers. On November 18, 1856, King wrote in his diary, "I bargained with Mr. Counts to live at the Rich place next year . . . [and] if either becomes dissatisfied we are to settle up and quit." In July, 1857, King recorded, "Counts has ruined his corn by ploughing it, a great Jack Ass;" and later in the year, Counts was fired.[43] In other instances, King was very fortunate in selecting his overseers, for three of the five men who worked for him in 1852 were still em-

---

Edwin W. King Diary, February 17, 1857, refer to the opening of the railroad. The entire road was not opened until July, 1857, however.

[41]See Davis, *The Cotton Kingdom in Alabama*, 118, for a map of the railroads in operation in Alabama in 1860. For an account of Alabama's early railroads, see Martin, "Internal Improvements in Alabama," *loc. cit.*, 127-205.

[42]Edwin W. King Diary, October 8, 1859, January 23, 1860.

[43]*Ibid.*, July 9, 1857. Other pertinent references to King's relations with his overseers are to be found in *ibid.*, October 27, 1857, and in Contracts with Overseers, in Edwin W. King Papers.

ployed in 1860. One reason for this was that they were paid good salaries: the overseer at the Bibb County plantation received $300 in 1852; the salary of the lower place overseer was raised from $235 in 1852 to $500 in 1860; and the home place overseer was paid $500 in 1859. In addition, the overseers received meat, bread, sugar, meal, and coffee, as well as a house, all of which was customary; and sometimes they were furnished "with a woman to cook and a nurse." The important task of the overseers was to direct the activities of the slaves and to make as much cotton and other produce as possible.[44] And in their treatment of slaves they followed the customs of their day, no better and no worse. The Negroes were adequately fed, clothed, and housed, and were worked regularly in the field and at specialized labor.[45] But as might be expected of a planter who owned 152 slaves, disciplinary problems often arose; and on occasion a slave was whipped either by King himself or by an overseer. However, there were no unusual incidents in this respect. A few Negroes ran away, but since Alabama was a long distance from non-slave territory, and the patrol system worked quite effectively in the state, they were recovered and punished.[46]

The work performed by the King slaves was of the ordinary type done on large plantations of the Alabama black belt. January was one of the busiest months. New land was cleared every year. After trees were felled, shingles were cut, rails split, fences constructed and repaired, and firewood split. Work was done on the public roads; logs, trash, and brush were piled and burned; ditches were dug; old cotton and corn stalks were either plowed under or pulled up and burned; cotton was ginned and hauled away to be sold; grain crops were sowed; hogs were killed and meat salted away; corn was shelled; gullies and washes were filled with brush; spinning wheels and looms were run; and great quantities of cotton seed and manure were hauled for fertilizing purposes. Toward the end of January, the plows were started in corn lands, and in February and March the corn was planted. In March and April,

---

[44]Edwin W. King Papers, *passim;* Edwin W. King Diary, February 9, 1852, February 17, 1853, July 22, November 18, 1856, April 25, June 14, November 10, 1859, March 6, 1860.
[45]Edwin W. King Diary, *passim.*
[46]*Ibid.,* October 21, 1857, May 26, July 16, 1859.

the slaves planted their own and the plantation garden plots. Cotton lands were usually ready for planting by April, and during this month and May the cotton was planted. As cotton came up the important job was to chop around it. In July and August, fodder was pulled, stacked, and stored away. Cotton picking began either in late August or early September and continued until the task was completed. Before the ginning was finished, it was usually time to begin with another year's work.[47] No records are available concerning King's interest in scientific farming, and for some reason he made no references to the subject in his diary. But his neighbors regularly experimented with crop rotations, fertilization methods, stock breeding, and even with irrigation.[48] King subscribed to numerous farm periodicals, and he must have attended some of the agricultural fairs and exhibits which were often held in the black belt region. Since he was in nearly every other respect a typical large planter of his locality, he must have experimented with new farming practices. There is no reason to believe that he butchered or mined his soil.

Among the crops produced at each of the King plantations were cotton, corn, peas, potatoes, wheat, oats, rye, barley, turnips, and peanuts. Vegetables of all kinds were raised; grapes, figs, apples, and peaches were grown; and goats, sheep, hogs, and chickens were raised. The most interesting practice followed by the younger King, however, was that of specializing in the production of one farm article at each of his plantations. The articles were then distributed wherever they were needed. For example, peas were raised particularly at the Mosley place, hogs at the Bibb County plantation, sheep at the Sarah E. King or lower place, goats at the Sanders place, and cows at the home place. But by no means was King self-sufficient in his plantation operations.[49] Like other planters, he bought numerous plantation supplies from merchants and through his factor, the articles being the same kind as those earlier purchased by his father. The following figures gleaned from hundreds of statements and receipted bills for plantation supplies among his correspondence and papers furnish some idea of his heavy expenses. The Sarah E. King plantation is not included in the tabulation.

[47]Ibid., passim.
[48]Hugh Davis Papers; William A. Jones Papers.
[49]Edwin W. King Diary, December, 1852-January, 1860.

	1853	1854	1855	1856	1857	1858	1859	Total
Dry Goods	$ 532.09	$ 711.08	$1,255.61	$ 778.28	$1,211.58	$ 994.56	$1,616.49	$ 7,099.69
Household Goods	519.25	847.57	508.70	30.40	—	32.82	69.20	2,007.94
Foodstuffs	188.54	554.87	452.77	1,169.45	1,996.45	584.38	1,269.91	6,180.37
Drugs	62.15	62.68	57.49	69.41	74.06	70.15	18.40	414.34
Livestock	—	—	900.00	135.00	165.00	—	—	1,200.00
Lumber	12.50	27.65	99.45	165.67	131.54	68.78	—	505.59
Farm Tools	—	193.32	155.65	71.22	99.00	231.57	130.08	880.84
Iron	—	84.97	32.37	53.61	—	211.59	33.80	416.34
Rope, Twine, and Bagging	244.12	316.26	363.09	854.06	255.09	376.05	47.55	2,456.22
Miscellaneous	123.02	215.59	299.82	662.39	211.27	174.35	167.66	1,854.10
	1,681.67	3,013.99	4,124.95	3,989.49	4,143.99	2,708.25	3,353.09	23,015.43

From 1852 until his death, King's Mobile factor was the firm of McDowell, Withers and Company, the same that had handled his father's business affairs in the years just before 1852. Complete statements submitted by McDowell and Withers of the younger King's annual business are available for the period from April 4, 1855 to February 23, 1860:[50]

Date	Receipts	Interest due on Balance and Receipts	Expenditures	Interest owed on Expenditures	Balance
Apr. 4, 1855					$24,584.63
1855-1856	$24,979.37	$2,438.25	$24,093.34	$623.10	27,285.81
1856-1857	17,146.19	2,075.44	13,024.32	403.58	33,079.54
1857-1858	13,345.84	3,183.43	14,155.43	600.34	34,852.64
1858-1859	18,370.05	3,060.09	26,424.64	528.29	30,396.43
1859-Feb. 23, 1860	16,817.64	2,343.83	34,000.87	658.19	14,871.84
	90,659.09	13,101.04	111,699.09	2,840.50	

Between 1852 and May, 1860, McDowell, Withers and Company sold all of King's cotton except 87 bales.[51] The cotton, sold in Mobile, always incurred the same kind of charges: freight, from Cahaba to Mobile,[52] usually $1 to $3 a bale; bill of lading, in nearly every case, 25¢ a bale; weighing, always 10¢ a bale; drayage, 10¢; wharfage, 8¢; storage, varying, depending on number of days in warehouses; and a commision of 2.5 percent paid to the factor on all sales. Fire insurance was always purchased, but on only four occasions was river insurance bought.[53] King's other relations with his factors were of the customary kind, including a close friendship. During his years as director of the family plantations, he annually produced and sold large numbers of bales of cotton; and records of a large portion of the sales in 1852 and from 1855 through 1859 are available. Of these crops, McDowell and Withers sold 2,025 bales for him, resulting in net proceeds of $104,614. Complete

---

[50]Edwin W. King Papers.

[51]Two sales were made in Selma, one through the firm of Sink and Milton, the other through J. E. Prestridge. Borden and Buck of Mobile also concluded two sales for King. Other than these few sales, totaling 87 bales, he concluded all of his cotton sales through McDowell, Withers and Company of Mobile. For the above mentioned 87 bales he received $5,019. *Ibid.*

[52]Until the Cahawba & Marion Rail Road was completed in 1857, King shipped goods and cotton by wagon from his home place to the town of Cahaba, and from there by river boat to Mobile. Edwin W. King Diary, January 13, September 7, 1857.

[53]*Ibid.*, October 23, 1851; Edwin W. King Papers.

reports of the sale of 1,725 of these bales are available. Their total weight was 934,476 pounds, charges for the sales amounted to $6,710, commissions were $2,521, gross proceeds totaled $96,846, and net proceeds were $90,135. The average price per pound amounted to $10.36¢, which means that the younger King, like his father, produced cotton at a fair profit.[54] He made money growing cotton forty years after Alabama became a state, thus proving that plantation slavery, in his case, was profitable at a time when his land was no longer virgin.

After Edwin W. King's death on August 10, 1860, the financial condition of the family estate became steadily worse. Before his death he had planted his 1860 cotton crops. They were sold by March 14, 1861, at which time, when all current debts were paid, the account with McDowell, Withers and Company showed a balance of $6,434 in the deceased planter's favor.[55] In previous years he had maintained a much more comfortable balance with the firm, this being the case despite the fact that the balance had decreased by more than 50 percent between March, 1859 and February, 1860. This decrease of balance with McDowell and Withers resulted from causes other than negligence or unprofitableness of slavery. King made heavy investments aside from those required by his plantation operations. A particular drain on his assets was excessively heavy personal loans to a spendthrift son-in-law, William P. Holman, and these loans were cancelled. Holman had been borrowing heavily for at least five years, even during the time he was courting King's daughter.[56] Holman was a spend-thrift who turned planter and failed because he was a wastrel and, unfortunately, he managed the King estate for about a year after King's death. Within the year, after selling the 1860-1861 cotton crops, the estate, under Holman's direction, showed a deficit for the first time in its history, the deficit with McDowell and Withers amounting to $7,410. Moreover, on his own account, Holman owed the same Company the sum of $6,824. One reason for this, in

[54]Edwin W. King Papers.
[55]McDowell, Withers and Company to Mrs. W. P. Holman, July 13, 1861, in Mrs. William P. Holman Papers (in possession of Miss Clara Barker, Marion).
[56]William P. Holman Diary, *passim;* Edwin W. King Diary, 1856-1860, *passim;* Perry County, Alabama, Will Book, III, 105-107.

addition to Holman's absolute lack of ability and judgment, was his purchase of numerous slaves at high prices.[57] When Holman died on May 28, 1861, operation of the family plantation was taken over by Mrs. Rhoda B. King, the widow of Edwin W.[58] This lady's business judgment was excellent, but she was unable to hold together her property because of the many problems created by the Civil War.[59] After the War, which violently disrupted and changed the plantation system throughout the South, Mrs. King was forced to curtail drastically her farming activities.[60]

---

[57]McDowell, Withers and Company to Mrs. W. P. Holman, July 13, 1861, and Bills of Sale and Statements of Accounts, all in Mrs. William P. Holman Papers.

[58]Rhoda B. King Papers (in possession of Miss Clara Barker, Marion). On December 28, 1864, Rhoda B. King was appointed to administer the estate of Mrs. Margaret King, the widow of Elisha F. King. Mrs. Margaret King died on September 23, 1863. Family Bible of Rhoda B. King Family.

[59]*Ibid.*

[60]The method of operation to which Mrs. Rhoda B. King and many other planters turned in the years following the Civil War is well described in the following agreement, made on November 17, 1868, concerning a portion of the "Rich place": "For the purpose of cultivating the plantation of Mrs. R. B. King, Known as the 'Rich Place,' during the year 1869, Mrs. R. B. King and Robert Liddell, make the following agreement, to wit, Mrs. King furnishes for culture one hundred and twenty acres of land more or less; four mules, to wit, Tobe, Molley, Morgan and Big Tom, for two of which she is to receive of Mr. Liddell thirty dollars each, for their years service; one waggon and plows and gear, the same to be returned in similar order at the end of the year; and half the feed for the mules; She will also advance one half the rations for the hands to be employed on the place to be reimbursed by the laborers out of their one third part of the nett proceeds of the crops of every kind, that may be produced during the year, and she will pay half the black smith bill for the use of the said place during the year. The said Liddell will give a special and generous superintendence to the plantation, and direct and control the laborers; He will furnish or pay for one half of the rations of the laborers, to be reimbursed from the nett proceeds of the crop that may be due them; He will furnish one half the feed for the mules, and pay one half the blacksmith bill; and at the close of the year will return all the farming implements used on the place, in the same order as received, ordinary wear and tear excepted, to said King. The laborers are to have one third part of all the crops that may be raised during the year, after paying all necessary and usual expenses in its preparation & transportation to market, and paying all advances for rations & other supplies. The said King and Liddell will divide equally all the cotton, corn, fodder, hay & potatoes that may be produced in the year 1869, after paying the laborers and all necessary expenses in and about the preparation and transportation to Market. It witness whereof we have hereunto [signed] this agreement in duplicate, this 17th day of Novr. A. D. 1868." To this agreement was affixed the signatures of two witnesses, James G. L. Huey and C. M. Huey, the signature of Mrs. R. B. King, and the mark (XX) of R. F. Liddell. Rhoda B. King Papers.

The King family furnishes some proof that a family could make profits from plantation operations.[61] Of course, profit in ante-bellum plantation management was a matter of degree, and a primary problem is what is meant by profit. Often, because of lack of complete records, it is impossible to determine precise expenditures and receipts and profits of planters. Particular cases, moreover, are dependent upon, among other factors, climate, soil, health and satisfaction and care of labor, and especially upon the personal characteristics of the plantation owner himself. Transportation facilities as well as time of shipment of produce to market also always influenced the net proceeds of a planter. In the same general locality some planters succeeded while their immediate neighbors failed. It is an established fact that one of the highest ambitions and highest attainments in the Gulf States of the Old South was to become a planter. So many planters did succeed that the occupation of a planter was highly admirable in their own eyes and minds and in the eyes and minds of thousands of persons who sought to become planters. Cotton planters, themselves, were engaged in the business of producing a very important commodity, indeed a commodity that comprised the greatest single export from the United States. Agriculture was a way of life, and certainly those people associated with agriculture believed that there was nothing shameful about it. Planters by no means entered farming activities with the intention of failing, and as for the profitableness of plantation slavery, despite changing attitudes toward the institution, it seems obvious that the institution would not have lasted for more than 200 years in the United States if it had been or was thought to be basically unprofitable. In regard to the Alabama black belt, the region happened to be one place where there was an excellent opportunity of gaining an exceedingly comfortable living through operation of a cotton plantation with slave labor during the three decades before the Civil War.[62]

---

[61]This conclusion is borne out by the records of the King family which the present author has examined and by the evidences of wealth still in the possession of the descendents of Elisha F. King.

[62]Despite the masterful studies of the subject of the profitableness of plantation slavery in such books as Ulrich B. Phillips, *American Negro Slavery* (New York, 1918), Charles Sackett Sydnor, *Slavery in Mississippi*, and Gray, *History of Agriculture in the Southern United States to 1860*, scholars will perhaps have

It is evident that Elisha F. King began his activities in Perry County a poor man and, despite the hard times of the Panic of 1837 and the middle 1840's, he died a wealthy man. His son inherited several thriving and prosperous agricultural establishments, free of debt; and he was financially solvent when he died. The Kings unquestionably were outstanding businessmen and managers. They raised and sold large crops of cotton and other produce and acquired extensive slave and other property holdings. In addition to very substantial monetary profits earned through their hard work, they lived comfortably, educated their children in approved style, contributed freely to various charities, and were leaders in their social circles. All of this, plus an undoubted sense of well-being and of leadership, resulted particularly from their farming activities. It was only when they ventured into business projects other than plantation management that they suffered financial setbacks.

More than one member of the King family became wealthy in Alabama, the wealthiest being General Edwin D. King, the millionaire brother of Elisha F.[63] In Marion, Alabama, there is a thought-provoking story still told about the General. He, it seems, was on tour by railway in Europe sometime before the Civil War, traveling by private car as was befitting a man of his eminent station. While passing through a small German state, troops of a local prince, it is said, attempted to eject King from his car in order that it might be occupied by the prince and his entourage. The General, thoroughly exasperated at this show of old-world effrontery but completely unawed by his titled adversary, exclaimed to the soldiers, "Money are power, and I are got it," and continued his journey in his car.

---

to be satisfied with determining if individual planters, those whose records are available, made or lost money with the much discussed Negro slave labor. The whole subject is of course a debatable one and is still very much alive, however; and we have "revisionists" among us, some of whom are "revising" the "revisionists." All this is good for the historical profession, and is an expression of "progress."

[63]The manuscript materials used in the preparation of this study prove beyond any doubt that General Edwin D. King was by far the wealthiest member of the King family in Perry County. He, himself, seems not to have left adequate records for an acceptable study of his activities. However, it is known that he, along with his brother Elisha F. King, was a poor man when he arrived in Alabama in the year 1819.

IV

A FAMILY DAYBOOK

Among the more valuable sources of information about actual living conditions in the Old South are documents known as day-books. In these collections are to be found such bits of information as favorite recipes, medical care, directions of all sorts aimed at making one's existence more bearable and interesting, and many other items. Individually the items of the typical daybook of the ante-bellum period are not of outstanding importance; but taken as a whole, especially if compiled over a lengthy period, and more particularly if brought together with some semblance of order, a well-kept daybook throws an enormous light on the social life of the period.

Many of the items of a typical pre-Civil War daybook reiterate the fact that everyday living in a rural and generally isolated environment was exceedingly crude. However, many of the items also show that some people of the Old South consciously sought to improve their existences and that in some respects they even reached a certain degree of cosmopolitanism. Much of what was included in the daybooks was based on trial and error and hearsay; much was copied from printed sources such as newspapers, agricultural journals, and medical books; a large portion of the information was gathered from friends and acquaintances; some was passed from father to son and mother to daughter. One such book was compiled by Martin Marshall, a South Carolinian who moved to Alabama and resided in the latter state for many years. Marshall was a man who is of interest to the historian because he and his family put together a magnificent daybook.[1]

Martin Marshall was born on May 4, 1782, in Richland County, South Carolina, near the present city of Columbia. His grandfather,

---

[1]Excerpts from this daybook, edited by the present writer, appeared as "Martin Marshall's Book: Introduction," *Alabama Historical Quarterly*, II, 158-168 (1940); "Martin Marshall's Book: Household Hints," *ibid.*, II, 318-330 (1940); "Martin Marshall's Book: Herb Medicine," *ibid.*, II, 443-459 (1940); "Martin Marshall's Book: Homemade Medicine," *ibid.*, III, 117-129 (1941); and "Martin Marshall's Book: Farming and Veterinary Practices," *ibid.*, III, 248-261 (1941).

John Marshall, moved to America from England, and by the year 1770 established a home in Richland County. John Marshall also operated a grist mill and acquired nearly 900 acres of land. William Marshall, the son of John and the father of Martin, operated the family mill and farm and followed the trade of weaver. William Marshall was not a man of wealth, although at his death in the year 1800 he owned about 925 acres of farm land, six slaves, a few cows, sheep, hogs, horses, and the usual goods and implements needed in the operation of a farm the size of his. Also listed among his possessions at the time of his death were spinning and weaving machines. His estate, excluding land, was appraised at $2,267. Young Martin Marshall thus did not have the advantages afforded by wealthy parents. During his youth he lived and worked with his father. He learned to read and write and very probably attended school for a short time. Of special importance to him, as a young man and later, was the training he received in several crafts. By his eighteenth year he had learned the skills of a mechanic, weaver and blacksmith. He was the third generation of the Marshalls in America to be a skilled craftsman.[2]

William Marshall's estate was sold within a few months of his death, the proceeds presumably being distributed among his ten children, of whom Martin was the oldest. Shortly thereafter Martin married Mary Blanchard, a neighbor, and then moved to Columbia. In Columbia he operated a blacksmith shop and also followed the trade of weaver, earning a living in this manner until the year 1808. In the latter year his wife inherited some property from one of her brothers, and since this property was soon converted into 17 slaves it is very likely that Marshall now turned to farming. One of the family traditions about him is that at this time he was saved from bankruptcy through the business judgment of his wife. He was not only a failure as a farmer, but he also gradually accumulated large debts; and these caused him to seek a new life in a new locality. Thus, in August, 1815, he sold what was left of his South Carolina property and moved to the southwest, choosing as a place to settle

---

[2]Information on the Marshall family has been furnished by various descendants of John Marshall, Martin's grandfather. Most of the information was supplied by the Reverend James W. Marshall, of Chattahoochie, Florida, who has brought together an excellent genealogical account of the family.

the Alabama River town of Fort Claiborne, a town which had been established in 1815 in the Territory of Mississippi. Fort Claiborne would soon be included in Alabama, which became a Territory in 1817 and a State two years later. Marshall remained in and near Fort Claiborne until his death in September, 1865.[3]

Following his arrival in the region which would become Monroe County, Marshall resumed his trades of blacksmith and weaver. Now he was successful, partially because Fort Claiborne at the time was a very prosperous little town. The town and the people in it benefited economically because it was located at a very favorable site on the Alabama River between Mobile and Montgomery, both of which were assuming their roles as important trade centers in the new state of Alabama. Fort Claiborne's population varied between 2,500 and 5,000 in the decade after Marshall's arrival. In the years from 1819 to 1826, while Cahaba, the little river town in Dallas County, was the capital of Alabama, the commercial importance of Fort Claiborne was enhanced because of its closeness to the seat of government.[4] Marshall enjoyed a secure life as a mechanic and blacksmith in these years, and by the year 1824 he purchased several town lots and hundreds of acres of farm land along the Alabama River.

Marshall's blacksmith and weaving businesses must have been helped by the attention that he attracted by some of the "new-fangled" ideas and practices he is said to have brought from South Carolina. For example, his descendents claim that he was the first person in the Fort Claiborne region to dig a well and the first to install a covered floor in his house. Family stories are still told of the wonder and amazement with which some people went to his house to see these innovations. He also began, if he had not already done so, writing notes about neighborhood affairs and the opinions of customers who patronized his shops. These notes, unfortunately,

---

[3]Martin Marshall's grave is located at Perdue Hill, Alabama.
[4]See William H. Brantley, *A Book about the First Three Capitals of Alabama: St. Stephens, Huntsville, & Cahawba* (Boston, 1947), 60-207; Summersell, *Mobile: History of a Seaport Town*, 10-24; and Williams, "Early Ante-Bellum Montgomery: A Black-Belt Constituency," *loc. cit.*, 495-509. For references to lands owned by Marshall, see Monroe County, Alabama, Deed Book (Office of the Probate Court, Monroe County Court House, Monroeville), A, 127, 131, 136, 138; *ibid.*, B, 42; *ibid*, D, 293, 458.

are lost. However, there is extant a family daybook which the Marshalls began keeping in April, 1802, a collection which was continued until Martin Marshall's death in 1865. Most of the materials included in the daybook were brought together after the family moved to Alabama. The original document, of approximately 450 pages, bore the title of "Martin Marshall's Book."[5]

The "Book" was prepared over a period of about 60 years, and it represents the interests of a man who was a mechanic, a weaver, a blacksmith, a planter, as well as a very inquisitive person who belonged to a family of exceedingly wide interests. Its contents were for Marshall's and his friends' use and edification. It dealt primarily with the serious business of surviving and making life more pleasant and bearable in a region which was only gradually evolving from a frontier status, a region which by the year 1850 would be included within the leading cotton state of the Old South. The "Book's" contents are indicative of the rather close ties that sometimes existed among rural Southerners, of their dependence upon each other, and of their cooperativeness and willingness to share information.[6]

Because of his activities as an Alabama businessman and planter, Marshall was able to make the necessary contacts to obtain many of the items entered in his "Book," and the broad range of items in the document indicates that its contents were gathered from many sources. Especially as a blacksmith, Marshall had ample opportunities for talking with many people and of obtaining a variety of information and hearsay from them. He undoubtedly picked up some knowledge of the customs of his adopted state both by observation and through gossip. Although he himself was not a widely traveled man, he must have learned many things from river travelers who

---

[5]The writer is indebted to the late Alexander J. Marshall, of Marion, Alabama, for permission to use "Martin Marshall's Book."

[6]"Martin Marshall's Book" is an outstanding example of a conclusion made by the president of the Southern Historical Association in 1938, when he was comparing such manuscripts with other, more readily available historical materials: "Of far more value may be some letter, or diary, or account book" which "has left a record which significantly throws some light on an otherwise unknown or incompletely understood phase of Southern history." Philip M. Hamer, "The Records of Southern History," *Journal of Southern History*, VI, 3 (1939).

passed through Fort Claiborne. Furthermore, one of the habits of Americans living in frontier regions and in other sparsely populated areas was to experiment with household or domestic practices, with medicine, with cooking, and so forth, and, if the results seemed successful or useable, to pass on information about them to neighbors and friends. Marshall followed this practice, too. Indeed, his interests were so varied that it would seem that he served as a sort of self-appointed information bureau for some of the people living in his community.

During most of the period of his residence in Alabama, Marshall had access to numerous newspapers, magazines, almanacs, medical journals, and other publications, and, as was the custom in bringing together a daybook, he and his family made hundreds of clippings from such printed sources and pasted the clippings in their "Book." In most cases when an item was clipped or was copied from a printed article, the family failed to indicate the title or date of the printed source. Thus, the sources of practically all of the clippings in the "Book" are unknown. However, those clippings which do designate a source are truly significant, for they were gathered from newspapers and other publications printed in nearly every state in the United States east of the Mississippi River. It seems quite evident that many of the household and family or domestic practices as described in the "Book" were known throughout much of the South and the eastern United States.

Presumably the Marshall family used the information contained in the clippings placed in their "Book." Moreover, in many cases, the clippings themselves show that the information included in them was submitted to editors by enterprising people who wished others to share in that information. Only a very cursory examination of ante-bellum publications is required to demonstrate that articles published under such headings as "Valuable Recipes" and "Useful Information" served a definitely useful purpose of spreading information about domestic practices. This popular pastime was particularly true of the Old South, one of the least populated of the settled areas of the country, as well as of the entire agricultural and quasi-frontier regions of the United States. Moreover, many Southerners, especially rural Southerners, retained very pronounced frontier characteristics during the years before 1860. Marshall would have been quite unusual if he had failed to take advantage of the opportunity to learn from these articles.

Marshall did not include in his "Book" any items in regard to housing as such, but he did show an interest in collecting numerous bits of information which are, perhaps, best described as "household hints." In caring for furniture and other household articles, he followed many of the practices that were common for his time and place. For example, furniture was given the appearance of "artificial mahogany" by planing the surface smooth, rubbing it with a solution of nitrous acid, and painting it with several coats of a solution of spirits of wine and carbonate of soda. When needed, the brilliancy of the finish was restored with an application of linseed oil.[7] Furniture was varnished with a mixture, in the ratio of two to one, of melted beeswax and spirits of turpentine applied with a woolen cloth.[8] If white spots appeared on furniture, they were removed through heating at the point of the spots with a warming-pan filled with coals and rubbing the spots with a piece of warm flannel.[9]

Another "item for housewives," a method of keeping a stove bright, was to paint a stove with a solution of weak alum-water and British-lustre. Broken china was mended with a "vicious paste" made of gum arabic and plaster of Paris. A paste said to be a "paste that is a paste" was concocted from an ounce of alum in a quart of warm water, and boiled with flour, powdered rosin, and two or three cloves.[10] Cement "as hard as marble & impenetrable by water" was made of "one part sand, two part ashes and three parts clay."

---

[7]This description of a method of making wood look like mahogany comes from a clipping of an unknown publication, a newspaper, book, or periodical, which Marshall pasted in his "Book." The title of the publication is unknown. Hereafter in this Chapter, when information comes from such a source, it will be cited as Clipping, Unknown Publication.

[8]This statement about the use of bees wax and spirits of turpentine on furniture appears in Marshall's own writing in his "Book." Where he obtained the information is unknown. However, rather than burden the reader with one *ibid.* after another by citing the "Book," it will suffice to state here that this Chapter, from this point onward, unless otherwise stated, is based on my own interpretation and presentation of the "Book" as Marshall himself, in his own handwriting, prepared it. Quotations, unless otherwise cited, are from Marshall's own words.

[9]Clipping, Unknown Publication.

[10]*Ibid.*

Oil paintings were cleaned with a sponge dipped in a solution of ammonia and water, while pictures and "paper hangings" were brightened by blowing off the dust with a bellows and wiping them downwards with half a loaf of bread, eight-day old bread, it was said, being best for this purpose. Stains and marks were removed from books by applying a solution of oxalic acid in combination with either nitric or tartaric acid.[11] Flat-irons were kept in useable condition through smearing them with melted suet and dusting them with unslaked lime.[12]

Like most rural or frontier families, the Marshalls were faced with the very practical problem of controlling pests, such as flies, ants, moths, fleas, bed bugs, and mice; and in their efforts either to control or kill these pests they utilized some very ingenious preventives. "An ant trap" was arranged by sprinkling sugar over a dry sponge and placing it where the ants were most troublesome. The ants were attracted by the sugar, the sponge was dipped in scalding water, the ants were drowned.[13] Flies were removed by placing in a room a plate filled with a mixture of powdered black pepper, brown sugar, and cream. Another preventive of flies, called by Marshall "a secret worth knowing," was to "boil three or four onions in a pint of water. Then with a gilding brush do over your glasses and frames and rest assured that the flies will not light on the articles washed." The Marshalls' method of controlling the approach of moths and caterpillars was: "wrap up yellow or turpentine soap in paper, or place an open bottle containing spirits of turpentine within the wardrobe. But as the smell of the latter may be unpleasant, sprinkle bay leaves, or wormwood, or lavendar, or walnut leaves, or rue, or black pepper in grains." Clothes were also sometimes protected against moths by sprinkling the clothes with a powder formed of pulverized cloves, cedar balls, and rhubarb. Bed bugs and fleas were prevented from infesting one's person, it was said, if he carried a few sprigs of penny royal in his pocket and from infesting his bed if it were painted with a mixture of one teaspoonful of quicksilver and the whites of six eggs. Mice and rats were killed by putting a mixture of plaster of Paris and flour where

---

[11]*Ibid.*
[12]*Ibid.* The date "7th April 1825" is written on the margin of this clipping.
[13]Clipping, Unknown Publication.

the rodents could eat it.[14] Marshall himself advised, "To destroy mice & rats, a plenty of good cats, feed them well, & they will perform well." On occasion he put "the plant dog's tongue" in places infested by mice, causing them "immediately [to] shift their quarters."

Since Marshall was a weaver, he included many items in his "Book" on weaving and on the dyeing of thread and cloth as well as the care of clothing. Scores of diagrams of cloth and of the operation of his looms appear in his "Book." Unfortunately, most of the diagrams have little meaning because they were patterns, or "drafts" as Marshall called them, either worked out by himself or collected solely for his personal use, and the directions as he recorded them are incomplete and incomprehensible. However, the fact that he included the diagrams in his "Book" indicates that he, like many of his contemporaries, worked at his loom and made his own cloth. Being a weaver, he of course had a special reason for an interest in the subject.

It is believed that Marshall used the common fly shuttle or hand loom since that was the type considered most acceptable during his day.[15] He was familiar with such processes and terms as cording, harness, drawing through the harness, temples, shuttles, spools, and so forth. He was adept at preparing cotton and wool for use through sizing, drying, carding, warping, winding, and beaming. His patterns must have been intricate, and they bore such interesting names as "huckaback," "double diamonds," "ducape," "nine snowball," "compass work," "Lady Rutland's feather," "spots and chains," "cross and circle," and "the world's wonder." Indicating that in his weaving, as in many other respects, Marshall was a borrower, some of his drafts were designated as "draft taken from Mrs. Garrett's counterpane," "draft from Mark's creek," "draft from Franklin," "a counterpane draft got at Fort Claiborne," "draft from Mrs. Agee," "draft from Mrs. McCall's bed cover," and "draft from Mrs. Crook." Some of the drafts were his own; many of them were borrowed; a few were brought to Alabama from South Carolina.

[14]*Ibid.*

[15]For an illustration of the type of loom that Marshall probably used, see J. & R. Bronson, *The Domestic Manufacturer's Assistant, and Family Directory, in the Arts of Weaving and Dyeing* (Utica, 1817), 53.

Whereas Marshall's drafts or patterns are quite unintelligible to the uninitiated weaver, his family's methods of washing clothes, dyeing cloth and yarn, and caring for clothing and shoes are readily understandable. Like most of its contemporaries, the family made its own soap and starches. Soap, according to one method, was made of six pounds of potash, four pounds of lard, and one-fourth pound of rosin.[16] A recipe for a "new soap" was "Take one pint of spirits of turpentine, one pint of alcohol, two pints of hartshorn, one ounce of gum camphor; shake them well together, then to one quart of soft soap [already made] add three tablespoonsful of this mixture."[17] As for dyeing and dye-making, it was said, "An ox's gall will set any color—silk, cotton, or woolen. . . . The colors of calico, which faded at one washing [can be] fixed by it."[18] Marshall's own method "to dye a good green" was: "Dye your yarn blue first, then dip it in yellow dye until you have as deep green as you wish—some dye the thread yellow first and then dip it in blue dye, which is best." To make a "beautiful blue," he learned, one should "take elder berries, mash them and press out the juice; to two gallons of juice add about one ounce of copperas and two ounces of alum. Dip the thread in this thoroughly, and air it, and the dye is set."[19]

Care of clothing and shoes was also an important consideration to the members of the Marshall family. They cleaned silk as follows: "One fourth of a pound of soft soap, one teaspoonful of brandy, one pint of gin and mixed well together. With a sponge, spread the mixture on each side of the silk without greasing it, iron on the wrong side, and it will look as well as new."[20] Ink was removed from cotton and linen by dipping the spotted part into melted tallow and then washing it,[21] while grease spots and mildew were removed by wetting the spots and rubbing in magnesia or chalk. Fruit spots were taken out of cloth by holding "the part over a

---

[16]Clipping, Unknown Publication, of the early 1860's, consisting of a reprint of a letter written by an unknown person residing in Oglethorpe County, Georgia, to the editor of a Virginia publication.

[17]Clipping, Unknown Publication, dated "7th April 1825."

[18]Clipping, Unknown Publication.

[19]*Ibid.*

[20]*Ibid.*

[21]*Ibid.*

lighted common brimstone match at a proper distance. The sulphurous gas, which is discharged, soon causes the spots to disappear." Iron molds in linen were treated as follows: "Hold the iron mould on the cover of a mug of boiling water, and rub on the spot a little juice of sorrel and salt, & when the cloth has thoroughly imbibed the juice, wash it in ley." Carriage wheel grease was removed from woolen clothes by rubbing the spots with fresh butter, laying on two or three strips of blotting paper, and ironing over the spots. A shoe-blacking, called "Liquid Japan," was made of treacle, lampblack, sweet oil, gum arabic, isinglass, water, spirit of wine, and an ox's gall;[22] a second blacking was concocted of ivory black, oil of vitriol, pulverized loaf sugar, and vinegar;[23] a third consisted of burnt wheat straw, molasses, sugar, vinegar, and oil. Boots and shoes were water-proofed with a solution of linseed oil, mutton suet, beeswax, and rosin.

Among its personal-care "recipes," the Marshall family's preparation of a "hair ointment" was particularly elaborate: "Take of castor oil, Bare's oil, Deer or Mutton suet, Essence or Oil of Roses, Equal quantity. And you may add Puccon root in proportion to the quantity of each. The above ointment will change the colour of the hair, if used every morning, to a black, or dark colour—and give a gloss to the hair, if managed properly."[24] The family also made its own perfumes, one method being to gather flowers, with as little stalk as possible, place the flowers in a jar of olive or almond juice, squeeze through a cloth the oil from the flowers, and mix with the oil "an equal quantity of pure rectified spirit."[25] Another concoction used by the Marshalls was an ointment for chapped hands, which was made as follows: "Scrape into an earthen vessel 1½ ounces of spermaceti and half an ounce of white wax; and six drachms of powdered camphor and four table spoonsful of the best olive oil. Let it stand near the fire until it dissolves, stirring it well when liquid. Before retiring put the ointment on the hands, also before washing them; use soap as usual."[26]

[22]*Ibid.*, dated "May 2, 1820."

[23]Clipping, Unknown Publication.

[24]Marshall obtained this "Hair Ointment" from a Mr. E. L. Howie, who obtained it from a Mrs. Prescott of Louisiana.

[25]Clipping, Unknown Publication, consisting of a reprint from an unknown issue of the popular *Scientific American*.

[26]Clipping, Unknown Publication.

The Marshalls also showed a very special interest in preparing and preserving foods, and in this respect, as in so many others, they were typical of their time and place. They presumably did not collect a large number of baking recipes, but the ones that were placed in their "Book" are quite intriguing, probably because they did not bother to write down very many of their plain, everyday recipes. Among the family's less elaborate recipes was one for "bachelor's pone," made as follows: "Three eggs well beaten, three half pints of milk, a piece of butter the size of an egg, tablespoonful strong yeast, and as much corn meal as will make the batter as thick as for muffins; scald half the meal with half the milk."[27] To make a "good biscuit" and have it "ready for the table in half an hour," one should take "One quart of milk, four even teaspoonsful of cream of tartar, two even teaspoonsful of carbonate of soda; the soda to be dissolved in the milk, and the cream of tartar to be thoroughly mixed with the dry flour, and a little salt. Mix it as soft as it can be baked."[28] A delicious "light bread," not to be cut "under twelve hours after baking" involved a ritual requiring four hours of preparation before the dough was baked. Muffins, made of fine flour, warm milk and water, yeast, and "a little salt," were baked after stirring the ingredients for fifteen minutes.[29]

To make sweet bread, Marshall said "Take ½ ounce of Pearl Ash, dissolve it in 2 table spoonsful of warm water—pour in one gallon of molasses first, then the pearl ash; add a little butter, and don't work the dough too much; roll it on a table, and form it into cakes." Another very interesting recipe, one for sponge biscuits, was "Beat the yolks of 14 eggs for half an hour; then put in 1½ pounds of beaten sifted sugar, and whisk it till it rises in bubbles; beat the whites to a strong froth, and whisk them well with the sugar & yolks; work in 14 ounces of flour, with the rhinds of two lemons grated. Bake them in tin moulds buttered, in a quick oven, for half an hour; before they are baked, sift a little fine sugar over them." Elaborate recipes also were followed in preparing other pastries, such as crumpets, rusks, cakes, custards, pies and "jumbles," the latter being made of sugar, butter, flour, eggs, and rose-water.

[27]*Ibid.*
[28]*Ibid.*, dated "7th April 1825."
[29]Clipping, Unknown Publication.

Like other rural families of their day, the Marshalls were faced with the serious problem of preserving foods for year-round use. Since climatic conditions in Alabama, that is, in the Deep South, demanded careful consideration of this problem if a family were to enjoy a variety of foods out-of-season, they filled many pages of their "Book" with descriptions of how to "can" and to "preserve." Plums, for instance, were "put up" as follows: "Take 1 pound of sugar, & 1 pint water; simmer it slow for half an hour. Then add one egg well beat (to clarify it), boil, or rather simmer it half an hour longer—then strain it—Return it to the kettle, add one pound of plums—Boil them until done—or say until the sour is out." This same method was followed in preserving peaches, but they, it was said, "should be steeped 12 or 14 hours in rum previous to their being boiled as above." Syrup for plums and peaches and other fruits was made of molasses or sugar house syrup, mixed with water and charcoal.[30] Figs and tomatoes were dried by pouring over them a weak ley of wood ashes, boiling them in syrup, and sprinkling them with pulverized sugar. Worms were kept out of dried fruits by placing the fruits in a bag and dipping them in scalding water.[31]

Other foodstuffs that were preserved included cabbage, flour, vegetables, fishes, and hams. Pickled cabbage, for example, was prepared as follows: "Shred red and white cabbage, or either; spread it in layers in a stone jar, with salt over each layer. Put two spoonsful of whole black pepper, and the same quantity of allspice, cloves and cinnamon in a bag, and scald them in two quarts of vinegar, and pour the vinegar over the cabbage, and cover it tight. It will be fit for use two days after." Flour was kept "sweet & wholesome any length of time" through adding to it a mixture of magnesia and carbonate of potash. "To pickle in brine," Marshall said, "A good brine is made of bay or alum, salt & water, thoroughly saturated, so that some of the salt remains undissolved; into this brine the substances to be preserved are plunged, & kept covered with it—Beans, artichokes, etc., may be thus preserved." Herrings and other fishes were also sometimes pickled in brine, but "to pre-

---

[30]Ibid.
[31]Ibid.; a reprint from an unknown issue of the *Southern Cultivator.*

serve fish by sugar" was a simpler way of keeping them, and according to Marshall it was necessary only to "open the fish, and apply the sugar to the muscular parts, placing it in a horizontal position for 2 or 3 days— . . . ventilate it occasionally to prevent mouldiness, if you wish to fry them."

Marshall also practiced several methods of curing and preserving hams. His most detailed method of curing, which he borrowed from a planter of central Alabama required that: "The pork should be perfectly cold before being cut up. The hams should be salted with fine salt, with a portion of red pepper, and about a gill of molasses to each ham. Let them remain in salt five weeks, then hang them up and smoke with hickory for five or six weeks. About the first of April take them down and wet them with cold water, and let them be rubbed with unleached ashes. Let them remain in bulk for several days, and then hang them in the loft for use."[32] And when pickling hams Marshall placed them in a cask and poured over them a brine made of water, salt, brown sugar, saltpeter, and saleratus, leaving them in the brine for at least three months. In preserving his hams from bugs, flies and skippers, all of which pests undoubtedly caused him much worry and some losses, numerous practices were followed. One was to cover the meat with charcoal; another consisted of dipping the meat in boiling ley and covering the fleshy side with pulverized black pepper; a third, which it was claimed would keep hams for seven years, was to smoke them, place them in bags, and fill the bags with "the very best sweet made hay."[33] Skippers in meat were destroyed, Marshall insisted, by beating elder leaves in a mortar, "adding a little water" to the juice, and spreading the concoction on the meat; that is, "rub the flesh side of the meat with the [elder] leaves thus bruised, and where small holes appear, pour in the juice."[34]

The making of wines, beers, brandies and rum was by no means a chief interest of the Marshalls, but there is no doubt that they brewed and concocted numerous kinds of drinks. Their "Book"

[32]Clipping, Unknown Publication, bearing the date "1850." The planter who used this method of curing hams was awarded a prize for his hams "at the recent Agricultural Fair in Montgomery county."

[33]Clipping, Unknown Publication.

[34]This item was copied from an unknown issue of the *American Farmer*, of Baltimore, and later of Washington.

is indisputable evidence that they utilized an almost unbelievable variety of beverages, wines and liquors for medicinal and other purposes. Moreover, if they had not indulged in the domestic manufacture of drinks and in what is sometimes called "social drinking," they would have differed from their class in their state and region. They purchased or manufactured strong drinks to use them as medicines; they made or bought others because they wanted to drink them. A pronounced temperance movement existed in Alabama during the ante-bellum period, but there is no evidence available that Marshall subscribed to it.

The Marshall "Book" contains almost as many recipes for beer as the total for all other strong drinks that the family made at home, perhaps because of the ease with which beers could be brewed. For example, a "table beer from sugar" was made as follows: "To 4 lbs. of coarse brown sugar, add 10 gallons of water; then put in 3 ounces of hops, and let the whole boil for three quarters of an hour, and work it as usual, with yeast. It should be kept a week or ten days before it is tapped, ..." To make hop beer, Marshall said, "Take ¼ lb. Ginger—6 ounces Hops, 1 Gallon Molasses, ¼ lb. Cream of Tartar. Mix well with 14 Gallons of cold water—Note—Boil the hops and Ginger together, strain them and pour the liquid in hot—Let it stand about two days—then bottle it tight and in 8 hours it will be fit for use." Another beer, surely a potent one, required more detailed preparations: "Pine tops of the Short Straw—China brier root—Red root—Sassafras root, Holly root or leaves, Molasses or Sugar, Yeast or Corn Meal—Take about an equal quantity of the above, for 5 gallons a Double handful of each—Boil them in Sufficient quantity of water, to make a decoction—and when cold—fill up a Demijohn, adding the yeast—When it has fermented sufficiently bottle it, or keep it Stopped close."

Marshall seems not to have been much interested in winemaking, for his legacy (his "Book") contains only two wine recipes, a blackberry and a grape wine.[35] On the other hand, there is no doubt that he was a brandy fancier. In making his brandy he placed thirty gallons of whiskey in a barrel, and to this he added one quart of unslaked lime, one-fourth of a pound of pearlash, and a

---

[35]Clipping, Unknown Publication.

piece of alum "as large as a hen's egg." These latter ingredients were pulverized and stirred together, added to the whiskey, and allowed to dissolve therein for two or three hours. In order to give the brandy "a beautiful color," it was "racked off," and two quarts of dried sweet apples were added which had been cut fine and scorched in a cast iron pan. Three gills of dulcified spirits of nitre and three gallons of Cognac Brandy were then added "to help the flavor materially;" and "to clarify it and render it perfectly clear," two ounces of isinglass which had been dissolved in boiling water were put in the barrel and stirred.[36]

Less elaborate than his brandy recipe, but perhaps equally significant, were Marshall's methods of preparing several other drinks. He made his own versions ("watered down" varieties) of Holland Gin, St. Croix Rum, and Jamaica Spirits by mixing small amounts of these commercially manufactured drinks, usually four gallons, with whiskey, usually twenty-six gallons of the latter.[37] Also, one of his several recipes for bitters, which must have been potent, was as follows: One ounce each of Columbo root, Gentian root, Orange peel, red sanders, Black Snake root, and Peruvian Bark, pulverized together and mixed with three pints of Jamaica Spirits, the mixture to "stand in the Sun for ten days" and then strained for use.

One of the special reasons for Marshall's interest in the domestic manufacture of alcoholic drinks was the medical uses to which he put them. Indeed, on the basis of the overall contents of his "Book," approximately one-third of which consists of prescriptions and methods of treating various diseases and ailments, it seems quite likely that his chief reason for bringing together his collection was to prepare a personal medical journal. The making of such a collection of prescriptions was a common undertaking with families of the Old South; and to the people, largely rural, living in such a region as Alabama in the ante-bellum period, home treatments of diseases were of great importance. Trained physicians were scarce at the time, and even trained ones were not very pro-

---

[36]*Ibid.*; a reprint from an unknown issue of the *Evening Journal* of Albany, New York.
[37]*Ibid.*

ficient in the work they performed.[38] Since few professionally trained doctors practiced in Marshall's region, he and the other people around Fort Claiborne relied upon their own resourcefulness, initiative, and inventiveness in treating diseases. Doing so, they were typical of the rural people of America of their day.

Some of the cures concocted by Marshall himself, as well as most of those that he collected, indicate that many pre-Civil War Southerners had the necessary inventiveness to combat almost any disease or ailment. Most of the treatments resulted from a trial and error process, and nearly every conceivable cure was attempted. This is not to say that all of them succeeded, for their success is unknown, and they are not recommended for modern usage, but it is to say that, sometimes in almost unbelievable ways, domestic cures of diseases were attempted. Any plant that was remotely suspected of possessing medicinal qualities was given a trial of one sort or another, the dual results being that few herbs escaped use and that some cures were effected. Marshall also used anvil dust from his blacksmith shop in preparing medicines. And as in the case of the other entries in his "Book," he copied some of his prescriptions from printed sources, such as newspapers, magazines, and medical journals. Many of his cures were his own; others came to him from neighbors and friends; some were picked up from Indian lore; some were brought to Alabama from Africa by Negro slaves. He practiced empiricism at its best, or worse.

On the basis of the number of cures described by Marshall, the most common ailments which interested him were dysentery, diarrhea, rheumatism, venereal diseases, cancer, coughs, ringworm, tetter, dropsy, and ulcers. It was to treat these diseases, as well as many others, that he and his contemporaries experimented. Preparation of medicines was a complicated, year-round procedure, with barks of trees and roots and plants being utilized while in season to make concoctions and salves and tonics for use throughout the year. Many of the treatments and prescriptions were so extremely horrible, both in preparation and administration, that the considered conclusion upon examining some of them is not

---

[38]See, for example, Martha Carolyn Mitchell, "Health and the Medical Profession in the Lower South, 1845-1860," *Journal of Southern History*, X, 424-446 (1944).

that they possibly succeeded but that the patients survived them. Nevertheless, Marshall did use the preventives and cures that he gathered and placed in his "Book." Since he lived to the advanced age of eighty-five years, a safe assumption would seem to be that his medicines did not kill him.

The medical lore collected by Marshall fell under three general categories: (1) herbs (2) prescriptions, ointments, cures, remedies and preventives, and (3) veterinary medicine. In listing herbs he indicated the medical properties of each one, the disease or diseases they were believed to cure, and how to prepare them for use; whereas in listing a disease for which he was seeking a cure, he described the method or methods of treating that disease. Except for the items on herbs, which were placed consecutively in the "Book," his items on medicine were scattered indiscriminately throughout his collection. This, then, was his method of arranging his information on medicine. In using it he could turn to an item on an herb and check its medical properties, or he could turn to an item on a disease and ascertain how he might treat it. However, he did not prepare an index to his "Book"; thus it could not be used conveniently or knowingly by anyone except him.

"Bearberry, Bear's whortleberry [or] wild cranberry," the dose to consist of "half a pint twice or thrice a day of a decoction made of the leaves, a handful to a pint," Marshall said, would relieve "the irritation of the stone gravel, & old cases of gonorrhea, menstrual discharges, also catarrhs and consumptions." A poultice made by boiling the roots of button snakeroot, it was averred, was "superior to any thing yet discovered in cases of gangrene and foul ulcers." The cinquefoil plant, boiled slowly in water or milk, sweetened with sugar, and administered by the teacupful three or four times daily, was recommended for dysentery and bowel complaints of adults. Dill, wrote Marshall, grew in his garden, and its seed, "in doses of one or two teaspoonfuls, are excellent to remove flatulent colics, and assist digestion." The common elder, its roots, bark, berries, or leaves, prepared in various ways, was used as an asperient medicine, as well as to combat colds, dropsies and eruptions of the skin, to reduce fevers, and to anoint burns. "The fresh root" of elicampane, "in ointment, or strong decoction," Marshall recorded, "is said to cure the itch." He also stated, "When unripe, figs, as well as the whole tree, yield an acrid milky juice, which externally applied is a mild caustic, and is uséd to remove warts, ring and tetter worms."[39]

These were by no means the only herbs utilized by Marshall and his contemporaries, but a few more examples must suffice here. Butterfly weed or pleurisy root was "good in violent colds and pleurisies" and in producing perspiration. Horse radish was judged to be an all-round medicine, since "when taken freely" it was thought to stimulate the nervous system, to be useful in treating palsy, dropsy, scurvy and rheumatism, and, concluded Marshall, "the root steeped in vinegar, will remove freckles of the face." Mistletoe, dried and pulverized, was said "to have cured epilepsy or fits." Peppermint was believed to be "a most valuable remedy," that is, "an excellent stomachic in flatulent colics, lanquors, hysteric cases, and vomiting." Samson snake root was "useful" in dyspepsia, indigestion, diarrhea and dysentery cases. An infusion of sassafras was employed "as a sweetner or purifier of the blood, in scorbatic, venereal, & cutaneous disorders, or where an acrimony of the fluids prevails." Boneset was another much used herb, for it was, according to Marshall, a "sudorific, antiseptic, carthartic, emetic, stimulant, etc." as well as an antidote for snake bites.

A method of preparing a diet drink for rheumatism, cachexy, dropsy, ague, cancerous ulcers, fever and worms was to "Take of walnut and Sassafras bark and red root equal quantities—Boil them in water until it is tolerably Astringent to the taste—Give from half a gill to a gill every hour until it purges, on the first day—Then give a sufficiency every day for three weeks to keep the bowels moderately laxative, unless the cure is performed in a shorter time." An unusual "recipe to cure a sore leg" was as follows: "Take cow's urine and boil it down to a Jelly. Wash the sore night and morning with soap and warm water, then cover the sore with a plaister of the Jelly spread on a rag. If the bone is effected, cut the leg off, if necessary." A tobacco ointment, for treating rheumatic or sciatic pains, was made as follows: "To 1 quart of wine add one pound of good Tobacco, steep it 24 hours then work it well in the wine and squeeze it out, then add a large handful of pennyroyal

---

[39]The descriptions of the herbs listed by Marshall in his "Book" appear in his own writing and without any indication of their sources.

and one pound of fresh butter, then stew out the wine, Strain it and bottle it for use."

In addition to using herbs as a base for his medicines, Marshall often prepared other concoctions by utilizing patent medicines as the chief ingredients, and on occasions he combined patent medicines with herbs and other articles. Here again he amply demonstrated both initiative and courage, initiative because he seemingly was willing to experiment with almost anything, courage because he took his own medicines. His "recipes," a sample listing of which shows the exceedingly wide variety of medicines which he made, included quinine pills, liquid laudanum, apodeldoc, tobacco ointment, itch lotion, basilicon ointment, febrifuge powders, tincture of rhubarb, charcoal poultice, tincture of alloes, lotion for scorbutic ulcers, tincture of myrrh, soda powders, elixir paregoric, and sedlitz powders.[40] Several of these are intriguing. Sedlitz powder, for instance, was made of rochelle salt, carbonate of soda, tartaric acid, and water. Itch lotion consisted of corrosive sublimate, crude sal ammoniac, and water. Elixir paregoric, as prepared by Marshall, was comprised of oil of anise, benzoic acid, powdered opium, camphor, powdered cochineal, spirits of wine, and water. Tincture of rhubarb, which was used as a laxative, consisted of rhubarb, cardamon seeds or ginger, and brandy or rum. A tincture of myrrh was made of 12 ounces of myrrh, 1 ounce of peach or cherry kernels, and 1 gallon of brandy or alcohol.

Among the many other ailments for which Marshall had various remedies were the following: yaws, sore throat, erysipelas, ear ache, whooping cough, sore mouth, colic, headache, croup, piles, cholera, small pox, toothache, scarlet fever, hiccups, diphtheria, corns, gout, jaundice, stammering, asthma, chicken pox, gravel, shingles, and tapeworm.[41] He also did not neglect the more common, yet painful or uncomfortable ailments which often prevail. For

---

[40]Marshall does not indicate the sources of his information as to how to prepare these medicines. However, one or more of the ingredients of these medicines usually consisted of patent medicines.

[41]Nearly all of Marshall's treatments of these ailments represent folk medicine as he practiced it. A small portion of the entries in his "Book" on these ailments consisted of unknown publication clippings. Marshall also obtained a few of his treatments from such well-known publications as the *Scientific American,* the *Saturday Evening Post,* and the Charleston *Mercury.*

example, his "recipe for a cold in the head" was to take at one dose one ounce of Epsom Salts and one-half an ounce of pepper tea mixed in eight ounces of water. To make teeth white, he said, "A mixture of honey with the purest charcoal will prove an admirable cleanser." Among his prescriptions for indigestion was one he received from a local physician, Dr. Caleb Lindsey: "Take 1 quart of clean Hickory ashes, and half a pint of clean soot, put it into a Jug, with One Gallon of water, and shake it often—After three or four days a wine glass full to be taken three times a day." A prescription for a "sick headache," also furnished by Dr. Lindsey, called for "2 grs. Blue Mass every 2 hours for five times, unless it operates sooner. Give 5 grs. Quinine every night, for 2 weeks." And "to cure baldness," that condition which comes to many men and which by many of them is considered a dreadful happening, Marshall concluded, "Rub the part morning and evening with onions until it is red, and rub it afterward with honey."

As has been mentioned, Marshall collected some items on veterinary medicine for his "Book," gathering them from agricultural journals, "horse doctors," or from the usual hearsay, experimentation, friends, and acquaintances. No evidence is available to show that he gave much attention to stock raising, but on the basis of the contents of his "Book" there is no question that he owned some cattle and that he was particularly interested in caring for his horses. Indeed, except for several brief items, including one on gapes in chickens and another on hen lice,[42] every item on farm animals in his collection was concerned with horses. In treating these animals he showed an ingenuity equal to that displayed in his medical care of himself, his family, and his slaves; and some of the treatments for horses differed from his other medical practices largely in the amount of medicine administered to his patients, human or otherwise, although not always for the same ailments, of course. On the other hand, some of his animal medications were much more drastic than those he used for humans.

---

[42]The item on gapes consisted of a clipping from an unknown publication. The item on hen lice, obtained from the *Saturday Evening Post,* advised feeding mashed onions and corn meal in water to hens to prevent lice. Marshall's conclusion about the latter practice was, "It has failed in Alabama."

His horses seem to have been bothered with three ailments in particular: colic, bots (resulting from larvae of botflies in the stomach), and scratches (a skin disease characterized by scabs, usually near the fetlock). To cure bots Marshall drenched his animals with various mixtures: sweet milk and molasses; red pepper, tobacco, and soap; vinegar and flour; onions; indigo, copperas, soot, salt, gun powder, salt petre, whiskey, and "old chamberley"; nitfly eggs and tobacco; slaked lime; dough and soap; or horse's hair and molasses. All this is further proof that Marshall was a medical empiricist. For "scratches in horses," several remedies were attempted, in each case the affected part being covered, either with slaked lime, strong brine, a solution of bluestone, copperas or borax, or with blue vitriol and hot tar.[43] For colic a horse was drenched with very salty water or a mixture of milk, molasses, and laudanum. Marshall was also interested in treatments of animals ailing with swinny, sore tongue, fistula, founder, farcy, coughs, bellows, spavin, bowel complaints, setfast, sore backs, staggers, and distemper;[44] and typical of his prescriptions for these ailments was the one for sore tongue: "Make a decoction of Black haw root, Redshank root & persimmon bark—Add alum, Borax, and Copperas—wash the tongue by means of a mop twice a day until cured—when cold after it, add vinegar, as much as the decoction."

As might be expected, Marshall also included in his daybook items on general farming practices, although for some reason he failed to put many such items in his collection. However, he was interested in such matters as transplanting, poultry manure, planting of various vegetables, and chicken feed.[45] Of more concern to him, on the basis of what he put in his "Book" for reference, was the farmer's perennial task of controlling the numerous pests and worms that destroyed his stock and plants. A method of fighting "the destructive ravages of the boll worm on cotton," he learned, was to destroy the stalks after the cotton was picked, the reason for this being, it was claimed, "that the worm deposits an egg in

---

[43]Marshall learned of one of the treatments for scratches from a reprint of an article from an unidentified agricultural journal published in Massachusetts, and another from a reprint from an unidentified Canadian newspaper.

[44]For the most part, the descriptions of these treatments appear in Marshall's "Book" as clippings from unknown publications.

[45]Clipping, Unknown Publication; reprints from the *Working Farmer*, of New York City, and of the Boston *Transcript*.

the stalk which remains there during the winter and produces a new worm next season."[46] Peach worms were controlled, it was said, by circling the trunks of trees with a shallow trench and pouring into the trench "very thick whitewash, made of fresh lime."[47] Several practices were followed in Marshall's efforts to "prevent birds from pulling up corn." One procedure was to soak the seed in a decoction of hen manure and fish brine, while another was to "steep" the seed in a "moderately strong solution" of copperas. "To catch all kind of varmin that live by blood," such as wolves, beaver and otter, all of which pestered his farm operations, he said, "Get 1 oz. of the Oil of Rodia or Rodium, 1 oz. of Oil of Aspur, 1 oz. of the Oil of Spike,1 oz. of oil of Olives or sweet oil, 1 oz. of Assafoetida [sic], 1 oz. of Beaver Castor. Mix a little of each in hog's lard, with the urine and seed of each animal you catch." This powerful, odoriferous mixture, it was believed, would attract the predators and kill them.

One of the Marshall "Book" items on farming, a clipping from an unknown publication and bearing the title "Hints to Farmers," is, perhaps, a clue to the interests and character of Marshall himself. To say the least, the item is in keeping with the truly amazing collection which he brought together over a period of sixty years; it is also a sort of catechism for good farming:[48]

A farmer should never undertake to cultivate more land than he can do thoroughly; half tilled land is growing poorer; well tilled land is constantly improving.

A farmer should never keep more cattle, horses, sheep or hogs than he can keep in good order; an animal in high order the first of December, is already half wintered.

A farmer should never depend on his neighbor for what he can, by care and good management, produce on his own farm; he should never beg fruit while he can plant trees, or borrow tools while he can make or buy them—a high authority has said, "the borrower is the servant to the lender."

A farmer should never be so immersed in political matters as to forget to sow his wheat, dig his potatoes and bank up his cellar; nor should he be so inattentive to them as to be ignorant of those great questions of national and state policy which will always agitate, more or less, a free people.

No farmer should allow the reproach of neglected education to lie against himself or family; if "knowledge is power," the commencement should be early and deeply laid in the minds of his children.

---

[46]Clipping, Unknown Publication, of a letter, dated September, 1852, written by a Joseph H. Martin to the editor.

[47]Clipping, Unknown Publication; a reprint from the *Horticulturist*, of Albany, New York.

[48]Clipping, Unknown Publication.

V

NEGRO "PECULIARITIES"

One of the most far-reaching aspects of thought in the Old South was the general belief among white Southerners that the Negro was not a member of the same species as the white man.[1] A popular contention was that Negroes possessed peculiarities which made them either susceptible or immune to certain ailments and diseases. Many professional physicians accepted and advanced the idea that Negroes were not the same physiologically and anatomically as whites. In the minds of many Southerners who justified slavery on ethnological grounds, there was no doubt that the Negro was inferior to the white. This ethnological justification of slavery exerted a powerful and long-lasting influence on the thinking of white Southerners. It also had some influence on the theories and practices of medicine in Alabama and elsewhere during the antebellum period. Just how much influence it had in these respects is unknown. There is not much evidence that Negroes were treated very differently from whites by their nurses, doctors and others, nor is there any reason to believe that surgeons cut differently into a man due to his color. There is, nevertheless, no doubt that there existed in the South a broadly accepted belief that the Negro differed from the white man. The idea was expressed in many forms and many places over a long period of time.[2] It was intimately associated with the ideology of white supremacy in the South. How this ideology came about and how it was popularized in Alabama is an interesting story, a story which, presumably, has never been told in detail.

---

[1]The contents of several paragraphs in this Chapter were included in "Plantation Medicine in the Old South," *Alabama Review*, III, 83-107 (1950), and have been rewritten here with the permission of W. Stanley Hoole and James B. McMillan, editors of the *Review*.

[2]Discussions of the ethnological justification of slavery may be found in William Sumner Jenkins, *Pro-Slavery Thought in the Old South* (Chapel Hill, 1935), 242-284, Arthur Young Lloyd, *The Slavery Controversy* (Chapel Hill, 1939), 228-242, and Harvey Wish, *George Fitzhugh, Propagandist of the Old South* (Baton Rouge, 1943), 35, 42, 298-300.

A very significant statement about so-called Negro "peculiarities" was made in the year 1820 by "FRANKLIN," an unknown correspondent of the *American Farmer* of Baltimore:

[Negroes] are less liable to the autumnal diseases than the whites, yet suffer *much more* severely from winter epidemics than they [the whites] do . . . *white* and *polished* surfaces let off heat slowly; whereas *black* or *rough* surfaces, radiate it freely. This is an admitted fact in chemistry and physiology. We know that liquids cool soonest in *dark* vessels, and retain their heat longest in bright ones. . . . The negro . . . was designed for the sultry regions of the torrid zone. His surface is therefore adapted to the ready escapement of internal heat. . . .

That they are then *really* more chilly, we cannot doubt, ... It therefore necessarily follows that they are more liable to diseases brought on by the cold of winter, than white persons. They are likewise more subject to disease on account of their greater exposure to wet and inclement weather.

How can the health of slaves be best preserved? We see that if they had a *white* skin, it would prove a security to them; but as we cannot "wash the Ethiop white," we must use such other means as may prevent the escapement of their heat. — They ought in the first place, to wear *woolens* next to their skin, instead of linen and cotton. Long woolen shirts would retain their heat, equalize the excitement, and secure them against the effects of wet work and rainy weather. These shirts should be *white* for reasons too obvious to need repetition. . . . When wet, negroes should dry by a good fire. They should also be allowed to sleep by a fire, if convenient: the *out* laborers especially.

By attending to this regimen, we feel no hesitation in saying, that a planter will greatly secure the health of his slaves.[3]

"FRANKLIN'S" remarks undoubtedly served as an important landmark in the development of one phase of southern ideology, and his opinion exerted great influence, not because it was, perhaps, the first such statement but because it became so widely circulated and accepted. The *American Farmer* was a very popular magazine.[4] Portions of the article by "FRANKLIN" were reprinted some years later, in 1839, in at least two other agricultural journals, the *Farmer's Register* of Virginia and the *Southern Agriculturist* of South Carolina,[5] which in their own right were read in many places.

---

[3]*American Farmer*, II, 242 (1820). For a discussion of the conceptions of several intellectuals on the subject of Negro ethnology in the years preceding the appearance of "FRANKLIN'S" article in the *American Farmer*, see John C. Greene, "The American Debate on the Negro's Place in Nature, 1780-1815," *Journal of the History of Ideas*, XV, 384-396 (1954).

[4]Albert Lowther Demaree, *The American Agricultural Press, 1819-1860* (New York, 1941), 19, 23-38, 117.

[5]*Farmer's Register*, VII, 372 (1839); *Southern Agriculturist*, XII, 492-493 (1839).

Moreover, during the period 1820-1860 the thoughts expressed by "FRANKLIN" were reiterated in innumerable forms throughout the South.

Another opinion about the Negro was offered by a physician who had practiced medicine in Africa, where he treated and examined numerous Negroes. One of his reports was that he had examined three dead Negroes and that he "found the stomach different from that organ in white people, both in size and structure. . . ." His conclusion was: "I think I am warranted in the supposition that the smallness of the negroes' stomachs, and the peculiar corrugations of their folds, are no less distinct marks of that race (insomuch as physical organization is concerned), than their thick craniums and prominent cheek bones . . . the stomach was below the ordinary size of that organ in Europeans, and its internal surface resembled in some degree a turtle's throat, from the extent of its corrugations." But this was not all. The doctor also said, "I discovered likewise, a difference in the skeleton, in two of these cases, each having six vertebrae of the loins, instead of five, and on examining the spines of many living negroes, I find the occurrence of six lumbar vertebrae very frequent. This accounts for the extraordinary length of the lumbar part of the back in so many negroes. That they are a distinct race I think is evident from these, and other peculiarities."[6]

In a series of two articles printed in 1839 in the *Southern Agriculturist*, Doctor W. G. Ramsay of South Carolina was quite positive that the Negro possessed certain peculiarities. His first article called attention to a number of "anatomical differences." The Negro, he said, did not possess "the fine forehead as in the European, which is caused by the frontal bone being shorter, and the parietal bones (the bones at the side of the head) less excavated, and smaller in the negro." Other Negro characteristics, continued the Doctor, were a high temporal ridge, "large and powerful" temporal muscles, large and strong mastication bones, "very thick" bones in the walls of the cranium, projected cheek bones, flat noses, slender anatomy of the trunk "particularly about the loins." As for the Negro's color, Ramsay stated, "We are almost tempted to believe that there must have been more Adams' than

[6]*Farmer's Register*, I, 665 (1834).

one, each variety of colour having its own original parent. The color of the skin of the negro gives him great advantage over the European's by enabling him to endure the heat of the sun with less suffering." He also held the following opinions: "Laziness is one of the great characteristics of the negro — . . . True bravery, love of liberty, ambition, and all the higher feelings to which the soul of man is heir to, belongs [sic] to the white man . . . . It is improbable, under any circumstances, that these two races of men can be made equal in moral and intellectual attainments, as to believe that by education, the bulldog may equal the greyhound in speed, or the mastiff rival the sagacious poodle." It was no accident that the white man was superior, said Ramsay, "but it is innate, implanted in him by the God of nature."[7]

Doctor Ramsay's second article had to do with "the differences as regards disease" among Negroes and whites, and here, just as in his first article, he expressed some conceptions that were broadly accepted in the South. The Negro, he continued, endured pain "with less apparent suffering" than the European, his "constitutional irritability is in many cases very great—slight wounds often produce troublesome ulcers," and he possessed "a peculiar liability to spasms, from very trifling causes, which, in most cases, would produce no injury amongst the whites." The Doctor also pointed out that plantation Negroes had been unaffected by the dengue fever, "which prevailed so extensively and universally at the South during the summer of 1828," and that they "were peculiarly exempt from miasmatic diseases, bilious, remittent, and intermittent fevers, which fatal diseases destroy so large a portion of the white population of the Southern States," but that they were subject to typhus fever and "Pneamonia typlodies" or "Bastard Pleurisy, as it is commonly called." In answer to the old question which would continue to trouble many people, white Southerners and others, "Do the races of men spring from the same original stock?" Ramsay concluded, "In investigating it we find ourselves wandering into regions dark and obscure, over which the torch of science sheds but a faint light, merely enough to convince us of our ignorance."[8]

[7]*Southern Agriculturist*, XII, 286-294 (1839).
[8]*Ibid.*, XII, 411-418 (1839).

Doctor Josiah C. Nott of Mobile was another leader among the Southerners who justified slavery on ethnological grounds. He was a student of Doctor Samuel George Morton, the famous craniologist of Philadelphia, who taught that races were diversified in their origin. Writing before Charles Darwin brought out his monumental *The Origin of Species* in 1859, Nott joined Morton and a large group of American and European scientists of the 1840's and 1850's in advocating the theory of the diversity of races, with the result that he, himself, became a world-renowned scientist because of his own extensive, diligent studies.[9] He first attracted attention in 1844 with two popular lectures which he delivered and published in Mobile.[10] His thesis, as he put it, was, "I set out with the proposition, that there is a genus, man, comprising two or more species—that physical causes cannot change a White man into a negro, and that to say that this change has been effected by a direct act of Providence, is an assumption that cannot be proven, and is contrary to the great change of nature's laws. . . . The White man cannot live in tropical Africa, or the African in the frigid zone. . . ."[11] The Negro, said Nott, differed from the Caucasian in that he had a smaller head, narrower forehead, projected upper jaw, thicker bones in the head, longer arm, flat and long thighs, and a different shin bone, calf, foot, and heel.[12] Being much interested in hybrids, of which he considered mulattoes an example, he wrote: "That those [Negroes] of unmixed extraction in the free States are not more liable to sickness or premature death, than the Whites of their rank and condition in society; but that the striking mortality, so manifest among the free people of color, is in every community and section of the country, *invariably confined to the Mulattoes*."[13]

In view of the many advances being made in the study of science as well as because of the broad acceptance of Biblical teachings which prevailed in America, including Alabama, during the 1840's,[14]

[9]Jenkins, *Pro-Slavery Thought in the Old South*, 261, 274.

[10]Josiah C. Nott, *Two Lectures on the Natural History of the Caucasian and Negro Races* (Mobile, 1844).

[11]*Ibid.*, 7, 19.

[12]*Ibid.*, 23-24.

[13]*Ibid.*, 30.

[14]Thomas Cary Johnson, Jr., *Scientific Interests in the Old South* (New York, 1936); Clement Eaton, *Freedom of Thought in the Old South* (Durham, 1940), 280-314.

it was to be expected that Nott would be severely criticized for his lectures. In April, 1845, a series of critical appraisals that would eventually devastate most of the Mobile doctor's theories was launched in the *Southern Quarterly Review* of Charleston, South Carolina, in an article written by Moses Ashley Curtis, a North Carolinian, who was both a botanist and Episcopal clergyman. This criticism was followed by many others, of course. Curtis wrote, "We think that the author [Nott] has done needless violence to the faith of those who have implicit confidence in the veracity of the Scriptures . . . we are persuaded, that natural causes are fully competent to the production of all the varieties of the human family." The question of physical differences of races, the reviewer added, was "not to be settled by remarking only the extreme physical *differences* but by giving due importance to the remarkable *resemblances* that occur between the several races." As for Nott, Curtis accused him of confused thought, begging the question, refuting himself, seeking an argument, and of being ill-informed. The Mobilian, concluded Curtis, was "a young man, too eager for taking rank among the savans [*sic*] to wait for a due digestion of his varied reading, too impatient for the slow toil of laying deep and sure the foundations of an impregnable reputation."[15] In other words, Nott was considered as an immature revisionist.

Doctor Nott showed himself to be a man of strong words and one who would not run from an argument by answering Curtis in an article printed in the July, 1845, issue of the *Southern Quarterly Review*. He stated that he, with "some fifteen or twenty" persons of various professions, had been invited to deliver a series of "popular lectures" in Mobile. He had given two lectures, which he had been forced to present briefly and without developing fully, for which he was being "taken rudely to task." He did not mind argument, but Reverend Curtis had "misplaced sentences, garbled and perverted meanings" in his criticisms of the lectures. The Reverend had "certainly *disputed,* though he has not *disproved, a single one* of the conclusions arrived at, if authorities be of any value," claimed Nott. In regard to his own support of the Scriptures, Nott averred: "We would have avoided this discussion, — it was forced on him. Contrary to his wishes or intention, it was made to assume a

---

[15]*Southern Quarterly Review*, VII, 386, 394, 411, 438, 447 (1845).

religious character, and he himself charged with views hostile to the truths of the Bible, — the Bible, for which he has ever had the highest veneration, and whose precepts, he trusts, he has never wilfully slighted. He has been wounded and injured by the unfairest imputations. . . ."[16]

Nott followed this first answer to Curtis with another phillipic in the same *Quarterly* in January, 1846, and again reiterated his belief in the diversity of races. Expounding at length on the subject of mulattoes, a subject which would intrigue him for many years, he said that they "presented many of the characters of hybrids, [and] corroborated very strongly this idea" that races were distinct species. Based on twenty years of study, he believed:[17]

1st.   That the Mulattoes are intermediate in intelligence between Blacks and Whites.

2d.   That they are less capable of undergoing fatigue and hardships, than Blacks and Whites.

3d.   That the Mulatto women are particularly delicate, and subject to a variety of chronic diseases.

4th.   That the women are bad breeders and bad nurses—many do not conceive—most are subject to abortions, and a large portion of the young die in the Southern States.

5th.   That the two sexes when they intermarry, are less prolific than when crossed on one of the parent stocks.

6th.   That Negroes and Mulattoes are exempt in a surprising degree from yellow fever.

In this article, Nott also accused Curtis of bringing up false issues and that he had "glossed over them . . . with clever fallacies." But this was not all that the aroused Nott had to say. Curtis, he argued, was guilty of "bravado" and had written an "unprovoked and ungenerous critique" and had raised "the blood-stained banner of blind fanaticism."[18] Upon reading Nott's diatribes, Reverend Curtis grew tired of the subject; thus, in the April, 1846, issue of the *Quarterly* he offered his last rejoinder. He had meant no injustice to the Doctor, he said, although he was positive that Nott had erred in some of his statements and that "some portions of the 'Two Lectures' were unjust, unfair, and erroneous. . ." On his part, stated the Reverend, he would not retract his own assertions. He con-

---

16*Ibid.*, VIII, 149-151, 190 (1845).
17*Ibid.*, IX, 45 (1846).
18*Ibid.*, IX, 55 (1846).

cluded, "We therefore take our leave of Dr. Nott. . . . It is with no unkind feelings that we now bid him adieu."[19]

Curtis' attack of Nott's lectures whetted the Doctor's appetite for debate, and, for this as well as the reason that he firmly believed in his theories, he continued after the year 1844 to develop his ideas on the diversity of races. In December, 1848, speaking from the Chair of Political Economy of the Louisiana University in New Orleans, he gave "Two Lectures on the Connection between the Biblical and Physical History of Man;" in July, 1850, the *Southern Quarterly Review* printed an article of his entitled "Physical History of the Jewish Race;" and in February, 1851, *DeBow's Review* of New Orleans published an article called "Diversity of the Human Race."[20] His best known works, however, in which he discussed the Negro as a distinct race and mulattoes as hybrids, were *Types of Mankind* (Philadelphia, 1854), on which he collaborated with George R. Gliddon, the archeologist, and *Indigenous Races of the Earth* (Philadelphia and London, 1857), which he edited. He thus became widely known as an ethnologist and anthropologist. However, his reputation as a scientist in these fields of study suffered irreparable harm with the publication of Darwin's *The Origin of Species* in 1859.

Nott denied the "unity doctrine" as taught by the Bible; he was also a firm advocate of the ideology of white supremacy. He was a scientist turned racist. In his book *Indigenous Races of the Earth*, one of his arguments was that "each type of mankind, like the several species of plants and animals, has its appropriate climate or station, beyond which it cannot travel, or acquire domiciliation, in any length of ages, ..."[21] On another occasion, in the course of a speech made in Mobile on the "Natural History of Man in Connection with Negro Slavery," he argued that slavery had been "bequeathed" to the South and that Negroes "stand at the lowest point in the scale of human beings" and were incapable of developing their own civilization or government. In this same speech he said, "It will not do to be guided by abstract notions of

[19]*Ibid.*, IX, 372, 391 (1846).

[20]*Ibid.*, XII, 265 (1849); *ibid.*, New Series, I, 426-451 (1850); *DeBow's Review*, VII, 377 (1849); *ibid.*, X, 130 (1851).

[21]*DeBow's Review*, XXII, 74 (1857).

liberty and slavery. We can only judge the future by the past; and as experience proves that the negro is better off in slavery at the South, than in freedom elsewhere, it is the part of philanthropy to keep him there, as we keep children in subjection for their own good."[22] At another time a writer in *DeBow's Review* agreed with him that the Negro was "a distinct race incapable of assimiliation or unassisted progress, ..."[23] In 1850 he wrote: "We do not doubt that individuals of inferior races, as Indians and negroes, are capable of receiving education and attaining what might be termed respectable mediocrity, when compared with the whites; . . . ."[24]

It was indeed true, as one writer expressed the thought, that Nott's theories "fell like a fire-brand in the midst of inflammable material,"[25] that is, that his speeches and articles and books helped bring about an explosive and vituperative debate between Southerners and Northerners on the subject of slavery during the 1840's and 1850's.[26] It would be quite unhistorical to claim that Nott was the first person to advance the belief that the Negro differed from white men. However, there is no question that, because of his Mobile lecture of 1844 and his other activities, he should be included, along with "FRANKLIN" for his 1820 article in the *American Farmer* and with Doctor W. G. Ramsay for his 1839 article in the *Southern Agriculturist,* among the very significant writers who helped lay the broad foundations for the belief among white Southerners that Negroes were different from and inferior to white men.[27]

The notions of Doctors Ramsay and Nott about the Negro were restated one way or another by many Alabamians and other Southerners during the late ante-bellum period. "J. A. C.," writing in the *Southern Quarterly Review,* was only one of the numerous correspondents of that magazine who chimed in with an ap-

---

[22]*Ibid.,* X, 329-332 (1851).
[23]*Ibid.,* VII, 377 (1849).
[24]*Southern Quarterly Review,* New Series, I, 450 (1850).
[25]*DeBow's Review,* IX, 244 (1850).
[26]For references to Nott's influence, see Avery O. Craven, *The Growth of Southern Nationalism, 1848-1861* (Baton Rouge, 1953), 259-260; Eaton, *Freedom of Thought in the Old South,* 309-310; Jenkins, *Pro-Slavery Thought in the Old South,* 275-284; Lloyd, *The Slavery Controversy,* 228-242.
[27]See, for example, Jenkins, *Pro-Slavery Thought in the Old South,* 256-257.

proval of the idea that Negroes were inferior to whites, claiming that "The African might be made a slave, because he was an infidel and a descendant of Ham." Another contributor to the *Quarterly* referred to the Negro as "so markedly our inferior," and said that "the literal and cramped interpretation of Genesis to which some would confine us, is utterly untenable," because "all races do *not* have the same abilities, enjoy the same powers, or show the same natural dispositions, and are not, therefore entitled to the same position in human society . . . the negro is fitted for his position, ..." Doctor John Y. Bassett, of Huntsville, Alabama, wrote that "the highest grade of civilization he [the Negro] ever reaches is in a state of slavery; which, when he quits, he falls, in a few generations, back towards his native state of savagism." Another Southerner argued, "It is scarcely now a subject of dispute that the black man is of inferior race to the white."[28] And the author of an article "The Black Race in North America," published in the *Southerner Literary Messenger* of Richmond, Virginia, concluded, "Two races so essentially different in character, intellect, habits, tastes, cannot occupy the same territory as equals. The inferior caste must be in subjection to the higher. And it is best for the former that it should be so."[29]

Martin W. Philips, a Mississippi planter who was also a Baptist minister, agreed with the old belief that a Negro could not stand cold and wet weather, saying, "Negroes cannot bear the same exposure to wet and cold that whites can, ... They require warmer clothing than whites, and better protection from the inclemencies of winter."[30] And the Negro's hair was of perennial interest to white Southerners, one of whom, in *DeBow's Review*, referred to Negro hair as "wool," concluding that this was evidence that the Negro was a "separate species of beings."[31] W. W. McQuire, editor of the *Alabama Planter*, stated, "The hair of the Caucasian, or white man, is an oval tube, with a large oval perforation; that of the

[28]*Southern Quarterly Review*, New Series, III, 337, 399, 407-408, 411 (1851); *ibid.*, New Series, IV, 130, 213 (1851).
[29]*Southern Literary Messenger*, XXI, 676 (1855).
[30]*Southern Cultivator*, V, 143 (1847). See also *American Cotton Planter and Soil of the South*, II, 293-294 (1858), and *DeBow's Review*, XXV, 571-572 (1858).
[31]*DeBow's Review*, IX, 231 (1850).

negro, oval but perfectly solid; that of the Indian, circular and perfectly solid."[32] Doctor George A. Ketchum of Mobile expressed the popular concept that Negroes lived longer than whites: "The colored population exceed the whites in longevity. The number of blacks dying from old age is nearly double that of the whites."[33] A Mobile editor argued that the Negro possessed a large liver and small lungs in comparison with white men and that he was thus slower than "the superior race." Accordingly, said the editor, white Southerners had learned not to force Negroes to work too fast, for "if they be made to move faster, they do not accomplish more; or accomplishing it, [they] do so at the sacrifice of their health."[34]

There was a common belief among white Southerners that Negroes were less susceptible to fevers than white men. For example, Doctor E. D. Fenner of New Orleans wrote, "It is a well-established fact that there is something in the negro constitution which affords him protection against the worst effects of Yellow Fever; but what it is I am unable to say." Fenner admitted that Negroes contracted yellow fever, "but less than the white man."[35] From Chinquepin Ridge, South Carolina, was circulated the following opinion: "Malarial influences act differently on different organizations. Of all the races of man, the Negro is best qualified by nature to brave these influences. Look at him under the burning sun in midsummer, in the rice field; he feels no inconvenience, for the heated ray is in relation with his skin and its function."[36] Another person, writing in the *Memphis Medical Recorder*, remarked that Negroes suffered from periodic fever more than any other disease but that they contracted it less often and less seriously than whites. Negroes, it was said, were less susceptible to yellow fever than whites because they were "perhaps, as a race, and certainly from their habits of life, less liable to gastric inflammation than the white race." Mulattoes, it was added, were increasingly liable to yellow

---

[32]*Alabama Planter*, V, 188 (1851).

[33]*DeBow's Review*, XI, 50 (1851).

[34]*Alabama Planter*, VI, 341 (1852).

[35]*DeBow's Review*, XVII, 42 (1854). See also *Southern Agriculturist*, IV, 472 (1831).

[36]*Farmer and Planter*, V, 255 (1854).

fever in proportion to their increase of white blood.[37]

"J. T.," the author of an article entitled "Negro-Mania—Race" published in 1852 in the *Southern Quarterly Review,* wrote at length on "the diverse peculiarities of the Caucasian and the negro." He agreed with Doctor Nott that residence, time, and location did not "change the Caucasian into the negro, — or the negro into the Caucasian,"[38] and summed up the white Southerner's popular ideas on the "physical diversities" of the two races:[39]

1. The head of the Caucasian is covered with hair, that of the negro with wool.

The hair of the Caucasian is oval in shape, in direction flowing or wavy and curled, and enters the epidermis at an acute angle. The wool of the negro is in shape eccentrically elliptical, or flat—in direction, crisped or frizzled, and sometimes spirally twisted—and, in inclination, issues out of the epidermis at a right angle.

2. The beard of the Caucasian is ample, that of the negro is scanty.

3. The complexion of the Caucasian is fair or white, that of the negro is jetty or black.

4. The face of the Caucasian is small or oval, that of the negro is broad, with projecting jaws.

5. The forehead of the Caucasian is vertical and expanded, that of the negro is receding and contracting.

6. The nose of the Caucasian is elevated, that of the negro flat.

7. The mouth of the Caucasian is usually small and gracefully defined, that of the negro large and ugly.

8. The lips of the Caucasian are thin and red, those of the negro thick and black.

9. The chin of the Caucasian is round and full, that of the negro retreating and ill-shaped.

10. The eyes of the Caucasian are distinct, clear, and pellucid in the iris, those of the negro are prominent, yellowish and dingy in the iris.

11. The heel of the Caucasian stands well under the column of the leg, that of the negro projects in the rear.

12. The skin of the Caucasian consists of two parts only, viz: the scarf skin and the true skin; that of the negro consists of three parts, viz: the scarf skin, the rete mucosum, and the true skin.

13. The cranium of the Caucasian measures usually, interiorly, from eighty-eight to ninety cubic inches, that of the negro measures, interiorly, only from seventy-eight to eighty cubic inches.

14. The general form of the Caucasian seems to be made up of rounded

---

[37]*Memphis Medical Recorder,* quoted in *DeBow's Review,* XX, 612-622 (1856).

[38]*Southern Quarterly Review,* New Series, V, 163 (1852). "J. T." was here reviewing John Bachman, *Negromania: Being an Examination of the Falsely Assumed Equality of the Various Races of Men* (Philadelphia, 1851). For another review of Bachman's book, see *Southern Literary Messenger,* XVII, 702-703 (1851).

[39]*Southern Quarterly Review,* New Series, V, 164-165 (1852).

columns and curved arches, compactly set together, and approaches the ideal expressed in the statues of Apollo and Venus. The general form of the negro is coarse, angular, loosely conjoined, and could never be taken as a model of art and excellence.

15. The Caucasian secretes more by the kidneys and less by the glands of the skin—the negro secretes more by the skin and less by the kidneys, and hence his disagreeable odour.

16. The sensibility of the Caucasian is high, quick, and active, that of the negro is low, sluggish and apathetic.

17. The nervous organism of the Caucasian is largely developed and exceedingly refined, that of the negro is less developed nor can it be regarded as equally refined.

"J. T." had still another idea, namely, that there existed certain "mental or physical diversities" between Negroes and whites. The Caucasian, he said, had developed attributes of "adoration, benevolence, conscientiousness, intellectual appetite, fame, speech, prudence, admiration, and reason, or causality." The Negro, he continued, "is neither originative, inventive nor speculative; he is roving, revengeful and destructive, and he is warlike, predatory and sensual." Conclusions reached from all this were:

The two are thus made separate and distinct, legitimately, by the will of God; whether we consider his will as expressed in nature, or as declared through the unquestioned curse denounced against Canaan; . . . . The animal [the Negro as a physical being] is inferior and though, perhaps, susceptible of some improvement and amelioration, under the direct training and example of the Caucasian, yet he can never be elevated into a being of a high order of intelligence . . . the physical and mental inferiority of the negro to the Caucasian can never be removed in this life; . . . the negro is a slave to the Caucasian for the same reason that the horse, the ox and the ass are subject to him—because of natural, unalterable, and eternal inferiority; . . . .[40]

Another writer, presumably an Alabamian, who showed an interest in Negro "peculiarities" was a correspondent of the Mobile *Tribune* and Mobile *Alabama Planter*. This man, writing under the pseudonym of "SCRAPS," was the author of a gossipy column about life in New Orleans, which he wrote for the pleasure of his Alabama readers. In one of his columns he discussed a speech presented at the Lyceum Hall in the Crescent City, March 10, 1852, by a visiting lecturer, a Doctor McDowell. According to "SCRAPS," the Doctor "branched out boldly" on the subject "The human races and the diversity of their origin, ... [His] chief object seemed to be to prove that the white man and the negro were of different generations. . . . He denied that Eve was the mother of the whole

[40]*Ibid.*, New Series, V, 165-175 (1852).

human race, and said that Moses didn't know anything about it. Men were as different in their origin as chalk from cheese." Mc-Dowell also exhibited skulls of the 'Opossum, Coon, Fox, Monkey, Ourang Outang, Hottentot, Ethiopian, Hindoo, New Zealander, Indian, and Caucasian, concluding "that there was a gradation from one to the other as regular as the steps of a ladder, ..." This demonstration intrigued "SCRAPS," who stated, "It was thought that he would try to show that the higher organisms had improved by regular gradation from the lower, but he didn't. He contended that there was no such thing as improvement in this lower world." In other words, the Doctor was a Nott man, his conclusion being: "The negro was anatomically different from the white man . . . there was a black fluid between the inner skin and the cuticle of the negro, which soap could not wash out nor cold dissipate, nor Attar of Roses sweeten." The lecture brought from "SCRAPS" the cynical report that it was "in some respects, most excellent, but not suited to this abolition atmosphere [in New Orleans]. It was too tough on the niggers by far. People here prefer going to the theatres; and would rather stay home to count three per cent a month, or to devise plans to cheat their neighbors."[41]

Two stories printed in the year 1855 in the *Daily Mail* of Montgomery furnish some proof that this popular newspaper also encouraged public approval of white supremacy and of the belief that Negroes possessed certain "peculiarities." One of these stories concerned a lecture on "The Negro Races" given in Petersburg, Virginia, by Professor Henry A. Washington of William and Mary College. Quoting from the Petersburg *Intelligencer*, the *Daily Mail* reported: "His object was to prove that the negro has always been, and ever will be, subordinate to the whites, and that, physically and intellectually, he is inferior to the latter." In regard to Negro slavery, it was said, "It has elevated him from the depths of barbarism and brutalism to a degree of civilization and usefulness, and happiness, which he never would have reached through any other instrumentality." In the words of the *Daily Mail*: "It is only necessary for learned Southern men to treat the subject of African slavery in a scientific and temperate manner in order to uproot the

---

[41]*Alabama Planter*, VI, 117 (1852).

errors that prevail on the subject at the North. . . . All that we have to fear is that Abolitionists will not read defences of African slavery."[42]

A second story in the *Daily Mail* demonstrating an unqualified sanction of the Nott school of thought was the newspaper's approval of J. H. Van Evrie's book *Negroes and Negro Slavery* (New York, 1855). The *Daily Mail* gave its full support to a statement in the preface of Van Evrie's book that the Negro was "a different and inferior species of man; . . . that it [this difference] is original, invariable, or indestructible, as long as the present order of creation itself lasts— . . . that so-called slavery is neither a 'wrong' nor an 'evil' . . . but that it is a normal condition, a natural relation, based upon the 'higher law,' and absolutely essential to the very existence of the inferior race." On its own account the *Mail* said of Van Evrie's book: "Its reason and logic are unassailable, ... The Doctor proves beyond all cavil or question, that the negro is physiologically and anatomically a totally and entirely as well as inferior being to the white man, ..." Quoting Doctor Samuel A. Cartwright, "a celebrated physician of New Orleans," the *Mail* added: "Every citizen who feels the least interest in the destiny of his country, or the welfare of twenty millions of his own people and race, should read this book. It so completely upsets every abolition argument, . . . that the simplest mind is convinced at once of the facts and errors in the whole question."[43] Here was the basic reason that so many physicians were interested in the Negro: they sought to prove he was inferior in order to prove that he deserved to be only a slave.

The above mentioned Doctor Cartwright was indeed "a celebrated physician." A Virginian by birth, he moved to New Orleans, where he became much interested in Negro medicine. He might have been termed a psychologist, a pathologist, and a psychiatrist, or even a psychoanalyst if he had lived in later years. In his discussions of the Negro he also demonstrated some keen humor, a trait which was ordinarily notable for its absence among Southerners who defended their "peculiar institution" of slavery. Doctor Cart-

---

[42]Montgomery *Daily Mail,* February 8, 1855, quoting Petersburg *Intelligencer.* The *Southern Literary Messenger,* XX, 333 (1854), refers to Henry A. Washington as "A learned and able Professor."
[43]Montgomery *Daily Mail,* October 31, 1855.

wright, at the same time, was an avid supporter of the belief in Negro "differences" and inferiority; furthermore, he was a forceful speaker and writer who expressed his beliefs in no uncertain terms on many occasions. He was not as original in his ideas as Doctor Nott, but he more than held his own among those physicians who popularized the ideology of white supremacy in the ante-bellum South. In 1858, for example, the Montgomery *Mail*, referring to him as "an eminent physician of Louisiana, and one whose reputation for learning, probity and natural intellect is not confined to the limits of the United States," quoted him as follows in regard to Guinea Negroes who had been brought into Virginia: " . . . in size, actions and grimaces, they resembled the ourang outang . . . the negro is not a white man with black skin, but a different being, differing in wants and conformation."[44]

Early in the 1850's Doctor Cartwright read before the Medical Convention of Louisiana a paper which he entitled "Diseases and Peculiarities of the Negro Race," a paper which he undoubtedly delivered both to entertain and instruct his listeners. Later it was published as a series of three little articles in *DeBow's Review*, which attracted wide attention and were quoted in many places, including newspapers in Alabama.[45] No editor seems to have appreciated the humor of the Cartwright paper; rather they earnestly and sanctimoniously approved of it because it followed the old line that Negroes had "peculiarities." Moreover, few people seem to have appreciated Cartwright's pathological approach to his subject. However, this appreciation would come later in the form of a lengthy series of articles published in the *American Cotton Planter*, an agricultural journal of Montgomery.

In his paper, Cartwright, so to speak, "pulled out all stops." The Negro, he said, differed in color, membranes, muscles, tendons, fluids, and secretions; a "prevading darkness" colored his brain, nerves, chyle, humors, bile and blood; and he differed in his bones, head, face, neck, spine, pelvis, thigh-bones, legs, feet, gastrocnemii muscles, gait, mouth, forehead, nose, lips, hair, brain, hearing, and sight. The Doctor added that Negro children were born "with heads like gourds, the fontinelles being nearly closed; and the

---

[44]*Ibid.*, April 2, 1858.
[45]See, for example, *Alabama Planter*, V, 257, 273 (1851).

sutures between the various bones of the head united—not open and permitting of overlapping, as in white children." According to Cartwright, the Negro was a slave "by nature, . . . unfitted from his organization and the physiological laws predicated on that organization, for the responsible duties of a free man, but, like the child, is only fitted for a state of dependence and subordination." This was "the great primary truth" in any consideration of the Negro.

Negroes, Cartwright continued, were unusually subject to certain ailments and diseases, particularly pleurisy, fevers, and, like children, to colics, cramps, convulsions, worms, glandular and nervous affections, sores, biles, warts, and scrofula. They also often contracted consumption, although not for the ordinary reasons or in the ordinary manner. Cartwright said: "The seat of negro consumption is not in the lungs, stomach, liver, or any organ of the body, but in the mind, and its cause is generally mismanagement or bad government on the part of the master, and superstition or dissatisfaction on the part of the negro. The patients themselves believe that they are poisoned; they are right, but it is not the body, but the mind that is poisoned."

That Cartwright was, among other things, a wit was shown by his discussion of two other diseases which he claimed were peculiar to Negroes. He, of course, coined his own terminology for these "ailments." The first one, in his words, was "Drapetomania, or the Disease Causing Negroes to Run Away." This affliction, he said, was "as much a disease of the mind as any other species of mental alienation." Its cure consisted, he added, in not permitting Negroes to raise themselves to the level of their master. If they became sulky or dissatisfied, the cause should be looked into and removed. Some masters followed a practice of "whipping the devil out of them." More attentive, humane, and kind, however, was the method of furnishing good food, clothing, and housing, as well as not overworking them, and keeping them in a position, as Cartwright put it, which God had intended, that is, a position "of Canaan or submissive knee-bender."

"Dysaesthesia, Aethiopia, or Hebetude of Mind and Obtuse Sensibility of Body—A Disease Peculiar to Negroes—Called by Overseers, 'Rascality,'" was the second Negro ailment described by

Cartwright. It was an ailment which, perhaps, deserves the description given to it by the Doctor:

From the careless movements of the individuals affected with the complaint, they are apt to do much mischief, which appears as if intentional, but is mostly owing to the stupidness of mind and insensibility of the nerves induced by the disease. Thus, they break, waste and destroy everything they handle— abuse horses and cattle, — tear, burn or rend their own clothing, and paying no attention to the rights of property, steal others, to replace what they have destroyed. They wander about at night, and keep in a half nodding sleep during the day. They slight their work, — cut up corn, cane, cotton or tobacco when hoeing it, as if for pure mischief. They raise disturbances with their overseers and fellow-servants without cause or motive, and seem to be insensible to pain when subjected to punishment.

"Dysaesthesia, Aethiopia," said Cartwright, was a common occurrence "on badly governed plantations," and it was a "complaint" brought on by idleness, slothfulness, uncleanliness, and indolence. Its cure, he concluded, was to keep the Negro busy, clean, and out-of-doors, and to treat him kindly. Then, "His intelligence restored and his sensations awakened, he is no longer the *bipedum nequissimus*, or arrant rascal, he was supposed to be, but a good negro that can hoe or plow, and handles things with as much care as his fellow-servants." So said Cartwright on "Dysaesthesia, Aethiopia."[46]

In his paper, Cartwright also made the point that Negroes were "almost entirely unnoticed in medical books and schools. . . . The little knowledge that Southern physicians have acquired concerning them, has not been derived from books or medical lectures, but from facts learned from their own observation in the field of experience, or picked up here and there from others." It was strange, he said, that no medical school in the United States had made "special provision" for instruction in medical treatment of Negroes, who were "differently organized in mind and body from any other people, and having diseases requiring peculiar treatment, ..." This situation could be remedied, he thought, through establishing courses of study in Negro medicine in schools of the South. A fuller knowledge of medical care of Negroes, he said later, was "to be found by cultivating comparative anatomy, physiology, history and ethnography."[47]

---

[46]Cartwright's paper may be found in *DeBow's Review*, XI, 64-69, 209-213, 331-336 (1851). See also *ibid.*, XI, 504-508 (1851), for some additional remarks he made on the same subject.

[47]*Ibid.*, XI, 65, 211-212, 508 (1851).

Because of the wide reception of his forceful writings, Cartwright exerted a profound influence upon many of the Southern physicians who wrote on the subject of Negro "peculiarities" during the 1850's.[48] One significant person who undoubtedly borrowed some of his ideas from Cartwright was Doctor John Stainbach Wilson, who, himself, wrote a series of articles, "The Peculiarities and Diseases of Negroes." The series was published from November, 1858, through December, 1860, in the *American Cotton Planter and Soil of the South,* a Montgomery, Alabama, periodical edited by Doctor Noah B. Cloud. The articles had every reason to attract attention. In the first place, the agricultural journal in which they appeared was a highly successful one, with a circulation of about 10,000, which meant that it, with the possible exception of the *Southern Cultivator* of Georgia, was the most widely distributed magazine in the South throughout the years before the Civil War. Moreover, the subject of the articles was extremely popular among Southerners, Doctor Wilson was competent from the Nott-Cartwright standpoint to present the subject in a manner highly acceptable to his readers, and Wilson already had a reading public since for several years before 1858 he had been editor of the so-called "Health Department" of *Godey's Lady's Book* and a corresponding editor of the *Savannah Journal of Medicine.* In 1860, while his series of articles was in progress, he brought out a very successful book: *Woman's Book of Health, A Work for Mothers and for Families on a Plan, New, Safe, and Efficient, Showing, in Plain Language, How Disease May Be Prevented and Cured Without the Use of Dangerous Remedies* (Philadelphia, 1860).[49]

Wilson's series on "Peculiarities and Diseases of Negroes" was the most extensive publication on the subject in the South before the Civil War, but he actually said little that had not already been said. His significant contribution was that he summarized many of the ideas and notions of "FRANKLIN," the Doctors Ramsay, Nott and Cartwright, and others, as well as many of the popular white opinions about the Negro which prevailed in the South in

---

[48]For references to Cartwright's activities, see Jenkins, *Pro-Slavery Thought in the Old South,* 247, 250, 254; Lloyd *The Slavery Controversy,* 243; and Wish, *George Fitzhugh,* 36, 42.

[49]*American Cotton Planter and Soil of the South,* V, 49 (1861).

the late 1850's. He was positive that Negroes differed from whites in their "wooly head, black skin, and shorter thicker muscles, and the longer sinews, . . . [and] with regard to the brain; . . ." that their breathing capacity was less than that of the white man; and that their "vital resistance and recovering or recuperative energies are comparatively feeble." Negroes, he insisted, had a lower type brain and were "more animal-like in their nature" than whites, and they were debased in their moral sentiments. Planters, he stated, should *"regard the defective heat-producing powers of the negro, . . . and endeavor to compensate for it by providing him with comfortable houses and a suitable supply of food and clothing."* In what was perhaps one of his more droll moments, he said, "Negroes, like hogs, are not remarkably cleanly;" therefore, planters were warned to prevent "the accumulated filth of years about negro cabins; . . . ." He held the confirmed belief that Negroes lived long because their owners sheltered them against many vices in which white men indulged. Having "no regrets for the past, and no anxieties about the future," so said Wilson, they were mentally prepared to enjoy good health.[50]

During the course of the publication of his first five articles, in the period from November, 1858, through July, 1859, Doctor Wilson received so much encouragement for what he was writing that he decided to enlarge on his articles and bring out a book on Negro medicine.[51] And in every month during the year 1860, one of his articles was printed in the *American Cotton Planter and Soil of the South.* He stated time and again that the Negro possessed certain special anatomical, physiological, mental, and moral traits. He recommended that slave cabins be built with openings near the top, "where impurities naturally tend to escape, ..." Clothing appropriate to the season, either cotton or wool, was advised in order to prevent wetness and colds. The Negro, the Doctor said, possessed "feeble heat generating powers," but he should by no means "be considered merely as a *walking furnace*, for the consumption of fuel in the form of food." He should be fed fat bacon, pork, corn, and peas because these "carbonaceous" foods generated heat. Molasses, sugar, and fruits were also excellent for him. Wilson

[50]*Ibid.*, II, 355 (1858), III, 67-68, 92-93, 197-198, 228-229 (1859).
[51]*Ibid.*, III, 311, 356, 358, 383 (1859).

maintained that since Negroes were "notoriously filthy" and "allied to *hogs* in their nature and habits," they should be given time to wash and mend their clothes and compelled to bathe at least once a week. Their cabins, it was believed, should be both whitewashed and so elevated "that a current of pure air can pass freely beneath; . . ." and cabin yards should be raked frequently.[52]

Believing *"that the natural stamina, the vital resistance, the enduring and recovering powers of the negro are inferior to those of the white man,"* Wilson was of the opinion that overwork short-ened the lives of Negroes. He recommended that there be no hard work on Sundays and that lights be put out every night at nine o'clock; otherwise masters "must expect to suffer loss in the sick-ness and premature decrepitude of their slaves." Negroes ought not to be forced to sleep on floors or benches, but should be furnished with cotton mattresses and woolen blankets. Wilson said, "During a residence of several years in the lower part of Alabama, we found that there were few nights sufficiently warm to render cover uncomfortable; . . . ." He also encouraged music, jubilees on holidays, corn-shuckings, and other such activities "in which negroes may be safely indulged that will add much to their enjoy-ment and thus tend to promote health." However, since Negroes possessed a "natural fondness for alcoholic liquors," the use of which, Wilson said, "predisposes to disease of every kind," such drinks, and coffee and tea, were advised only for medicinal pur-poses. He commented that "from natural fickleness, from that strength of passion always dominant in inferior animal nature, . . . [Negroes] are very prone to violate their marriage obligations, . . ." and therefore should have their marriage relations magnified and made more binding by a religious ceremony. Slaveowners could "promote the happiness of their negroes, and consequently their health" by respecting family affections, never separating families, furnishing a cabin to each family, and furnishing each family a garden patch for its own use. Wilson remarked that a great mistake was made by some planters in not clothing "little negroes," since such a practice brought on chills, fevers, congestions, inflammations, and bowel complaints. Having little regard for mulattoes, he con-cluded: "the jet black, shiny, unadulterated, greasy-skinned, *strong-*

---

[52]*Ibid.*, IV, 46-47, 79-80, 126-128, 173-176, 222-224 (1860).

smelling negro is the best every way, after he has been in the country long enough to undergo proper training, and get rid of some of his native African notions."[53]

Doctor Wilson closed his last article in December, 1860, with an announcement of a book, "The Plantation and Family Physician," which would consist of between 500 and 600 pages. His book, he said, would be more thorough and complete than the "imperfect and hastily written articles" which had been carried in the *American Cotton Planter and Soil of the South*. But the book was never printed. Wilson's plans were interrupted by the coming of the Civil War, although as late as the year 1863, he still hoped to publish it. In that year, while serving as a surgeon in the Confederate Army, he brought out a sixteen-page booklet, *The Southern Soldier's Health Guide*, on the cover of which appeared the advertisement: "Now ready for the press. The plantation and family physician; a work for families generally and slave-owners specially: . . . By John Stainbach Wilson, M. D. This work is now ready for the press, and will be published as soon as the war is over. . . ."[54]

Wilson's hopes of winning the war and of printing his book on plantation medicine were doomed when the South lost its military fight. After Appomattox there no longer existed the urge among Southern planters to support such a publication as the Doctor's. They had lost their earlier intimate and economic solicitude for the Negro. A new day in white-Negro relationships had arrived. Now there existed a Negro Problem instead of a Slave Question. Many Southerners continued to think of the Negro as different from the white man; to have done otherwise would have been contrary to their history and their custom. This concept had worked itself into the *mores* of a majority of contemporary white Southerners. The belief had helped cause a Civil War; it would be debated for more than a hundred years; it would be declared untenable by the United States Supreme Court in the year 1954; it was a question that forced its way into the main stream of American history.

---

[53]*Ibid.*, IV, 223, 270-272, 319-320, 366-368, 415-416, 463-464, 510-512, 557-560 (1860).

[54]John Stainbach Wilson, *The Southern Soldier's Health Guide* (Richmond, 1863).

VI

THE CRUSADE FOR AGRICULTURAL REFORM

Because of the great and abiding interest in the production of cotton and other money crops in the Old South, there has developed a persistent conception that the people of the region were only slightly interested in such matters as scientific farming and improvement of their land.[1] Indeed, since cotton was so important, serious consideration of other farm activities in the Cotton Belt from Georgia to Texas is supposed to have been practically nonexistent. This stereotyped interpretation is by no means correct, for there is abundant evidence available to prove that the late ante-bellum South, including Alabama, possessed many promoters and crusading practitioners of "modern" scientific farming. Among the best known and most outspoken of these publicists were planters of cotton and editors of newspapers and farm journals.[2] But because many of them were large planters who gave much of their time and attention to producing cotton, there has developed a broadly accepted belief, even one of ridicule, that they were merely playing at scientific farming, that they were "book farmers" or gentleman farmers entirely unaccustomed to dirt, and that they were not serious reformers at all.

Historians have not been tolerant of Old South planters as crusaders for agricultural reform. However, the truth of the matter is that most planters were at one time small farmers who had known hard physical work intimately and that they, themselves, most particularly realized the need for and practiced diversification. Many

---

[1]Some portions of this chapter were first published under the titles of "Noah B. Cloud's Activities on Behalf of Southern Agriculture," *Agricultural History*, XXV, 53-58 (1951), and "Agricultural Societies in Ante-Bellum Alabama," *Alabama Review*, IV, 241-253 (1951), and are reproduced with the permission of Edward E. Edwards, the late editor of *Agricultural History*, and of W. Stanley Hoole and James B. McMillan, the editors of the *Alabama Review*.

[2]Elizabeth McTyeire Essler, "The Agricultural Reform Movement in Alabama, 1850-1860," *Alabama Review*, I, 243-260 (1948); Demaree, *The American Agricultural Press, 1819-1860*. See also James C. Bonner, "Genesis of Agricultural Reform in the Cotton Belt," *Journal of Southern History*, IX, 475-500 (1943).

planters and others gave much more than lip service to crop rotation, hillside ditching, contour plowing, use of fertilizers and farm machinery, breeding of stock, and numerous other advanced agricultural practices.[3] They were little different from agricultural reformers the country over. This is not to say, however, that white Southerners before the year 1861 were similar to other white Americans in their culture, economic life, intellectual interests, and politics. Such an interpretation would be based on fancy rather than historical facts.

One of the Old South's reformers, indeed one of the most energetic promoters of improved agriculture in American history, was Noah B. Cloud, of Macon and Montgomery Counties, Alabama. And Cloud was so important in the agricultural reform movement in ante-bellum Alabama that the story of that movement can be properly understood and appreciated only after a study of his activities. More than any Alabamian he was the leader of the reform movement in his adopted state. Born in 1809, he was a native of Edgefield District, South Carolina. After training as a physician at the well-known Jefferson Medical College in Philadelphia, from which he graduated in 1835,[4] he moved to Alabama in 1838. Thus he arrived in Alabama at a time, as has been seen, when cotton culture was coming to dominate farm and plantation activities in the state. However, he did not move to the state for the purpose of opening up a large plantation in order to produce large bales of cotton with a large force of Negro slaves. He was different from many of his contemporary emigrants in that he turned immediately to a study of better farming practices. The result was that he established himself as a highly respected and recognized leader in the extensive movement in agricultural reform in his region and even in the nation. Having wealth and earning more, he was free to pursue his interests.[5] He did more for Alabama's economic betterment than any of his contemporaries.

---

[3]*Ibid.*; Avery O. Craven, "The Agricultural Reformers of the Ante-Bellum South," *American Historical Review*, XXXIII, 302-315 (1928).

[4]John McK. Mitchell, Dean, School of Medicine, University of Pennsylvania, to the author, November 27, 1950; *Harper's Weekly*, II, 756 (1858); Thomas P. Abernethy, "Noah B. Cloud," in Allen Johnson, Dumas Malone, and Harris E. Starr, eds., *Dictionary of American Biography*, 21 vols. and index (New York, 1928-1944), IV, 232.

[5]Montgomery *Alabama Journal*, June 4, 1850.

If Cloud had died during the Civil War, he would very possibly
.be remembered as a state hero, both for his pre-War activities and
his death during the War; but since he lived on for a decade after
1865 and became a Scalawag, he died something of a scamp in the
eyes of many Alabamians. However, his politics were not altogether
unusual and it is more than likely that what he did after 1865 he
did for what he considered the good of his state. The modern
historian of the South does not consider all Scalawags to have been
dishonest. Cloud's politics are not hard to understand; and he
acted as did many other men of his generation. Before the Civil War
he was an active member of the Whig party; he was also a Unionist,
but at the same time he was a Southerner, showing this by serving
as a Confederate surgeon during the Civil War. After the War he
affiliated with the Republican party in Alabama; thus he became a
Scalawag. Still very much interested in promoting Alabama's agricultural and industrial resources, he corresponded frequently with
the United States Commissioner of Agriculture. He also wrote a
series of newspaper articles entitled "The Industrial Resources of
Alabama," thereby helping to create a Commission of Industrial
Resources. He sponsored immigration to Alabama, and became the
state's first Commissioner of Immigration. Continuing his long-time
interest in public education, he won election as State Superintendent
of Education in 1868. Two years later he was elected to the Republican state legislature, where he reiterated his earlier support
of an agricultural and mechanical college, this time under the provisions of the famous Morrill Act passed by the Civil War Congress
in Washington. He lived to see the establishment of the A. and M.
College at Auburn in 1872. He unquestionably did more for the
good of his state than the men who maligned him for his politics and
who accused him of being a thief.[6]

Cloud died in 1875, a time when neither he nor any other
Scalawag was not likely to receive eulogies from the recently

---

[6]Peter A. Brannon, Alabama Department of Archives and History, to the
author, August 31, 1950; *Alabama Planter*, VIII, 297 (1854); *Harper's Weekly*,
II, 756-757 (1858); and the following Montgomery newspapers: *Daily
Advertiser*, September 27, 1872; *Daily State Sentinel*, August 24, September 4,
October 9, 24, November 2, 9, 1867; *Weekly Journal*, May 24, 1851; *Weekly
Mail*, October 19, 26, 1870. See also the Tuskegee *Macon Republican*, August
19, 1852.

revived Democratic press of his State. He was buried almost un-announced despite the fact that from 1842 until 1861 his name had appeared thousands of times in Alabama newspapers and elsewhere throughout the South. Several contemporary newspapers, although critical of his postwar political affiliations, which, indeed, were not at all unusual for old-line Southern Whigs, did praise him for his charitableness and kindheartedness.[7] One editor described him as "a man of considerable ability and an earnest advocate of agricultural improvement."[8] In view of his long and diligent labor on behalf of his state and region, this is a very niggardly understatement of fact, despite the course of events and feelings of white people in Alabama following 1865. A more charitable appraisal is supplied by Cloud's home-county newspaper in 1858, at a time when he was a Unionist. It is worthy of note, however, that again his political sentiments were not overlooked: "The doctor, though most worthy in all the relations of his life, except his politics—which are awful—will, after all, stand or fall by his labors for the good of agri-culture. . . ."[9] So be it, and this is as it should be.

Cloud's agricultural crusade began with and was most consist-ently marked by the contention that the South concentrated excessively on cotton production and that too much land and labor were utilized in the process. After reading widely on the subjects of science and their application to agriculture, especially from the writings of Sir Humphrey Davy and Baron Justus von Liebig, two world leaders in the crusade for better farm methods, Cloud inaugurated his experiments in 1840 on a 3-acre portion of his farm located on Uchee Creek in Russell County, Alabama. The region until only recently had been Indian country. In 1843 Cloud

---

[7]Montgomery *Daily Advertiser*, November 6, 1875; Montgomery *State Journal*, November 7, 1875; Selma *Southern Argus*, November 12, 1875; Talladega *Our Mountain Home*, November 10, 1875.

[8]Greensboro *Alabama Beacon*, November 13, 1858.

[9]Tuskegee *Republican*, December 2, 1858. For some pertinent references to Cloud's activities and reputation as an advocate of agricultural reform, see *American Cotton Planter*, I, 19 (1853), III, 50 (1855); *DeBow's Review*, XIV, 193 (1853); Macon *Daily Telegraph*, December 15, 1860; Montgomery *Weekly Advertiser and State Gazette*, October 18, 1858; Prattville *Autauga Citizen*, November 10, 1853; *Report of the Commissioner of Patents, for the Year 1859, Agriculture* (Washington, 1860), 29; *Soil of the South*, II, 370, 371, 376 (1852); *Southern Cultivator*, X, 85 (1852), XII, 316 (1854).

sold his farm, known as "Planter's Retreat," moved to what he called "La Place" in Macon County, and settled down to farming and the practice of the medical profession.[10] From Planter's Retreat and La Place he poured out over the South and the eastern United States accounts of his experiments and ideas on agriculture. The result was an accomplishment equalled by few men in United States history.

Cloud's original purpose, as explained by himself, was to replace the "kill and cripple, and every way injurious system" of cotton culture practiced in many areas of the South.[11] At another time he stated: "My object in these experiments has not been to augment the crop of cotton, either per hand or per the aggregate, already too great, but an entirely new and improved system of culture, predicated upon the principle of scientific and enlightened policy, to curtail the immense capital engaged, under the destructive system of our country, in its production, to one-third of its present enormity."[12] Because he had different ideas and attacked without mercy an established system of cotton culture, Cloud attracted much attention, much praise, and some scorn. The so-called "Cloud System," nevertheless, became one of the most talked about and popular subjects in his region. Alabama was fortunate to have attracted a man of Cloud's interests and abilities.

Fundamentally, Cloud was a soil builder. Employing an amazingly few acres of poor "forked-leaf, black-jack, pine barren" land, as he called it,[13] he literally plastered it with homemade fertilizer. Collection of barnyard manure, cotton seed, pine straw, leaves, wood scrapings, muck, barks, trash, table and garden scraps, and other refuse was an almost incessant activity of his small corps of slaves. These materials for his fertilizer were first scattered in stock lots, then gathered and dumped in a pit, from where they were washed by means of sunken conduits through a series of pits

[10]*Alabama Planter*, VII, 325 (1853); *Southern Agriculturist*, New Series, III, 339, 388-389 (1843); *Southern Cultivator*, X, 37-39 (1852); Tuskegee *Macon Republican*, May 29, 1856. See also Unpublished Census Returns, 1850, Schedule 1, pp. 164-165, 209, 211, 213, Schedule 2, p. 27, and *ibid.*, 1860, Schedule 1, pp. 75, 79, Schedule 2, p. 38.
[11]*Southern Agriculturist*, New Series, III, 15-19 (1843).
[12]*Ibid.*, III, 339 (1843); *Southern Cultivator*, I, 121-122 (1843).
[13]*Southern Cultivator*, I, 12-13 (1843).

after being "aged" in each pit for several fortnights. This manure making and its utilization were considered basic in Cloud's system; and although he introduced the use of Peruvian guano in Alabama in the early 1840's and consistently recommended it as well as manufactured restoratives, he always placed emphasis on preparing and depending upon his own concoctions.[14] In this phase of his activities, except as to substances utilized as soil builders, he adapted earlier practices made popular in Virginia by Edmund Ruffin, the "calcareous manure" advocate.[15]

Another of Cloud's recommendations was to fallow land one year preceding its use for cotton. Before planting he also leveled his fields, measuring each acre into 2,940 hills or squares upon which 400 to 500 bushels of compost were hauled and dumped into small, equal amounts in the squares. In order to distribute the substance equally, it was then broadcast with shovels, raked, and plowed under deeply. The cotton seeds were rolled in leached ashes or sand, placed in rows 5 feet apart, and covered "lightly and carefully" with hoes. After the cotton came up, the middles were plowed, and the grass was chopped. By July 1, the stalks usually stood to a height of from 5 to 6 feet, and a homemade sweep was run through the middles to kill the new grass. Afterwards the fields were chopped "about in places" one time only.[16] This system, under which 5,989 pounds of seed cotton per acre was produced in 1842, was, according to Cloud, "an *infallible insurance* of 5,000 pounds of superior staple per acre."[17]

The first public announcement of the "Cloud System" was made in 1842 and 1843 in a series of letters published in the famous *Cultivator*, of Albany, New York. Soon the letters were reprinted

---

[14]*American Cotton Planter*, January, 1853-December, 1856; *American Cotton Planter and Soil of the South*, III, 336-337 (1859); Montgomery *Weekly Alabama Journal*, April 10, 1852; Unpublished Census Returns, 1850, Schedule 2, p. 164.

[15]See especially Avery O. Craven, *Soil Exhaustion as a Factor in the Agricultural History of Virginia and Maryland, 1606-1860* (Urbana, 1926). Ruffin's first *Essay on Calcareous Manures* was published in 1821; additional essays appeared until the year 1852.

[16]*Southern Agriculturist*, New Series, III, 147-152 (1843); *Southern Cultivator*, I, 12-13 (1843).

[17]*Southern Cultivator*, I, 12-13 (1843). See also *Southern Agriculturist*, New Series, III, 15-19 (1843).

in several southern agricultural journals and newspapers, and as might be expected in a region where many planters mined their land for quick profits, the system created a sensation.[18] Cloud became the subject of an extensive debate, with most participants favoring his suggestions. For example, his methods were endorsed, halfheartedly, by the Monticello Planters' Society of Fairfield District, South Carolina, and more fully by the Fishing Creek Agricultural Society of Fort Mitchell, Alabama. He was commended by Thomas Affleck, soon to be a well-known scientific farmer, who had just moved to Mississippi from Cincinnati, where he had been junior editor of the *Western Farmer and Gardner.* The *Southwestern Farmer* of Raymond, Mississippi, concluded that Cloud had instituted "the only feasible plan of improving our system of cotton culture we have seen recommended for years. . . ."[19] On the other hand, Cloud's "check system" was roundly condemned by the Nashville *Agriculturist* and called "preposterous" by a correspondent of the *Southwestern Farmer.*[20] In 1847, a leading agricultural reformer, Martin W. Philips of Edwards, Mississippi, who must have been one of the most prolific letter writers in American history, and who had at first favored the system, reported it to be "a complete failure, and had I the sense that scientific men have I could have foreseen my error."[21] Following an acrimonious and very intriguing correspondence, however, Philips and Cloud became fast friends, and Philips soon admitted that the Alabamian had had an exceptional success as a cotton producer.[22]

Cloud never retracted any claims made by himself or others in support of his system. In 1851 he boasted: "I commenced in 1840, laying my plans for a radically improved plan of plantation economy, and the result has been, to me, entirely satisfactory—as the present condition of my farm demonstrates."[23] At the later

---

[18]*Ibid.,* III, 147-152, 338-340 (1843), IV, 50-57 (1844).

[19]Quoted in *ibid.,* III, 199-200 (1843). See also *ibid.,* III, 183-188, 420-425 (1843), IV, 320-323 (1844); Greensboro *Alabama Beacon,* March 5, 1852; and *Southern Cultivator,* II, 55-56 (1844), V, 68 (1847), X, 206 (1852).

[20]Quoted in *Southern Agriculturist,* New Series, IV, 58-59 (1844).

[21]*Southern Cultivator,* V, 109, 155-157 (1847), VI, 35-36 (1848).

[22]*Report of the Commissioner of Patents, for the Year 1849, Agriculture* (Washington, 1850), 151.

[23]*Southern Cultivator,* X, 37 (1852).

period he owned only six working slaves. From 1853 until 1861 he filled the pages of his *American Cotton Planter* (later the *American Cotton Planter and the Soil of the South*) of Montgomery, Alabama, with descriptions of his practices.[24] As will be seen, this journal became one of the most popular and influential of its type in the South. In 1857, Cloud's contributions were further publicized and recommended by J. A. Turner, ex-editor of a Georgia periodical, the *Plantation*. Cloud's own explanations of his system were incorporated as Chapter 2 in Turner's *Cotton Planter's Manual*, one of the most widely popular and searching collections of information on cotton available to farmers in the Old South.[25] A reasonable conclusion is that the system, or plan as it was often called, influenced the activities of many ante-bellum cotton producers. Certainly the "Cloud Plan" enhanced immensely its originator's reputation and following.

Perhaps Cloud's most important contribution to the cause of agriculture was publication of the *American Cotton Planter*. He was the chief contributor to the magazine but was aided very materially, after 1857, by his successive horticultural editors, Charles A. Peabody and Robert Nelson, two outstanding leaders in their field.[26] His publication was liberally supplied with letters and articles by prominent agricultural reformers throughout the South, including Martin W. Philips, James M. Chambers, Norbonne B. Powell, John Stainbach Wilson, Garland D. Harmon, Thomas Affleck, and Edmund Ruffin. Hundreds of contributions from anonymous writers, plain farmers, and large planters were also printed. Among the readers of these various articles were numer-

---

[24]See *American Cotton Planter*, II, 217-218, 242-244, 276-278, 308-309, 340-342, 373-375 (1854), III, 20-23 (1855), IV, 89-91, 123-124 (1856), and *American Cotton Planter and Soil of the South*, IV, 363-364 (1860). See Unpublished Census Returns, 1850, Schedule 2, p. 164, for a reference to Cloud's slaves.

[25]This *Manual*, published by C. M. Saxton, of New York City, was highly praised by such southern publications as *DeBow's Review*, XXIII, 108 (1857); Macon *Georgia Journal and Messenger*, February 11, 1857; *North Carolina Planter*, III, 36-38 (1860); and *Southern Cultivator*, XV, 127-128 (1857).

[26]*American Cotton Planter and Soil of the South*, II, 377 (1858), III, 25 (1859); Cahaba *Dallas Gazette*, November 21, 1856; Eufaula *Express*, December 9, 1858; Montgomery *Daily Mail*, November 20, 1856.

ous Alabamians, who of course benefited, as did the other followers of the magazine.[27]

The *American Cotton Planter* was begun in January, 1853, with a circulation of less than 500 copies. First printed by a jobber in Montgomery, it was soon turned over to the press of the Montgomery *Advertiser and State Gazette,* the largest and "neatest" newspaper in Alabama. Cloud was so successful in his own publishing venture that he became a co-owner of the *Advertiser* in June, 1856, sole owner the next year, and he retained part ownership as late as September, 1859.[28] Peculiarly enough, here was an ardent Whig partially owning and even editing the leading Democratic newspaper in the home state of William L. Yancey! Be that ludicrous fact as it may, Cloud's excellent agricultural journal consistently increased in popularity, as shown by the fact that in January, 1859, after having been merged for three years with the *Soil of the South* of Columbus, Georgia, ten thousand copies of the periodical were being printed for circulation.[29] Also, as was customary among such publications, the *American Cotton Planter* was quoted widely by other southern journals, thus spreading its influence greatly beyond its own readers.[30] A comparison of its format, content, and circulation with that of such journals as the *Farmer's Register,* the *Southern Planter,* the *North Carolina Planter,* the *Southern Agriculturist, Soil of the South,* the *Southern Cultivator,* the *Alabama Planter,* and *DeBow's Review* shows that it was a leader in the South.[31] Moreover, it suffers not at all in comparison with similar magazines printed throughout the United States.[32]

---

[27]*American Cotton Planter* and *American Cotton Planter and Soil of the South, passim.*

[28]*Harper's Weekly,* II, 757 (1858); Montgomery *Advertiser and State Gazette,* October 29, 1856, March 24, 1857, January 5, 1858, September 28, 1859; Tuskegee *Macon Republican,* June 12, 1856.

[29]See, for example, Macon *Journal and Messenger,* December 29, 1858.

[30]See, for example, the files of the *Alabama Planter* of Mobile, *DeBow's Review* of Louisiana, *Farmer and Planter* of South Carolina, *Southern Cultivator* of Georgia, as well as the *Arator* and the *Farmer's Journal,* both of Raleigh, North Carolina.

[31]These journals were among the better agricultural publications of the Old South.

[32]See, for example, *American Agriculturist* (New York), *American Farmer* (Baltimore), *Cultivator* (Albany, New York), *Genesee Farmer* (Rochester, New

As for Cloud, his editorials and articles indicate that he had few contemporaries who were more earnestly engaged in the crusade for such causes as railroads, manufacturing, direct trade with Europe, defense against abolitionism, and southern medicine, to mention a few of his interests. He and his correspondents, many of whom were Alabamians, including dirt farmers, overseers, women, and planters, persistently agitated for all phases of agricultural reform: crop rotation, diversification, blooded stock, horticulture, fertilizers of all sorts, hillside ditching, horizontal plowing, drainage, fences, housing, clothing, Negro management, education, an agricultural college in Alabama, and government aid to agriculture. One of Cloud's long-time interests was humane care of slaves. He possessed a flair for writing and at times a pen dipped in venom, and he was both hard-working and colorful.[33] Few men have managed to crowd so many useful activities into a lifetime.

Newspapers and journals throughout Alabama and the South lauded Cloud and his journal from 1853 to 1861, which means that Cloud's work as a promoter of agricultural reform must have been known not only to his own readers but to thousands of other families. Contemporary opinions of Cloud and the *American Cotton Planter* prove without question that Cloud was indeed significant in his field of activity and that there existed a broad interest and support of the reforms advocated in the *American Cotton Planter*. In support of Cloud's projected journal, the *Alabama Planter* of Mobile stated, December, 1852, "This work promises to be of incalculable value to the southern agriculturist, ..."[34] In January, 1853, a Montgomery editor boosted Cloud's magazine by remarking, "We are pleased to be able to state that its permanency is placed beyond all doubt, by the large subscription list with which it has commenced, and which is daily augmenting."[35] From Mobile came the suggestion that "our people can sustain a publication of the kind, and it is their duty to do it."[36] A Huntsville newspaper

York), *Homestead* (Hartford, Connecticut), *New England Farmer* (Boston), and *Prairie Farmer* (Chicago).

[33]*American Cotton Planter* and *American Cotton Planter and Soil of the South, passim.*

[34]*Alabama Planter*, VII, 29 (1852).

[35]Montgomery *Weekly Alabama Journal*, January 29, 1853.

[36]*Ibid.*, February 19, 1853, quoting the Mobile *Tribune.*

stated that the magazine was "full of instructive and useful matter. We hope to see it succeed. Our farming friends should sustain, heartily sustain it."[37] From Montgomery it was announced, in February, 1853, "that subscribers to the work are pouring in, and that the indications are that it will receive a *living* support."[38] A Prattville newspaper boasted, in March of the same year, "Each number comes to us improved in some respect, and, we doubt not, it will ere long surpass all other journals of the same kind published in the South." It was "obligatory," added the editor, that "this noble enterprise" be supported by the people of Alabama.[39] These sentiments were echoed from Cloud's home county of Macon: "Dr. Cloud's valuable monthly is again upon our table. The dish he serves up for March [1853] is by no means inferior to those to which we sat down during any of the preceding months, and the accessories are better."[40]

On and on went the praise for Cloud and his journal through the years 1853 to 1861. A Montgomery editor, in extolling the journal, boasted that "Its editor is just the man to make it the best Agricultural paper in the world."[41] In April, 1853, the *Southern Cultivator*, certainly without suspecting that the *American Cotton Planter* would some day rival the *Cultivator* for the position as the most widely circulated magazine published in the South before the Civil War, reported that Cloud's periodical "may now be considered as a 'fixed fact.' It is conducted with much talent and industry, and is well worthy of a liberal support."[42] Similar good wishes came from Georgia's other significant agricultural journal, the *Soil of the South*, "The Doctor [Cloud] has a wide spread reputation, and we hope may have a circulation fully commensurate with the merits of his work. Success to the *American Cotton Planter*."[43] Cloud's "valuable journal," said the Auburn *Gazette*, "is steadily increasing in interest, and we hope but few of our readers

---

[37]Huntsville *Southern Advocate*, February 23, 1853.
[38]Montgomery *Advertiser and State Gazette*, February 12, 1853.
[39]Prattville *Autauga Citizen*, March 24, 1853.
[40]Tuskegee *Macon Republican*, March 24, 1853.
[41]Montgomery *Weekly Alabama Journal*, March 12, 1853.
[42]*Southern Cultivator*, XI, 114 (1853).
[43]*Soil of the South*, III, 497 (1853).

are deprived of its excellent teachings."[44] And of special interest was an editorial appearing in the Selma *Reporter* early in 1853:

The *American Cotton Planter* for May contains much instructive matter. We are particularly struck with an able essay on the policy of the cotton growing states. The writer gives a faithful picture of the gradual impoverishment of our lands, and suggests a remedy for this and other evils. The first error to be corrected, says he, is the planting of more land than can be cultivated, and at the same time improved. A large portion of labor should be devoted to ditching, draining, building, raising stock and provisions, etc., etc. Manufactures should be encouraged by vigorous measures. The most effective of these measures, says the writer, would be to prohibit the further introduction of slaves except such as might be acquired by actual residents through marriage, or such as might be brought in by bonafide immigrants settling among us, and with the restriction that they should not be sold or hired for a term of years, unless under process of law. This would stop the drain of money, encourage white immigration, foster manufactures, etc.[45]

In its late years, as in its first year of its existence, the *American Cotton Planter* and its editor received an almost unbounded support from southern newspapers and agricultural journals, thus indicating that Cloud's periodical was no mere short-lived fad. In 1857, after Cloud's journal was united with the *Soil of the South* and was issued under the title of the *American Cotton Planter and the Soil of the South*, an Alabama writer advised: "Every farmer ought to have it, if it cost $10 instead of $1. We ought to have a statute in our penal code, making it a penitentiary offence for an Alabama planter to be without the 'Cotton Planter.' It is just as necessary to him as a good wife."[46] In January, 1857, the magazine was also eulogized by J. J. Hooper, editor of the Montgomery *Daily Mail*:

We congratulate our friends [the editors of the *American Cotton Planter*, Noah B. Cloud and Charles A. Peabody] on the *great* improvement of the work. It is as elegant in typographical arrangement and execution as the most fastidious could desire, the general style being far superior to that of most agricultural periodicals; . . . . Besides the good reading, its pages are embellished with fine wood engravings, illustrative of subjects of interest to the stock and fruit raisers! . . . . Dr. Cloud informs us that subscribers pour in *by hundreds,* and if the influx continues for a few weeks it will place the Planter, in point of circulation, among the first publications of its class in the Union. Let every man who desires to see a real progress in our section, lend it a helping hand![47]

---

[44]Quoted in Montgomery *Daily Alabama Journal,* May 2, 1853.
[45]Quoted in Montgomery *Tri-Weekly Journal,* May 25, 1853.
[46]Wetumpka *Spectator,* January 15, 1857.
[47]Montgomery *Daily Mail,* January 7, 1857.

"In our estimation," says another Alabama editorial of March, 1857, Cloud's magazine "is the most valuable publication of the kind we have ever seen, ... It is not filled as some suppose, with vague and impracticable theories, but with practical common sense suggestions perfectly comprensible [*sic*] and intellible [*sic*] to the most novitiate farmer."[48] Since Charles A. Peabody, who was a resident of Russell County, Alabama,[49] was the horticultural editor, the magazine had two very "able editors." The journal was described in August, 1857, as "a gem, unsurpassed by any in the Union."[50] And while praising the magazine, one editor made the following pertinent remarks:

It [the *American Cotton Planter*] enforces the doctrine that farmers should raise at home every thing necessary for the operations of their farms—leaving the cotton crop a clear profit. There can be no successful farming unless an abundant supply of provisions be produced. Without this the planter's machinery moves slowly and heavily.— With poor horses and mules—badly fed negroes, no man can work to advantage. This must be the case if corn has to be bought; everything is then stinted. But if large corn crops are planted, you have fat mules and horses—slick negroes—fine looking cattle, furnishing plenty of milk and butter, and also plenty of fat hogs. It won't do for planters to raise cotton to buy mules and horses, and hogs, and flour and oxen, etc. Try it and you will soon find out.[51]

As already mentioned, many articles from the *American Cotton Planter* were reprinted in newspapers and magazines, which means that Cloud's journal was quite influential both in his own state and elsewhere in the South. Amply supplied with excerpts from the journal in some instances were such Alabama newspapers as the *Sumter County Whig* of Livingston, the Huntsville *Democrat*, the *Macon Republican* of Tuskegee, and the Greensboro *Alabama Beacon*.[52] These and other state newspapers sometimes literally filled their pages with reprints of articles and illustrations from the *American Cotton Planter*. Three North Carolina agricultural maga-

---

[48]Grove Hill *Clarke County Democrat*, March 12, 1857.

[49]Montgomery *Daily Mail*, October 6, 1857.

[50]Jacksonville *Republican*, August 19, 1857.

[51]Carrollton *West Alabamian*, October 21, 1857.

[52]See, for example, the Greensboro *Alabama Beacon*, April 24, 1857; Huntsville *Democrat*, April 7, 1853; Livingston *Sumter County Whig*, January 25, 1853; and Tuskegee *Macon Republican*, July 13, 1854. See also the Carrollton *West Alabamian*, October 28, 1857; Florence *Gazette*, November 12, 1858; Gainesville *Independent*, October 10, 1857; Grove Hill *Clarke County Democrat*, November 6, 1856; Tuscaloosa *Independent Monitor*, June 18, 1857; and Wetumpka *Dispatch*, August 7, 1857.

zines that frequently quoted at length from Cloud's journal were the *Arator*, the *Farmer's Journal*, and the *North Carolina Planter*; and the editor of the South Carolina publication, *The Farmer and Planter*, also was a regular patron.[53] *DeBow's Review* of New Orleans and the *Southern Cultivator* carried dozens of articles that appeared originally in the *American Cotton Planter*.[54]

Cloud abundantly deserved his excellent reputation as a promoter of agricultural reform. As much as any man in the South, and perhaps in the United States, he warranted the compliment in 1859 that he was one "of the old veterans in the cause of our country's salvation. . . ."[55] A little newspaper in Alabama also remarked, December, 1860, a few months before the *American Cotton Planter* suspended publication, that "Dr. Cloud's agricultural and horticultural monthly, . . . still holds its place among the agricultural works of the country. The Doctor is one of the most enterprising men to be found anywhere, and the pages of his work give evidence of the fact."[56] Cloud must be accorded an equal place beside Edmund Ruffin, Daniel Lee, John Stuart Skinner and the other outstanding agricultural reformers of the South during the pre-Civil War period. If he had accomplished nothing else, his skilled editorship of his magnificent agricultural journal would in itself have been more than enough to warrant the conclusion that he was one of the very outstanding advocates of economic reform in the ante-bellum South.

One reason for Cloud's strong influence was the fact that he was addicted to conventions and meetings. In May, 1852, he was an active delegate at the Southwestern Industrial Convention in New Orleans. He was principal secretary at the Southern Commercial Convention in December, 1856, at Savannah. At the Montgomery Commercial Convention of 1858 he was a member of the committee on local arrangements. He attended numerous

---

[53]*The Arator*, III, 781 (1857); *Farmer's Journal*, III, 135-138 (1854); *North Carolina Planter*, I, 68-69 (1858); *Farmer and Planter*, V, 6 (1854), X, 11-13 (1859).

[54]See, for example, *DeBow's Review*, XVIII, 59-60 (1855), and *Southern Cultivator*, XII, 381-382 (1854).

[55]*Southern Cultivator*, XVII, 142 (1859).

[56]Gainesville *Independent*, December 15, 1860.

Whig conventions in Alabama during the early 1850's. He engaged in the activities of Masonic conventions, of at least one temperance gathering, and at stockholder and barbecue meetings of the Decatur and Montgomery Railroad, all of his state. For several years he was closely associated with the Alleghany Copper Mining Company.[57]

A highlight of Cloud's career was his support of the cotton planters' conventions, which were widely popular in the Old South. From 1851 to 1854 he was energetically involved in the work of these conventions, serving for two years as secretary. Strangely enough, until recently these planters' conventions have received very little attention as a factor in southern history. However, beginning in the year 1839, in some of their proposals for regional economic and social causes, they most definitely were forerunners of the better-known southern commercial conventions, about which so much has been written. The planters' conventions also significantly expressed the sectional feelings sometimes known as southern nationalism. The first one met in Georgia in 1839; two others convened in Alabama in 1845; their heyday was in the 1850's, during which decade approximately twenty meetings were held in Florida, Georgia, Alabama, South Carolina, Mississippi, Tennessee, and Louisiana. Their chief purposes were to establish southern direct trade with Europe, to obtain higher and less fluctuating prices for cotton, and to emphasize scientific farming.[58] On all these scores, Cloud for four years was one of their most unflinching spokesmen. At one of the conventions, in Montgomery in May, 1853, he was materially involved in establishing a so-called Agricultural Association of the Slaveholding States, which he had proposed as early as 1847. For two years Cloud published in his agricultural journal and elsewhere, accounts of the Association's interests and activities. He was secretary, as already mentioned, and his *American Cotton*

---

[57]*Alabama Planter*, VI, 179-180 (1852); Mobile *Register*, quoted in Livingston *Sumter County Whig*, May 25, 1852; Savannah *Daily Republican*, December 9, 1856; Tuscaloosa *Independent Monitor*, April 2, 1859; Tuskegee *Macon Republican*, May 22, 1851, April 21, 1853, April 20, 1854; and the following Montgomery newspapers: *Advertiser and State Gazette*, December 17, 1856, August 12, 23, 28, September 8, 1858, October 19, 1859; *Daily Mail*, December 11, 1856, March 16, 1859; *Daily Post*, April 17, 1860; *Weekly Advertiser*, December 12, 1860; *Weekly Alabama Journal*, April 24, May 15, 1852.

[58]Jordan, "Cotton Planters' Conventions in the Old South," *loc. cit.*

Planter was the official publication of the organization.[59]

While working with the Agricultural Association of the Slaveholding States, Cloud was mainly responsible for bringing together at Columbia, South Carolina, in December, 1853, what is believed to have been the most outstanding regional gathering of scientific farmers which met as a body in the entire history of the Old South. That particular convention, lasting six days, discussed such matters as botany, chemistry, education, horticulture, landscaping, grasses, cotton, and slavery, each discussion being led by an expert on the subject. However, in 1855 the Association merged with the southern commercial convention in order more effectively to promote direct trade with Europe; and at the same time its support of scientific farming was assumed by state agricultural societies.[60] It was more than a mere coincidence that Cloud was instrumental in creating an active Alabama State Agricultural Society at the precise time that the Agricultural Association of the Slaveholding States ceased to exist.

But this Alabama State Agricultural Society was by no means solely the work of Cloud, for it was the earlier growth of local and county groups that created an urge for a state society (the first of which was briefly in existence in the early 1840's only to be revived in 1852 and reorganized in 1855). These state organizations, in turn, encouraged the founding of additional local clubs.[61] So many societies were established that Alabama's support of them compares quite favorably with Virginia's and Georgia's, the two states generally recognized as leaders in the movement in the ante-bellum South.[62]

[59]Gray, *History of Agriculture in the Southern United States to 1860*, II, 925-927, mentions briefly the cotton planters' conventions.

[60]*Alabama Planter*, V, 345, 394 (1851), VII, 204 (1853), VIII, 49 (1854); *American Cotton Planter*, I, 81, 305 (1853), II, 66, 276 (1854); *DeBow's Review*, XVII, 491 (1854); Montgomery *Weekly Alabama Journal*, September 27, 1851, November 6, 1852; Prattville *Autauga Citizen*, May 5, 1853; Tuskegee *Macon Republican*, September 18, November 13, 20, December 4, 1851; *Soil of the South*, I, 151 (1851); *Southern Cultivator*, V, 182-183 (1847), XI, 273 (1853).

[61]*American Cotton Planter*, III, 40-50 (1855); Mobile *Daily Advertiser*, January 30, 1852; Montgomery *Weekly Alabama Journal*, November 13, 1852; *Southern Cultivator*, XIII, 57 (1855).

[62]James C. Bonner, "Profile of a Late Ante-Bellum Community," *American Historical Review*, XLIX, 663-680 (1944); Charles W. Turner, "Virginia Agricultural Reform, 1815-1860," *Agricultural History*, XXVI, 80-88 (1952).

Two local societies were organized in Alabama in the late 1820's. The first was established in Monroe County, September, 1828, to combat the so-called "tariff of abominations" which was so unpopular in the South. Although the society's main purpose was to complain about the tariff, it also resolved "to promote the culture of some staple production suited to our climate, and which directs the attention of planters from the growing of cotton now produced in excess."[63] Presumably, this society was soon abandoned. The second organization, which seems to be the original scientific society in the state, was chartered in Greensboro in 1828, and held its first regular meeting the next year. While celebrating its first anniversary of operation, in September, 1830, its president, Doctor Robert W. Withers, described its objective as follows: "To excite and keep alive, that state of activity and enterprise into which our necessities have driven us—to direct the agricultural interests of our southern country, into more useful and profitable channels . . . than can be done when all are exclusively devoted to one object [cotton raising which had] long ceased to remunerate its cultivators with any thing like a fair equivalent for their labor. . . ." Otherwise, he said, Alabama would suffer from worn-out lands as had Virginia, the Carolinas and Georgia.[64] After several years' operation, including the staging of two fairs in the early 1830's, this Greensboro Society was discontinued until 1850, at which time it was revived and became one of the most active in the state.[65]

Few clubs seem to have functioned in Alabama during the 1830's; rather, they first became prominent during the 1840's.[66] Among those that were active in the latter decade were the Society of Fort Mitchell, in Russell County, whose members demonstrated much interest in applying chemistry to farming; the Talladega Agricultural and Mechanical Association, which functioned for about five years; the Monroe and Conecuh Society, which encouraged its

[63]Tuscaloosa *Chronicle*, October 18, 1828.

[64]*American Farmer*, XII, 241-243 (1830).

[65]*Alabama Planter*, IV, 230 (1850); Greensboro *Alabama Beacon*, August 16, 1851, August 13, 1858.

[66]It seems that the only club that was active enough during the 1830's, other than the one in Greensboro, was the Agricultural Society of South Alabama, which had its headquarters in Montgomery. Montgomery *Daily Post*, July 21, 26, 1860; *Southern Agriculturist*, New Series, II, 281-292 (1842).

members to ameliorate their land by employing fertilizers and deep plowing; the Clarke County Society; and the Chunnenuggee Horticultural Society, of Macon County.[67] However, the most interesting one of its type in the 1840's was the Barbour County Agricultural Society, which held its meetings alternately at Glenville and Eufaula. Among the subjects that it studied were fall plowing, fertilizing, horticulture, mechanical arts, deep plowing, the potential of cotton seed as a manure, value of oxen for farm purposes, management of slaves, raising and fattening hogs, and the advantages of an agricultural press. Members also considered the question of how much food to ration to slaves "when they have free access to vegetables and milk."[68] Such activities led W. W. McGuire, editor of the *Alabama Planter*, published in Mobile, to write in August, 1849: "we have . . . among us scattered here and there, a number of the most intelligent and practical agriculturists, ... By the organization of county agricultural societies, with a rule for holding annual state fairs at some suitable place, all this intelligence and practical skill might be brought together and made common property for the good of all."[69]

The decade of the 1850's was the "golden era" of agricultural societies in Alabama; and it is believed that neither before nor since has so much interest in them existed in the state. Functioning in the years from 1850 to 1861 were at least thirty organizations representing every section of the state. Typical local clubs were established at Robinson Springs, Eufaula, Catoma, Benton, Selma, Union Springs, LaFayette, Greensboro, Lynchburg, Linden, Tuscaloosa, and Mobile. Among the county groups were those in Dallas, Chambers, Montgomery, Lowndes, Autauga, Choctaw, Lauderdale, Madison, Pickens, and Limestone.[70] Subjects of interest to the

[67]*Alabama Planter*, III, 154 (1849); *Report of the Commissioner of Patents, for the Year 1850, Agriculture* (Washington, 1851), 459-462.

[68]*Southern Cultivator*, IV, 143-144 (1846). See also *ibid.*, I, 134-135 (1843), III, 76-78 (1845), IV, 113-114 (1846), V, 76-78 (1847).

[69]*Alabama Planter*, III, 312 (1849).

[70]*Ibid.*, VIII, 169 (1854); *American Cotton Planter*, I, 268-271, (1853), II, 275 (1854), III, 221 (1855), IV, 93 (1856); Cahaba *Dallas Gazette*, June 19, 1857, April 8, 1859; Carrollton *West Alabamian*, August 15, 1855; Florence *Gazette*, March 13, 1861; Huntsville *Southern Advocate*, November 16, 1853, November 4, 1858; Montgomery *Advertiser and State Gazette*, August 20, 1853; Montgomery *Alabama Journal*, July 16, 1850, April 15, 1853; Prattville

Lowndes County association were representative. Its members studied "the introduction of new implements, animals, trees and seeds, and such other matters as may promote the interests of the society."[71] Most of the clubs held regular meetings, fairs were conducted less frequently, and programs of the meetings ordinarily centered around discussion of such problems as general farm management, small grains, red clover as a soil builder, methods of reclamation, and so forth. Overcropping of cotton was frequently lamented. Fair exhibits, for which very elaborate premiums were sometimes awarded, included field crops, cattle, hogs, sheep, horses, poultry, vegetables, fruits, needle work, rugs, wax work, flowers, and fine arts. As many as 200 premiums were on occasion awarded at the local and county fairs.[72]

Two of the most active organizations in ante-bellum Alabama were the Mobile and the Chunnenuggee horticultural societies, the latter of which drew its members from the region near the town of Union Springs and from the population scattered throughout Chunnenuggee Ridge. The Ridge was a large area of table land commencing about forty miles southeast of Montgomery. The Mobile club was organized in 1853 to encourage production and display of such objects as flowers, vegetables, poultry, and needlework and other home prepared articles. At its second fair, in 1854, it attracted more than 5,000 spectators and participants, and by the year 1860 was a leading annual social event in the state.[73] Mobile drew the crowds, but Chunnenuggee more than held its own in other respects, particularly with its fairs, which were exciting

---

Autauga Citizen, September 29, 1853, May 24, 1855; *Soil of the South,* I, 117-118, 164-165 (1851), II, 307-308, 318 (1852), IV, 66 (1854); *Southern Cultivator,* IX, 3-4 (1851); Tuscaloosa *Independent Monitor,* May 6, 1858. One of the better Alabama newspapers for information on the state's agricultural history is the Greensboro *Alabama Beacon,* of which the issue of March 28, 1851, is a good example.

[71]Cahaba *Dallas Gazette,* April 8, 1859.

[72]*Alabama Planter,* IV, 273, 298, 417 (1850); *American Cotton Planter,* I, 224, 268-271, 286-287 (1853); Florence *Gazette,* October 24, 1860; Greensboro *Alabama Beacon,* August 20, 1852; Montgomery *Alabama Journal,* August 20, 1853; Montgomery *Weekly Advertiser,* October 3, 1860; *Soil of the South,* II, 378 (1852).

[73]*Alabama Planter,* VII, 81, 211 (1853), VIII, 177, 193 (1854); *American Cotton Planter,* IV, 311-312 (1856); Montgomery *Daily Post,* May 14, 1860; *Soil of the South,* V, 127 (1855).

and sometimes almost breath-takingly beautiful and inspiring. Founded in March, 1847, by Norbonne B. Powell, a Virginian who, before he moved to Alabama, presumably lived for a short time in Talbot County, Georgia,[74] the Society eventually developed a fair ground consisting of a 5-acre plot, landscaped and planted with choice flowers, shrubbery, and fruit trees. Summer houses, arbors and trellises abounded, and in the center of the grounds was a circular pavillion, forty feet in diameter, "with luxuriant roses and delicate jassamines [sic] climbing upon it."[75]

Shown at the monthly and annual fairs at Chunnenuggee were numerous exhibits. Forty-two prizes (both first and second) were announced for the 1851 fair. At the annual exhibition of May, 1855, premiums including pitchers, vases, goblets, cups, saucers, bowls, knives and forks were awarded for such items as vegetables, flowers, strawberries, hot-house plants, bead work, laces, oil paintings, quilts, wax flowers, hams, butter, breads, preserves, pickles, and soaps. The next year 68 premiums valued at from $1 to $8 were announced, and committees were appointed to judge vegetables, strawberries, flowers, needlework, and miscellaneous and discretionary articles and essays. According to a visitor to the 1856 fair, "the display in the floral and horticultural department was singularly rich and varied—forming a delightful adjunct with the manifold charms of the group of joyous fair [women] who arranged and mingled with them. Among the flowers were many rare and choice varieties, which attracted much admiration and interest. . . . In the preparation of conserves, pickles, preserved fruits, etc., it was also apparent that the housewives of that community excel. There was also a fine display of plantation tools and agricultural implements."[76]

---

[74]Southern Agriculturist, VI, 327-328 (1833), quoting the Southern Planter. Daniel Sayre, the editor, states in his Tuskegee Macon Republican, May 6, 1852: "[Powell] is a noble specimen of the fine old Southern gentleman, christian and patriot. He is now, possibly, near the close of a long and useful life, surrounded by a large family of descendants who have profited by his example and his precepts, equally esteemed and beloved by all who know him, and benefiting by his well-informed intellect, and his enlarged hospitality."
[75]Southern Cultivator, XII, 195 (1854).
[76]Montgomery Weekly Alabama Journal, May 10, 1856. See also the American Cotton Planter, III, 125-126 (1855), IV, 126 (1856), and the Tuskegee Macon Republican, March 13, 1851.

In addition to the exhibits the Chunnenuggee fairs offered many other attractions. Horse shows were sometimes held, and visitors enjoyed picnics, magnificent dinners, dances and concerts. There was also available a large area planted with tall shrubs in such a manner that young lovers could enter the maze and lose themselves from sight. Featured also were speakers, usually a politician and either a scientist or an agriculturist. John Forsyth of Mobile reminded his listeners in 1851 that Americans were still "a nation of pioneers," a race that was restless and possessed "a panting spirit of adventure and love of change," but complimented the Chunnenuggee people for having made homes of their residences and beautifying the "Ridge."[77] In 1853, Wylie W. Mason of Auburn told his audience that the sciences of geology, mineralogy and botany were necessary tools of the farmer, and in an oratorical flourish typical of the times concluded that chemistry was of the greatest utility, saying, "we must school ourselves in the halls of Chemical learning and research; our offerings must be laid upon her altars; we must consult her oracles."[78] The next year a speaker presented an exceedingly glowing account of the importance of horticulture from the time of the ancient Hebrews and Persians to the time of mid-nineteenth century America. In 1855, Clement C. Clay, the famous Alabama statesman, urged the people of his state to turn more from cotton production to manufacturing, to a varied agriculture, and to timber culture, mining, and so on. From Columbus, Georgia, there came a statement in the spring of 1856 that the officers of the Chunnenuggee Society had "elected as their anniversary orator, Governor H. V. Johnson [of Georgia]. . . . A rich treat may be anticipated, and we hope a large crop may be there to enjoy it."[79]

Few Alabama garden or horticultural groups have equalled the Chunnenuggee Society for showmanship, accomplishments, and publicity. It was eulogized by leading newspapers and journals of the period and by visitors who came from Alabama and other

---

[77]*Soil of the South*, I, 124-127 (1851).

[78]*Ibid.*, III, 527 (1853).

[79]*Ibid.*, VI, 103 (1856). See also *American Cotton Planter*, III, 209 (1855); *DeBow's Review*, XVIII, 725-728 (1855); Huntsville *Democrat* November 8, 1855; Soil of the South, III, 641-644 (1853); and Tuskegee *Macon Republican*, April 26, 1855.

southern states to attend its functions. The editor of the Tuskegee *Macon Republican*, April 24, 1851, remarked, "These annual Fairs at Chunnenuggee are always occasions of the most pleasant kind, and that of the present year is going to be much more so than any former one." In anticipation of the 1852 exhibition, the same editor stated, April 22 of that year, that the fairs were "extremely popular, and well attended, ... Every thing to please the eye, from pretty flowers to pretty women, will be present; whatever is most agreeable to the palate; and also whatever is most captivating to the ear." This editor's considered opinion, on May 6, 1852, was that "This was the first time we had ever been present at these annual Fairs, . . . but we shall take care how we miss another." Noah B. Cloud wrote in 1855, "we can assure our readers that a day or two cannot be spent more agreeably than at Chunnenuggee during the period of the Society's Fair."[80] Another editor stated in 1854,

. . . Some few years since, a few families from Georgia settled a place in Macon County, Ala., called Chunnuynuggee Ridge. They carried with them, the refinements of education, and a lingering love of home. — No sooner had the sturdy oaks fallen beneath the 'woodman's axe,' than the memories of early years prompted them to plant the fruit and flower in their places; neighbors gave to each other, frequently met and compared specimens, finally formed themselves into a Society for horticultural improvement [in 1847], and annually hold a floral festival in May, ... The influence of that neighborhood Society and its annual festivals, upon the rough material around it, can hardly be estimated.[81]

Still another report was that the Chunnenuggee inhabitants could "drink pure water, breathe pure air, enjoy uninterrupted health, and educate their children in all the refinement of city life without exposure to the city's attendant vices."[82] Partly through the presence of their Society, the people of the area are said to have "made the wilderness blossom like a rose;"[83] and the Society's influence undoubtedly was also felt by the adjacent black belt.

Several of the agricultural societies in ante-bellum Alabama crossed county lines. The membership of one of them, the Muscogee and Russell County Society, was made up of Alabamians and Georgians, and after the year 1852 it was known as the Georgia

---

[80]*American Cotton Planter*, III, 113 (1855). See also *Southern Cultivator*, XII, 195-196 (1854).

[81]*Soil of the South*, IV, 26 (1854).

[82]Montgomery *Daily Mail*, March 23, 1859.

[83]*American Cotton Planter*, I, 114 (1853).

and Alabama Agricultural Society. Its headquarters and the site of its fairs was Columbus, Georgia. Led by their very energetic secretary, George A. Peabody, members studied cotton prices, drainage methods, cultivation of the peanut, and other subjects.[84] Another very important club was the Agricultural and Horticultural Society of Western Alabama, whose supporters came from Marengo, Greene, Clarke, Perry, Pickens, Choctaw, Mobile, Bibb, Tuscaloosa, Sumter, and Washington Counties. This organization functioned for only about three years before the year 1861, but it conducted splendid fairs at Demopolis in 1859 and 1860. In arranging its original fair, which drew nearly 9,000 people, its members spent $10,000, and the occasion was so successful that one editor reported that visitors were "in ecstacies with what they saw."[85] A Tuscaloosa newspaper even exclaimed that *during the entire five days of the Fair, we did not see a single drunken man, or know of a brawl or disturbance in all that vast assemblage!* If this be true, the Demopolis fairs were indeed unusual; they also were almost as elaborate as the fairs held by the state society in the same period.[86]

In the late 1850's North Alabama also sponsored two intrastate societies. Beginning in 1857, Decatur was for four years the scene of fairs which featured various kinds of animals. A Huntsville editor, for example, stated that the stock at the 1857 Decatur fair "was very fine . . . [and] it evinced that, in this respect . . . the people of Limestone, Morgan, Lawrence, Lauderdale and Jackson [Counties] are alive to their duty and interest." He hoped that the show "was a mere commencement—the inauguration of a new era in agricultural, mechanical and other pursuits in North Alabama."[87] His wishes were partly realized, for almost immediately a charter was obtained from the state legislature for the North Alabama Agricultural and Mechanical Association, which for three years promoted better farming in its region. In November, 1858, a rival

[84]*Soil of the South,* I, 15-16, 138 (1851), II, 307 (1852), III, 386-389, 421-422 (1853); *Southern Cultivator,* VIII, 108 (1850), X, 310 (1852).
[85]Gainesville *Independent,* November 12, 1859.
[86]Tuscaloosa *Independent Monitor,* November 12, 1859. See also *ibid.,* September 10, 1859; Greensboro *Alabama Beacon,* December 2, 1859, November 9, 1860; and Montgomery *Daily Mail,* November 22, 1858.
[87]Huntsville *Southern Advocate,* October 8, 1857.

society, the Tennessee Valley Agricultural and Mechanical Association, with headquarters in Tuscumbia, was also organized. The Tuscumbia 1859 fair was attended by 4,000 people, and on that occasion and in 1860 its exhibits consisted primarily of farm animals. Undoubtedly, many North Alabamians took part in both the Decatur and Tuscumbia societies and fairs.[88]

Among the organizations in Alabama during the late ante-bellum period, the most important was the State Agricultural Society, whose chief promoter was Noah B. Cloud, who presided at the Society's organizational meeting in January, 1852, and was thereafter its leading booster. In 1853, as has been mentioned, Cloud began publishing his *American Cotton Planter*, and through it, the official journal of the Society, he agitated for a more effective club than the one originally established. In January, 1855, again in Montgomery, he presided at a gathering of Alabama's leading agriculturists, at which time the Society was reorganized and put on a working basis.[89] From the latter date until the Civil War, the organization was one of the most highly publicized and influential of its type in the South. Under the guiding hand of Cloud, its permanent secretary and spokesman, the State Agricultural Society served both as a clearing house for information on scientific and practical farming and as an advocate of local societies. The state society's leadership other than Cloud was also excellent. Its first president was Isaac Croom of Greensboro, one of the most successful scientific farmers and stock raisers in the Old South; its treasurer was Charles T. Pollard, who, in addition to his interest in agriculture, was the leading railroad builder in ante-bellum Alabama.[90]

The Society demonstrated an absorbing interest in the usual subjects which attracted so much attention among similar organi-

---

[88]*Ibid.*, January 28, 1858, October 26, November 2, 1859; Florence *Gazette*, November 5, 12, 1858, November 2, 1859, October 17, November 7, 1860.

[89]*Alabama Planter*, VI, 51 (1852); *American Cotton Planter*, I, 31 (1853), II, 242, 371-372 (1854); *DeBow's Review*, XVIII, 613-615 (1855); Mobile *Daily Advertiser*, January 15, 1852; Montgomery *Daily Mail*, January 8, 1855; Montgomery *Weekly Alabama Journal*, January 31, 1852; *Southern Agriculturist*, New Series, II, 281, 337-351 (1842); *Southern Cultivator*, XIII, 57 (1855); Tuskegee *Macon Republican*, January 4, 1855.

[90]Croom and Pollard are mentioned and honored in glowing terms by many of Alabama's newspapers of the 1850's and by southern agricultural journals in the period 1840-1860.

zations of its time and region, such as deep plowing, use of fertilizers, horticulture, management of slaves, hillside ditching, crop rotation, farm machinery and mechanical arts, stock breeding, introduction of new seeds and grasses, drainage methods, agricultural education, and government aid to agriculture.[91] These subjects were discussed at great length and publicized quite thoroughly through the columns of newspapers and magazines and through private correspondence. One of the Society's chief interests and activities, however, was its state fair; and its executive committee began immediately to make plans for a fair in the fall of 1855. Shortly after the Society was organized, overtures were made to "the corporate authorities of Montgomery, Mobile [and] Selma" for financial assistance to purchase land for a fair ground. In May, 1855, the Montgomery City Council granted the sum of $2,500 to the Society for its use; two members of the Society agreed to lend additional funds needed to purchase a site for its grounds and to pay other necessary expenses; and by August an appropriate site on the bank of the Alabama River north of Montgomery, near the railway station, was obtained; and several buildings were immediately put under construction.[92]

Beginning in 1855 with a small building called the "Industrial Palace," the physical plant of the state fair grounds was developed into one of the most complete and elaborate of its type in the Old South. The site, thirty acres in size, fenced and planted in part in Bermuda grass, and containing board walks, was "a large and perfectly level plateau of land . . . many feet above the river, . . . as level as a dining table, and dotted here and there with willow, oak, elm, gum and pine."[93] The "Industrial Palace" was enlarged eventually into a structure containing 14,500 square feet of floor space. The main structure, built in 1856, was an amphitheater 176 feet in diameter, which seated 10,000 people. In the center of the amphitheater was a stand for both judges and musicians. Hundreds of stalls were built to accommodate the animals which

[91]See the files of the *American Cotton Planter* and the *American Cotton Planter and Soil of the South.*

[92]*American Cotton Planter,* III, 179, 241-242 (1855); *DeBow's Review,* XVIII, 613-615 (1855).

[93]Montgomery *Daily Mail,* September 11, 1855.

were placed on display; and there was a half-mile track for trotters and gamblers. As the fair grew in size and popularity from year to year, several small buildings and numerous tents were erected to furnish shelter and space for exhibits and for pieces of equipment owned by the Society. In 1858 the grounds and buildings were valued at $20,000; and by this date, through gate receipts and a gift of $5,000 from the State Legislature, the Society was clear of debt.[94] One editor wrote in 1855 that the fair ground was the most elaborate he had "ever seen or 'read about.' "[95] Charles A. Peabody, the Alabama-Georgia horticulturist and a widely traveled man, concluded that "in its appointment, and general arrangements of the grounds and buildings, . . . [the 1856 Alabama fair] surpassed any Fair we ever witnessed."[96] Facilities at the fair grounds for handling crowds were indeed so adequate that the site was utilized as an encampment, under the name of "Fort Jefferson Davis," during the Civil War.[97]

An almost endless number of exhibits was presented at the Alabama state fairs. Animals shown included horses, brood mares, trotters, pacers and colts; mules; camels; Southdown, Merino, Saxon and Cotswald sheep; Devon, Durham, Aldernay, Ayrshire, milk, beef and working cattle; Essex, Suffolk and other hogs; Bantam, Shanghai and Brama Pootra chickens; ducks; Sumatra geese; tur-

---

[94]*Ibid.*, September 24, 1855, quoting Eutaw *Observer; Acts, General Assembly of Alabama* (Montgomery, 1856), 342-343; *American Cotton Planter,* IV, 82, 305-306 (1856); Montgomery *Daily Mail,* November 8, 1856, November 17, 1858; Montgomery *Tri-Weekly Mail,* July 8, 1856; *Soil of the South,* VI, 227 (1856); *Southern Cultivator,* XIV, 122 (1856), XVI, 26 (1858); Tuskegee *Macon Republican,* October 4, 1855.

[95]Prattville *Autauga Citizen,* September 27, 1855. For references to the facilities at the fair ground, see the following Montgomery newspapers: *Advertiser and State Gazette,* November 28, 1855; *Daily Confederation,* November 8, 1858; *Daily Mail,* January 30, 1852, November 12-15, 1856, November 19, 1857, November 3, 1858; *Daily Messenger,* November 10, 1856; *Tri-Weekly Mail,* July 8, 1856; *Weekly Advertiser,* November 23, 1859, November 7, 1860; and *Weekly Alabama Journal,* January 17, 31, November 13, 1852, January 11, November 24, 29, 1855, November 15, 1856. See also the *American Cotton Planter,* II, 371-372 (1854), III, 18-19, 49-50, 146 (1855), IV, 209, 275-276; *DeBow's Review,* XVIII, 613-615 (1855), and *Harper's Weekly,* II, 756 (1858).

[96]*Soil of the South,* VI, 365 (1856).

[97]Greensboro *Alabama Beacon,* May 17, 1861; Montgomery *Daily Post,* September 5, 16, 30, October 4, 1861.

keys; pigeons; and many others. Among the farm implements displayed were cotton gins made by the famous Alabama industrialist, Daniel Pratt, and other manufacturers. Shown also were wagons, buggies, carriages, harnesses, plows, harrows, threshers, grain fans, corn shellers, straw cutters, and other equipment made in Alabama and many other states. Additional manufactured articles exhibited included cloth, jeans, blankets, bricks, stoves, pianos, books, sewing machines, and even a self-revolving fan attached to a rocking chair. This latter very intriguing contraption was recommended for a person taking his ease and for rocking babies to sleep. Hundreds of women participants at the fairs exhibited rugs, quilts, hats, dresses, embroidery, flowers, wax fruit, paintings, wines, brandies, and foods of all kinds. The exhibits were judged, sometimes by as many as 500 or 600 judges serving on 50 or more committees; and premiums averaging about $3,500 in value were awarded each year. Most of the premiums were worth approximately $20 to $25, the highest ones of $50 each being reserved for the best cotton gins and for Alabama-built steamboats. Ordinarily the premiums consisted of pitchers, goblets, and plates.[98] Medals were awarded in 1860 and were described as follows: "On one side practical plantation economy is neatly illustrated, and on the other the chart of the State, encircled with a wreath of corn, cotton and wheat [and the medal] is engraved in the most tasteful style."[99] Cotton was by no means the only interest of either the visitors or the promoters of the fairs.

Agricultural exhibits and competition for premiums were only part of the attractions of the fairs. A very energetic Montgomery theater offered some of its leading plays and actors during fair weeks, including John Wilkes Booth in the "Apostate" in 1860. Military companies paraded, bands played, the Legislature adjourned, and Montgomery merchants displayed their choicest wares.

---

[98]Montgomery newspapers contain hundreds of references to exhibits and to premiums awarded at the fairs during the 1850's. See also, for example, the files of the *American Cotton Planter and Soil of the South,* as well as the following: Cahaba *Dallas Gazette,* December 5, 1856, November 25, 1859; *Report of the Commissioner of Patents, for the Year 1858, Agriculture* (Washington, 1859), 92; Troy *Independent American,* November 16, 1859; and Tuscaloosa *Independent Monitor,* November 11, 1858.

[99]Montgomery *Daily Post,* October 12, 1860.

Dinners and balls and dances were held in private homes and in public halls throughout the city. The dances were especially popular and were always crowded, so much so that one young man once concluded, "The ladies were so considerate as to go unhooped (most of them), for which they deserve a vote of thanks."[100] Conventions were held by manufacturing, railroad, political, and temperance promoters. Stephen A. Douglas, after being greeted with a barrage of eggs, spoke from the Capitol steps during the 1860 fair, to little avail, of course. And at the fair ground itself there was always much to see and to hear. Members of the State Agricultural Society presented lengthy lectures on various aspects of farming. There also were Chinese jugglers; collections of Indian curiosities; beauty contests; fat ladies; skeleton men; and a Negro child, perhaps Siamese twins, "with two heads, four arms, and four legs."[101] In 1858, "two 'monkey shows' were on the ground—[and also] the 'hairy woman' and the 'double head girl,' besides a liquor shed where mean whiskey was vended. . . ."[102] From 1857 to 1860, a tournament, with "knights" and courts of honor and "fair ladies" and trophies for outstanding horsemanship, were features of the fair. In some respects the fair took on a carnival air before it was finished by the coming of the Civil War.[103]

Numerous attendants at the state fairs spoke eloquently of the popularity of the occasions and of the crowded conditions which prevailed. Daily attendance in several instances amounted to more than 12,000 people. In 1856, for example, "the Fair Grounds was a Babel of confusion. Every thoroughfare was jammed. Nothing less than the impetus of a strong arm could force a passage through the solid mass of human beings."[104] Speaking of the crowds in 1859, one observer wrote, "where they staid I cannot imagine, for

---

[100]Montgomery *Daily Mail*, November 14, 1856.

[101]Huntsville *Southern Advocate*, December 3, 1856.

[102]Tuscaloosa *Independent Monitor*, November 11, 1858.

[103]See Prattville *Autauga Citizen*, November 6, 1856, November 26, 1857, October 25, 1860; Tuskegee *Republican*, November 4, 1858, November 24, 1859; and the following Montgomery newspapers: *Advertiser and State Gazette*, November 16, 1857; *Daily Confederation*, November 2, 1859; *Daily Post*, October 29, 1860; *Daily Messenger*, November 12, 1856; *Weekly Advertiser*, November 23, 1859; and *Weekly Alabama Journal*, October 17, November 19, 1856.

[104]Montgomery *Daily Mail*, November 13, 1856.

every place was full, and many of them could not have gone to sleep at all."[105] Since Montgomery's population was only 8,843 in 1860,[106] and since the little city's population was possibly almost doubled by visitors to the fair, housing was indeed a severe problem and a problem never solved satisfactorily. But crowds of people continued to come and enjoy the occasion. The following magnificent description has been left by a visitor in 1856:

> We half wish that the Fair were an 'established institution'— . . . always in progress—like the Court of Chancery, always open—and that we might be always there. It was no pageant . . . but a most interesting, elevating, inspiring exhibition—a social reunion—a great popular holiday. . . . It was a scene to be daguerreotyped on the heart of humanity—to be 'set in a historical frame work' full of suggestions to a thoughtful patriot. There we were, old and young—politicians, merchants, lawyers, doctors, farmers—men, women and children—priest, editors and people—rich and poor—city bred and 'sun burnt sicklemen,' pedagogue and pedlar—buoyant, impulsive, generous youth and bright, innocent, radiant, fresh blown, blushing beauty; —Age . . . was there in gravity and awful counsels. There, too, were widow and widower, with wink and wile—the young old bachelor and the old young maid. There we were, all, and all delighted.[107]

Anticipating the 1859 fair, a young man of Montgomery wrote, "There will be a crowd of articles exhibited, . . . there will also be a crowd of legislators, politicians, candidates, rich people, visitors from all parts of the world, editors, fortune-hunters, pleasure-seekers, loafers, pickpockets, black-legs, and . . . pretty women."[108]

During the years before the first fair was held in 1855, Alabamians and other Southerners were certain that such an exhibition would bring many economic benefits. A Mobile editor was of the opinion that a fair would aid immeasurably in developing his state's resources. From Georgia came encouragement from two of the South's leading agricultural editors, Charles A. Peabody of the *Soil of the South* and Daniel Lee of the *Southern Cultivator*. When Lee learned that Alabama contemplated a fair, his conclusion was that "Here We Rest" was no longer an appropriate motto for the state. A correspondent of a Montgomery newspaper argued that "surely there is no subject more worthy of the attention of a great

---

[105]Tuskegee *Republican,* November 24, 1859. See also *Southern Cultivator,* XVI, 26 (1856), and Tuscaloosa *Independent Monitor,* November 11, 1858.

[106]*Eighth Census of the United States, 1860, Population,* 9.

[107]Montgomery *Weekly Alabama Journal,* December 13, 1856.

[108]Tuskegee *Republican,* November 3, 1859.

and prosperous people."[109] Another opinion, expressed in March, 1855, was that agricultural societies and "industrial exhibitions and fairs" were "certainly the best means yet devised for rural districts, thinly populated, as is the case in the planting States, for stimulating, etc., causing planters to interest themselves in agricultural improvements."[110] Other editorial comments on the eve of the first fair were "Those of us who have nothing of superior qualities to exhibit on the occasion should nevertheless go, and imbibe the spirit of the age in improvements of all kinds" and "we anticipate a mighty revolution by this means, ..."[111]

Once the fairs were begun the state's editors gave them their almost undivided support and painted glowing accounts of what they saw. Although the modern student of history can not reach a sound conclusion in regard to the precise economic benefits of Alabama's early fairs, there is no doubt that contemporary observers were positive that the fairs brought great improvements in agriculture. Widely circulated expressions of approval were that fairs "have contributed more to our vigorous growth as a nation, than all the gold California can pour into the country for ages;" that wherever they were held, one could find "the greatest amount of thriftiness and prosperity;" and that they encouraged a spirit of inquiry, competition among exhibitors, and imitation among those who witnessed the accomplishments of others.[112]

Other opinions were that pleasure and profit resulted from the fair, that there was no type of public activity which satisfied the interests of so many classes of society, and that the exhibitions increased prosperity. One person argued, "Is a man interested in a draft [of] oxen? He sees, at an agricultural fair the finest specimens of the kind, becomes eager to possess a yoke of them, and if he has the means, introduces them into his section, and arouses

---

[109]Montgomery *Daily Mail*, December 11, 1854. See also *Alabama Planter*, III, 329 (1849); *Soil of the South*, III, 567 (1853); *Southern Cultivator*, XIII, 282 (1855).

[110]*American Cotton Planter*, III, 87 (1855).

[111]These quotations are, respectively, from the Troy *Independent American*, October 24, 1855, and the Eutaw *Observer*, quoted in the Montgomery *Daily Mail*, September 24, 1855.

[112]*Genesee Farmer*, quoted in Montgomery *Daily Mail*, September 27, 1857.

the emulation of his neighbors."[113] Noah B. Cloud wrote that the fair was on the side of science and against "old fogyism" and "stupid opposition" to improved agriculture.[114] In a report to the United States Commissioner of Patents in 1858, Cloud, who was better acquainted with Alabama agriculture than any man in his state, concluded:

> The most important benefit resulting from our Society is the spirit of land improvement, by 'horizontalizing' and fertilizing, which is prevalent among our planters. Stock is also better, horses, mules, milch cows, and superior breeds of swine. We are giving much attention to diversifying our crops, combining to a proper extent farming, grazing and stock purposes, with planting. An evident and large increase has been exhibited in all our agricultural products for the last few years. . . . In the manufacture of 'domestics,' such has been the advance that we are amply compensated for all our trouble and expense.[115]

Alabama did indeed make some noteworthy agricultural accomplishments during the 1850's. The acreage of improved farm land increased from 4,435,614 in 1850 to 6,385,724 in 1860, and farm values rose from $64,323,224 to $175,824,622. Among the thirty-three states in 1860, Alabama ranked second in cotton production, third in sweet potatoes, fifth in domestic manufactures, seventh in peas and beans, and tenth in value of livestock and slaughtered animals. On the basis of population, Alabama was one of the outstanding farm states in the Union.[116] In many respects she was the leading agricultural state in the Gulf of Mexico region. And there is no reason to doubt that the agricultural society and fair had something to do with her attainment of this leadership.[117]

But Alabama was by no means the only slave-holding state to show a broad interest in farm improvements through support of agricultural journals, societies and fairs during the 1850's. Every state had its group of promoters. Every state possessed an active

---

[113]Montgomery *Weekly Alabama Journal*, October 25, 1856. See also Gainesville *Independent*, October 30, 1858; Montgomery *Daily Post*, October 12, 1860; Prattville *Autauga Citizen*, November 29, 1855.

[114]*American Cotton Planter and Soil of the South*, IV, 386 (1860).

[115]*Report of the Commissioner of Patents, for the Year 1858, Agriculture*, 92.

[116]*Agriculture of the United States in 1860, Compiled from the Original Returns of the Eighth Census* (Washington, 1864), xlvii-xlix, lxxiv, lxxxi, xciv, cxxvi, 186-187; *A Compendium of the Ninth Census* (Washington, 1872), 688, 690.

[117]For an appraisal of American fairs in general, see Wayne C. Neely, *The Agricultural Fair* (New York, 1935).

farm press; from Maryland to Texas to Kentucky and Missouri there were thriving agricultural societies and fairs; and many of the states created Boards of Agriculture and conducted geological surveys for agricultural purposes.[118] Everywhere there was talk of and some application of crop diversification and scientific farming. It is a well-known fact, of course, that many of the states and some of the sub-regions of the South did not practice self-sufficient farming. But it is of some value to mention once again that the slave-holding states, when taken as a whole, comprised one of the most self-sufficient agricultural regions in world history. Agriculture, not cotton, was king in the Old South. Partial proof of this condition are the facts, recorded in official census returns, that in 1860 the region produced all of the country's cotton, sugar and rice, 80% of the tobacco, and much more than its ratio of the corn, sweet potatoes, beans, peas, hemp, flax and livestock, practically all of the domestic manufactures, and 30% of the wheat. Credit and distribution facilities were quite inadequate for an altogether successful and well-balanced agriculture in the Old South, but a revolution was quite definitely in the making from a production standpoint by the year 1860.[119]

Diversification in agriculture continued, of necessity, from 1861 to 1865, more so than previously because of the demands of a live-at-home procedure brought on by the Civil War. During this period cotton was of less basic importance to its immediate producers than at any time in the history of the United States. Prices for farm produce were high, of course, but so was the inflation, and shipments outside of the South became less and less as the War dragged on and on. The era just after the Civil War is still another story, for Alabama and many other southern farmers then became involved, more than before 1861, in a vicious one-crop system. Post-war conditions and attitudes have led to an erroneous belief

---

[118]*American Cotton Planter and Soil of the South*, IV, 337 (1860); *Carolina Cultivator*, I, 204 (1855);*DeBow's Review*, XIII, 103 (1852), XIV, 334-335 (1853); *Farmer's Journal*, II, 5 (1853); *Soil of the South*, II, 380 (1852); *Southern Cultivator*, VIII, 144 (1850), IX, 75 (1851), XII, 285 (1854), XIV, 176 (1856), XVI, 289 (1858).

[119]For a discussion of the changes that occurred in agriculture in the northern states after the year 1860, see Louis B. Schmidt, "The Agricultural Revolution in the United States, 1860-1930," *Science*, LXII, 585-594 (1930).

that at no time until the twentieth century have southern farmers been actively interested in diversification of crops. This belief must be erroneous if the work of Noah B. Cloud, his state society, the state fair, and local societies are dependable criteria for a study of ante-bellum agriculture in Alabama. The only tenable conclusion seems to be that the state's history in the 1850's was marked by a deep interest in a program of balanced farming.

Because of such pre-Civil War accomplishments it is likely that Alabama and the South would have continued to evolve a fully developed program of diversified farming along with other portions of the United States, if a disrupting war had not come. But the troubles of the period 1860-1875, money-grasping merchants, share-cropping, the crop lien system, a dependency on cotton more pronounced than before 1860, selfish Bourbon politicians and concern with white supremacy, all helped to set back the southern agricultural reform movement more than a generation. Furthermore, commercial fertilizer was no more a complete panacea in Alabama than elsewhere. From 1865 to 1896, southern farmers and others sought to promote their interests through the Patrons of Husbandry, the Greenback Movement, the Farmers' Alliance, and the Populist Party.[120] Finally, it was only through state and federal agencies with their money, educational campaigns, and trained personnel, that scientific farming in the modern sense was developed. This new order of things was more advantageous to the farmer than the old one under the leadership of privately organized societies; and it provide better for his three basic concerns, production, distribution, and credit.

Twentieth century developments in American farm practices have caused many moderns to forget that present day agriculture rests quite solidly on numerous basic methods and interests advo-

---

[120]Several books of use on the southern farmers' movement after the year 1865 are Solon J. Buck, *The Agrarian Crusade; A Chronicle of the Farmer in Politics* (New Haven, 1920); John B. Clark, *Populism in Alabama* (Auburn, 1927); Allen J. Going, *Bourbon Democracy in Alabama, 1874-1890* (Tuscaloosa, 1951); Stuart Noblin, *Leonidas La Fayette Polk: Agrarian Crusader* (Chapel Hill, 1949); Williard Range, *A Century of Georgia Agriculture, 1850-1950* (Athens, 1954); Alfred C. True, *A History of Agricultural Education in the United States, 1785-1925* (Washington, 1929); and C. Vann Woodward, *Origins of the New South, 1877-1913* (Baton Rouge, 1951).

cated before 1860. It is a little known fact, for example, that hundreds of Alabamians and other Southerners as early as 1851 supported programs similar to the sub-treasury plan of the Farmers' Alliance of the 1880's, as well as the controlled market, the ever-normal granary, and regulated prices of the "New Deal" of the 1930's and afterwards.[121] The ante-bellum plans failed mainly because of lack of government support, state and national; the same plans enjoyed some success in the twentieth century because of both government and political support. That the ante-bellum South, including Alabama, was interested seriously in balanced farming is not altogether a strange notion. The intriguing historical fact is that the effort in ante-bellum Alabama reached its peak at the precise time when the state, along with Mississippi, led the United States in the production of cotton.

---

[121]Jordan, "Cotton Planters' Conventions in the Old South," *loc. cit.* For references to the growth of the so-called "Florida Plan," which was an effort of southern planters to promote their economic interests, see, for example, the *American Cotton Planter*, I, 183-186 (1853), Montgomery *Tri-Weekly Journal*, May 6, 1853, and Tallahassee *Florida Sentinel*, August 5, 1851. See also Weymouth T. Jordan, " 'The Florida Plan': An Ante-Bellum Effort to Control Cotton Sales," *Florida Historical Quarterly*, XXXV, 205-218 (1957).

VII

THE INDUSTRIAL GOSPEL

One of the best-known facts about ante-bellum Alabama is that it was not a manufacturing state. Cotton mills were among its most active industrial enterprises, but the state had only fourteen cotton goods factories producing articles valued at $1,040,147 in 1860. Mobile, the state's metropolis with a population of 29,258, employed only 764 persons in its little factories in the same year. Farmers numbered 68,638 in 1850 and 67,743 in 1860, thus showing where the state's chief economic interests lay.[1] However, this is not to say that agriculture was the state's only interest.

Every part of the state possessed numerous zealous and sometimes fanatical persons who agitated in behalf of manufacturing. The state might not have many factories when compared with either the northern states or southern states such as Virginia, Georgia and North Carolina,[2] but the crusaders for industry, over and over and year after year, called on Alabamians to turn to manufacturing. A host of men, especially newspaper editors, passionately argued for factories at precisely the time when the state was dominated by agriculture. To say, as some twentieth century scholars have said, that the Old South, including Alabama, neglected to publicize its manufacturing or to agitate for additional factories, is to miss one of the leading aspects of the history of the region.[3] Alabamians shared in the Southern crusade for industry for two reasons in particular: (1) they sought a diversified or balanced economy, and (2) they wanted factories, just as they

---

[1]*Hunt's Merchants' Magazine,* XXII, 199 (1855); *Manufactures of the United States in 1860; Compiled from the Original Returns of the Eighth Census* (Washington, 1865), xxi; *Eighth Census of the United States, 1860, Population,* 659-680; *Statistics of the United States, Including Mortality, Property, etc.,* in 1860; . . . (Washington, 1866), xviii.

[2]*DeBow's Review,* XVI, 11 (1854), XVIII, 113-114 (1855).

[3]Many general histories of the United States barely mention the subject of the ante-bellum Southern interest in manufacturing. However, the subject has been surveyed in Herbert Collins, "The Southern Industrial Gospel before 1860," *Journal of Southern History,* XII, 386-402 (1946), and Phillip Davidson, "Industrialism in the Ante-Bellum South," *South Atlantic Quarterly,* XXVII, 405-425 (1928).

wanted a diversified agriculture, in order to be economically independent of the North.

There is much reason to believe that Alabamians sought economic independence of the North more than they sought self-sufficiency, although it is perhaps true that the two aims were so emotionally entertwined that they could not be separated. The remarks of a Huntsville editor in 1849 serve as a case in point. Anticipating Henry Grady, the prominent and much-quoted advocate of industry in the New South, the Huntsville editor was quite passionately upset at his region's economic dependence upon the North. His remedy for the salvation of the South was manufacturing, of course. He said:

The South *has* a remedy, which, if properly used, would work a wonderful change, in Northern aggressive sentiments. *Let the South learn to live at home!* At present, the North fattens and grows rich upon the South. We depend upon it for our entire supplies. We purchase all our luxuries and necessaries from the North. We do not depend upon ourselves. We do not encourage enterprise, skill and industry at home; but give the preference to that of the North. With us, every branch and pursuit in life, every trade, profession and occupation is dependent upon the North. For instance, the northerners abuse and denounce slavery and slaveholders, yet our slaves are clothed with northern manufactured goods, have northern hats and shoes, work with northern hoes, and other implements, are chastised with northern made instrument[s], are working for northern more than southern profit. The slaveholder dresses in northern goods, rides a northern saddle with all the other accoutrements, sports his northern carriage, patronizes northern newspapers, drinks northern liquors, reads northern books, spends his money at northern watering places, crowds northern fashionable resorts, in short, his person, his slaves, his farm, his necessaries, his luxuries—as he walks, rides, sleeps, loafs, lounges, or works, he is surrounded with articles of northern origin. The aggressive acts upon his rights and his property arouse his resentment—and on northern made paper, with a northern pen, with northern ink he resolves, and resolves in regard to his rights! In northern vessels his products are carried to market—his cotton is ginned with northern gins—his sugar is crushed and preserved by northern machinery—his rivers are navigated by northern steamboats; his mails are carried in northern stages; his negroes are fed with northern bacon, beef, flour, and corn; his brandy toddy is cooled with northern ice; his land is cleared with a northern axe, and a yankee clock sits upon his mantle piece; his floor is swept by a northern broom, is covered with a northern carpet, and his wife dresses herself in a northern looking glass; his child cries for a northern toy, crows over a northern shoe, and is perfectly happy in having a northern knife; his son is educated at a northern college, his daughter receives the finishing polish at a northern seminary, his doctor graduates in a northern medical college; his schools are supplied with northern teachers, and he is furnished with northern inventions and notions.[4]

---

[4]Huntsville *Advocate,* quoted in Wetumpka *Daily State Guard,* April 6, 1849.

Echoing full approval of these sentiments, a Wetumpka writer remarked, "We, too, say the South has her remedy, if her people will only set about to accomplish it. Let the people of the South with one voice declare to-day, that they will produce *all articles* of their consumption. . . . This course," he reiterated, "would encourage our industrious mechanics, produce domestic wealth, and consequently effect more good than fifty southern Addresses, or twenty thousand southern indignation meetings."[5]

These two men were preceded during the late 1830's and the 1840's by scores of fellow Alabamians who preached the gospel of industry in their state. A correspondent of the Mobile *Alabama Planter* fervently maintained, "We possess in the south [and Alabama] all the elements of a great manufacturing country," especially raw materials, labor, coal, and iron.[6] While praising a cotton yarn and wool carding factory near Tuscaloosa, another writer boasted that the company was located at a place with enough water power to operate 10,000 spindles. Already, he added, ". . . the prospects of the company as to profit, are exceedingly flattering. Their sales are brisk, ..."[7] On another occasion cotton mills in the vicinity of Tuscaloosa were said to be paying dividends of 18 to 24 per cent to their investors.[8] When the establishment of a paper mill in Tuscaloosa was announced in 1846, a local booster proclaimed, "Tuscaloosa will soon attain a degree of prosperity which she has never hitherto enjoyed. If proper use be made of the natural resources within the reach of her enterprise, a bright destiny will reward the exertions of her citizens."[9]

Iron manufacturing was started in Bibb and surrounding counties during the early 1830's, and this was looked on as the beginnings of a great industry. A Mobile writer pointed out that the region was rich in ore, that its supply of bituminous coal was large, and that its water power was unlimited.[10] John M. Moore, of Benton County, was reported to be producing "first rate" iron

[5]Wetumpka *Daily State Guard*, April 6, 1849.
[6]*Alabama Planter*, III, 305 (1849).
[7]Tuscaloosa *Monitor*, May 30, 1838.
[8]*Ibid.*, quoted in *Niles' National Register*, LXXII, 260 (June 26, 1847).
[9]Tuscaloosa *Monitor*, quoted in Tuscumbia *North Alabamian*, August 14, 1846.
[10]*Alabama Planter*, quoted in *DeBow's Review*, III, 585 (1847).

castings "superior to Eastern and Western castings for toughness and standing the fire."[11] Another story, from a Shelby County iron-maker, was, "Our Furnace is in full blast and bids fair to do well. . . . We are making from ten to twelve thousand pounds of pig iron per day, and will soon be ready to do any and all sorts of casting. . . . Our ore yields from 50 to 60 per cent., and is wholly inexhaustible."[12] The geologist, Michael Tuomey of the University of Alabama, reported that the state's coal and iron deposits bordered on the fabulous.[13] Recognizing the signs of a blossoming industry in the state in the late 1840's, Charles C. Langdon, editor of the Mobile *Daily Register,* concluded emphatically that the only way Mobile could ever be "great and prosperous" was to "become a manufacturing city."[14] He made this statement at the very time when Alabama was the leading cotton-producing state and Mobile the second ranking cotton exporting city in the United States.[15]

Alabama's promoters of manufacturing were much more active and outspoken during the 1850's than they had been in the 1840's. One reason for this, obviously, was that more factories were established, which, since they demonstrated some of the more desirable advantages of an industrial economy, created a demand for additional factories. In other words, manufacturing begat manufacturing.

A second, and more important, reason for the increased pace of the industrial gospel during the 1850's was that Southern nationalism became more pronounced. It was indeed with passion that a leading Mobile newspaper printed the following widely quoted diatribe in 1850: "We frankly tell you that, so far as we are concerned, we *despise the Union, and hate the North as we do hell itself.*"[16] Bordering on the violent, this psychological condition incited a greater desire for manufacturing or anything else which would strengthen the South. One may as well carry this latter interpretation to a certain conclusion, namely, that many influ-

[11]Wetumpka *Argus,* quoted in *Southern Cultivator,* IV, 8-9 (1846).

[12]Wetumpka *Daily State Guard,* March 10, 1849.

[13]Tuscaloosa *Independent Monitor,* August 24, 1847.

[14]Mobile *Daily Register,* October 30, 1849.

[15]For an account of the rise of Mobile as a cotton port, see Jordan "Ante-Bellum Mobile: Alabama's Agricultural Emporium," *loc. cit.*

[16]*Sentinel* (Columbus, Georgia), quoted in Mobile *Daily Advertiser,* November 13, 1850.

ential Alabamians during the late 1850's and early 1860's reached a point of so despising the North that they not only sought factories in order to render themselves economically independent, but they also convinced themselves that they should fight a preventive war in an effort to "protect" what they believed to be their "rights." Among the reasons that a group begins a preventive war are its beliefs that it is superior to the potential enemy and that the enemy should be attacked before he is ready to defend himself adequately. These reasons, perhaps, should be included among those that caused the Confederacy, from its headquarters in Montgomery in 1861, to decide to fire on Fort Sumter.

For all that, all of the hot-heads were not on the secession side. For example, an Alabama Unionist in a letter to the Florence *Gazette* said that a non-Unionist "could not get a meal's victuals or a bed to sleep on at my home. My dogs should not bark at him. If I was to catch a buzzard eating the carcass of a disunionist, I would[n't] shoot it. They are the last of all creation; fit for nothing but to be winked at by negroes, kicked at by mules, gored by bulls, and butted by rams."[17]

In actuality, except for more frequent references to sectionalism and southern nationalism, the arguments presented by Alabamians in favor of manufacturing during the 1850's were about the same as those advanced previously. For instance, an Alabama correspondent of *DeBow's Review* complained, "No state in the Union possesses to a greater degree materials for a proud independence, than does Alabama. . . . Too much time is given to the *growing* of cotton. . . . How long, with all the advantages which God has given her, shall Alabama remain in the background, with her countless millions of wealth buried beneath her soil?"[18] Another person, in referring to the Warrior River area, bragged, "The coal is there, the water-power is there, the timber is there; and, we think, the iron is there. The facilities for collecting them together, so that each may support and make the other more valuable, are almost or quite unsurpassed."[19] A propagandist of ship-building as an industry for South Alabama declared that labor was cheap, that

---

[17]Florence *Gazette,* quoted in Mobile *Daily Advertiser,* April 8, 1851.
[18]*DeBow's Review,* XIV, 67-68 (1853).
[19]*Ibid.* XI, 82 (1851), quoting *Alabama Planter.*

the supplies of timber in the region, including pine, white-oak, live-oak, cypress, juniper and white cedar were scarcely touched, and that these advantages, as well as the area's "unquestionable health," made it an ideal place for ship-building. Since the state possessed countless advantages for industry, proclaimed the *Alabama Planter,* "We shall presently have a revolution which no man is able to calculate the consequences of."[20] Another booster called attention to the fact that Alabama was the best watered state in the Union, and in his exuberance trumpeted that there was enough water at Wetumpka alone "to work up more than half the cotton made in the plantation States!!!"[21] Gasconading in a similar vein, one person hoped that Lauderdale County would become "the Lowell of the South," for, he blustered, "She has the water power, [is] free from disease, [and has] fuel, labor, capital, and practical knowledge. And there is no limit to the demand for all that she can manufacture."[22]

Iron-making was an activity that whetted the ambitions of many of Alabama's economic crusaders during the 1850's. The fact is that not much iron-making took place,[23] but this did not retard the exultation of the promoters, for, to them, the state's iron deposits were unquestionably the means of a new kind of El Dorado. A mountain of iron in Fayette County, for instance, was vaunted as follows: "On the sides, ledges of ore crop out from the summit to the base. From the ledges, with a sledge hammer, one man can burst up from the ledges, two to three tons of ore per day."[24] Also, after a rolling mill was set up near Columbiana, a local newspaper trumpeted, "This place combines all the facilities for the successful prosecution of the iron business. . . . The best of ore, almost on top of the ground, an abundance of wood, a plenty of fire-proof clay close at hand, any quantity of bituminous coal, together with excellent springs of water, all combine to render

---

[20]*Alabama Planter,* IV, 288 (1850). See also *DeBow's Review,* XIX, 611-613 (1855).

[21]*Soil of the South,* I, 118 (1851).

[22]Huntsville *Advocate,* quoted in *Hunt's Merchants' Magazine,* XXXVII, 111 (1857).

[23]*DeBow's Review,* XVIII, 109 (1855); *Hunt's Merchants' Magazine,* XL, 758-759 (1859).

[24]Huntsville *Southern Advocate,* December 25, 1856.

it the most valuable property in the Union."[25] The Elyton *Alabamian,* of Jefferson County, stated prophetically, "Come along, gentlemen, and examine our iron ore, rich variegated marble, inexhaustible beds of bituminous coal, and mountains of Spanish brown and lime rock, . . . and you can hardly fail to be struck with the advantages afforded for turning all these minerals to immense profit. Now is the time to make good investments."[26] Far-sighted, too, was a Tuscaloosa newspaper when it advised the establishment of a rolling mill in Alabama for the purpose of manufacturing iron and iron rails for railroads, saying, "Iron can be furnished for all the railroads that can ever be built in the State, for all time to come, . . ."[27]

But, Alabama's industrial crusaders of the 1850's had a reason for industrial development other than the mere encouragement of manufacturing and the stolid matter of earning dividends on investments. The editor of a Montgomery newspaper wrote: "It will afford us special pleasure, at all times, to chronicle the establishment of cotton, or any other kind of manufactories in Alabama. In such enterprise we recognize the right step towards independence of the North on the part of the South, and the proper mode to place our section in the commanding position which it ought to occupy. With the raw materials at our door, plenty of water and steam power actually wasting and no lack of suitable hands, it is worse than folly to continue to pay tribute, yea, the profits of our labor, to sections of the Union that really are seeking our destruction by all constitutional and unconstitutional means."[28] This was said in the year 1860, but it represents a culmination of what had been said countless times throughout the 1850's. A few examples will suffice to demonstrate that this fixation indeed existed.

Speaking of a cotton factory in Mobile, a citizen of that city said, "This is the kind of non-intercourse which we recommend." Factories, he added at a later date, were "one of the main pillars of Southern independence," and "We must diversify our labor, build

---

[25]Columbiana *Chronicle,* quoted in Talladega *Democratic Watchtower,* May 2, 1860.

[26]Elyton *Alabamian,* quoted in Montgomery *Daily Mail,* March 19, 1858.

[27]Tuscaloosa *Independent Monitor,* April 16, 1859.

[28]Montgomery *Daily Post,* April 18, 1860.

up factories and forges, if we desire real independence."[29] The Talladega quarries were lauded as follows: "One such enterprise as this will do more towards establishing the independence of the South, than all the indignation meetings that can be drummed up in the State."[30] A cotton factory at Autaugaville, it was affirmed, was another example of the manner by which the South was "gradually freeing herself from northern bondage."[31] Industrial crusaders repeated and repeated the argument that Alabama needed factories in order to "sustain" itself against the North. From Clarke County came the admonition: "Let us, as Southerners, encourage and support as far as lies in our power, the enterprise and industry of our section. By doing so we generally get a better article, and, besides, have the consolation of the reflection that our money is in the pocket of one friendly to us and to our institutions."[32] A writer in Selma pleaded for a ship-building company in Alabama, arguing that the state should stop buying ships from abolitionists and others who "squint awfully that way." He concluded, "We can never have independence while we pay so much tribute to other States and countries."[33]

Despite her overpowering interest in becoming economically self-sufficient and economically independent of the North, Alabama developed only a small amount of manufacturing before the Civil War. Mobile and Montgomery were the only cities worthy of the name. They had the state's best systems of police, schools, city streets and urban transportation, and the most active churches, theaters and other entertainments, as well as the most outstanding physicians, poets and other writers, musicians, dancing teachers, housing, and hotel facilities. There were some evidences of an embryonic factory system in the two cities, but despite their advantages of population, finances and labor, neither of the two places developed into distinctive manufacturing centers. Montgomery was the governmental nucleus of the state as well as the commercially-minded trade hub of the Black Belt; Mobile was an agricultural

[29]Mobile *Daily Advertiser*, May 11, 23, October 3, 1850.
[30]*Ibid.*, October 11, 1850.
[31]*Alabama Planter*, V, 166 (1851).
[32]Grove Hill *Clarke County Democrat*, January 31, 1856.
[33]Selma *Reporter*, quoted in Montgomery *Advertiser and State Gazette*, April 9, 1856.

emporium, whose chief economic interest concerned the shipment and sale of cotton. Montgomery and Mobile were, of course, the social capitals of the state.[34]

The way the state manufactured cotton goods and farm implements serves as an excellent key to its industrial activities in the ante-bellum period.[35] Instead of building up some large manufacturing enterprises in Mobile and Montgomery, as might have been done if the water power in those two cities had been more useable, the entrepreneurs of the state chose to develop a number of little manufacturing villages in the north central portion of the state. Such communities as Autaugaville, Scottsville, Tallassee and Prattville were set up as manufacturing towns because they were located near the fall lines of rivers. These villages were the prototype of ante-bellum Alabama's industrial enterprise. None of them developed into large communities when compared, for example, with the factory towns of New England, but they were among the largest and most active of their type in Alabama, and Alabamians were inordinately proud of them. Newspaper editors and other public spirited persons boasted of the goods, largely cotton goods and farm implements, turned out in the villages; it was argued that such villages helped make the South self-sufficient; and throughout the 1840's and 1850's, additional villages were sought after fervently.

Scottsville, situated not far from Centerville in Bibb County, and near the Cahaba River, became a village which was "devoted exclusively to manufactures." Operation of a cotton yarn and wool carding factory in a brick building three stories high and 90 by 44 feet in size was begun in the community in 1837 by the Tuscaloosa Manufacturing Company. An early report stated, "About twenty hands are employed—all white—some males, some females—some large, and some small."[36] The company "got to work" with a capital of only $37,000, and for four years operated at a loss.

[34]Jordan, "Ante-Bellum Mobile: Alabama's Agricultural Emporium," *loc. cit.*; Summersell, *Mobile: History of a Seaport Town, passim;* Williams, "Early Ante-Bellum Montgomery: A Black Belt Constituency," *loc. cit.*

[35]Richard W. Griffin, "Cotton Manufacture in Alabama to 1865," *Alabama Historical Quarterly,* XVIII, 289-307 (1956).

[36]*Niles' National Register,* LIV, 258 (June 23, 1838).

Daniel Scott, one of the founders of the company, obtained control of the factory, and he, by the year 1858, managed to develop his organization into a rather profitable and active business. His first profit of $2200, which was realized in 1841, "was expended in a family of negroes to work in the factory," and the value of this family later increased to $10,000. By the year 1841, the sum of $40,000 was paid into the company as capital stock; every year thereafter a dividend of at least 10 per cent was declared. Capital stock in 1858 amounted to $117,000; operatives, most of them women, numbered over 100; and the Scottsville enterprise was considered a great success. The editor of the Selma *Sentinel* reported, "The company owns 3000 acres of land and all the buildings on the place, which consist of the factory, a large hotel, the store, blacksmith, wheelwright and boot and shoe shops, a saw mill, grist mills, large flouring mill, a church and a large number of cottages. . . ." He concluded, proudly, "So much for enterprise, governed by steadiness, perseverance and skill."[37]

The Autaugaville Manufacturing Company was organized in August, 1848, opened for business in July, 1850, and within a year after beginning operations, Autaugaville had a population of 400. The town was located on Swift Creek, "four miles from Vernon, on the Alabama River, and fourteen miles west of Prattville." In early 1851 the factory building was a fire-proof brick structure, 150 by 50 feet; its capital stock amounted to $78,000; its machinery was valued at $40,000; and plans of expansion envisaged 3,000 spindles and 100 looms turning out 4,000 yards of osnaburgs, shirting, and "all kinds of thread and yarn" per day. One of its boosters wrote, "A tract of land containing 800 acres, is under control of the stockholders; and, according to an act of the Legislature, no kind of ardent spirits is allowed to be vended within two miles of the premises. . . . The number of hands required is only 120, and all of these [most of them women] are Southern laborers, taken from the immediate vicinity."[38]

DeBow's Review reported, in 1851, that "Autaugaville has grown up in the woods during the past two years," while the *Soil*

---

[37]Selma *Sentinel,* quoted in Florence *Gazette,* November 5, 1858. See also *DeBow's Review,* XII, 694-695 (1852), XXV, 717 (1858), and *Hunt's Merchants' Magazine,* XXXIX, 755 (1858).

[38]*Alabama Planter,* V, 82 (1851); *DeBow's Review,* X, 560 (1851).

of the South, of Columbus, Georgia, carried an article by an Alabamian, "J. A. W.," stating that the little community had helped make Autauga County into "the *Banner* county of the State, ..." The Company, it was said, was turning out articles as good as "the best 'Lowell.'"[39] A Mobile agricultural journal praised the Autaugaville Manufacturing Company as follows: "The prices are as low, and in our opinion lower, than the same qualities can be laid down for in Mobile, from the North or East. Merchants, we are sure," it was added, "will promote their own interests by purchasing these goods."[40] Autaugaville, then, was a typical manufacturing village. It was small; it was located at the fall line; it produced cotton goods for local and regional consumption; its workers were native white women for the most part; its owners prohibited use of liquor by its employees; and it was acclaimed as a promoter of Southern nationalism.

Accounts of the village of Tallassee Falls were marked by ecstasy more than anything else. This was not true of the earlier descriptions of the place, but it did become the case during the 1850's, after a cotton mill began to thrive there. *Niles' National Register* reported, sedately, in April, 1844, "Preparations are making to begin an extensive spinning and weaving establishment at the Tallapoosa Falls in the neighborhood of Tallassee."[41] Operation of a cotton factory was begun two years later by the Marks and Barnett Company, and thereafter the supporters of the Company and the town were filled with joy. In 1853, for example, the Company advertised its holdings ("with Water Power and Town Site at the Falls of the Tallapoosa River, on the west side") as follows:

Our situation seems especially designed by nature for a large manufacturing city. We do not hesitate to say that our place possesses greater advantages than any other in the South, and we believe greater than any in the Union. Our Dam and Race are built of rock, laid in hydraulic cement. We have only a portion of our water power controlled, but enough to drive 50,000 spindles. The first floors of our buildings are 56 to 60 feet above the highest freshets, our works not disturbed by high or low water. The Fall is 50 feet in 800, with immense power and certainty of stream. The place is unsurpassed for health, and of close proximity to a rich planting country; in fact, nature seems to have

---

[39]*DeBow's Review.* X, 461 (1851); *Soil of the South,* I, 117-118 (1851).
[40]*Alabama Planter,* VI, 333 (1852), V, 166 (1851).
[41]*Niles' National Register,* LXVI, 87 (1844).

been lavish with advantages which stand inviting man to improve.[42]
It might seem that this was enough to say in praise of the site, but it was a mere beginning; it was nothing more than an advertisement beseeching investments in the area.

Of much more interest than the above advertisement was an inspired, poetic description of Tallassee by a writer in the Montgomery *Advertiser and State Gazette*. The falls, he said, were "beautiful and romantic." The land on the west side of the river was covered with "excellent pine timber, sufficient to supply all the demands of the surrounding country and the young village springing up immediately at the Falls." The falls, he went on, were marked by both "their singular beauty and extraordinary facilities for manufacturing purposes. . . . If we regard these Falls for their wild, enchanting scenery, we are confident that they cannot be surpassed in any part of the *United States, South*." The factory, which had been erected in 1846, was capable of working about 40 looms and 1500 spindles. Also, a new enterprise known as Barnett, Gilmer and Company was making many improvements, not the least of which was a "noble" and "substantial" building of rock masonry. The building, he said, "has already been carried four stories high in front, and on the side next to the river presents a massive adamantine wall, of more than one hundred feet perpendicular altitude. Its entire length is 217 feet—width 57—height in front 50. When filled with machinery (as it soon will be) it is calculated that it will run about 10,000 spindles, will require at least 400 looms, and will give employment to about 400 additional hands." But this was not all that the observer had to pass on to his readers. He was literally overwhelmed by the savage beauty of the falls and the river, although he was no more enthralled than thousands of sight-seers would be in the future. He wrote, lovingly:

The river immediately at the Falls is divided into two rather unequal parts by a small rocky island, the larger division being on the western side, though the greatest perpendicular fall of water is undoubtedly on the opposite side. Above this insulated mass of rocks are several smaller, and one or two larger islands, embowered in the richest verdure imaginable. . . . After sweeping around these fairy islands, the water is gradually concentrated towards the upper extremity of the rocky island before spoken of; then gliding away with increased velocity, each division, as if daring the other to the dreadful conflict, rushes

---

[42]Montgomery *Advertiser and State Gazette*, November 8, 1853. See also *Southwestern Baptist* (Montgomery, Alabama), November 18, 1853.

furiously on its mad career, leaping from shelf to shelf with deafening roar. Dashing now from side to side, 'midst foam and spray, it comes whirling through the broad cliffs and broken passages to the deep chasms below; then boiling and surging along the rocky ramparts, the confused waters are again united, and passing rapidly under the west arch of the bridge, immediately spread out, broad, deep and placid, as if to compose themselves before they proceed on their journey to the ocean.[43]

Of all the manufacturing villages in Alabama, and indeed of the entire South before 1860, Prattville was the most notable. The amazing developments there, a little place whose population amounted to 582 whites and 263 Negroes in 1855,[44] were primarily the work of Daniel Pratt. This man Pratt, along with Noah B. Cloud, stood out as an extraordinary advocate of Alabama's and the South's economic betterment; and Alabama had much reason to be proud of these two adopted sons. Cloud, as has been seen, was an inveterate sponsor of agricultural improvements; indeed he was one of the most active publicists of scientific agriculture in the South. However, there was a striking difference between Cloud and Pratt. Doctor Cloud became so involved in his promotional work that it became his chief activity; he was so busy preaching that he did not have time to practice fully what he was preaching. He was a journalist-farmer as well as a practicing farmer. Pratt, on the other hand, was a man of action, who, with his own mind and efforts, created what was truly an unusual business enterprise at his little domain of Prattville, Alabama, located on Autauga Creek, thirteen miles west of Montgomery.[45] By 1850, Autauga County was operating 5,962 spindles, twice as many as any other county in Alabama, and of these Pratt was running 2,682 in his factory, the Prattville Manufacturing Company. His cotton goods, osnaburgs, a cheap, coarse cloth for slave use, was said to be as good as similar goods from Massachusetts.[46] In 1860, Alabama was the leading cotton gin producing state in the Union, with 178 hands working in 16 factories turning out gins valued at $434,805. Pratt's gin factory at Prattville manufactured about one-fourth of these machines.[47]

[43]Montgomery *Advertiser and State Gazette*, December 29, 1853.
[44]Tuskegee *Macon Republican*, May 17, 1855.
[45]*DeBow's Review*, II, 153-155 (1846).
[46]*Alabama Planter*, IV, 298, 305 (1850).
[47]*Agriculture of the United States in 1860*, p. xxxvi; *American Cotton Planter and Soil of the South*, I, 156 (1857).

Pratt was eulogized for his accomplishments more than any other businessman in the lower South in the years immediately before the Civil War, for here was a man after the heart of the Southern nationalists. And these eulogies serve several purposes to the student of history. They demonstrate unequivocally that Southerners wanted manufacturing, that they were proud of what they had, and that they wanted more. Furthermore, the eulogies furnish some excellent information as to Pratt's activities. Several examples of the praise showered on him, including the following one from the Mobile *Tribune* of 1851, will suffice to illustrate the feelings of representative editors toward their subject:

Mr. Pratt is a native of Temple, New Hampshire. He was brought up to the trade of a carpenter and on the completion of his apprenticeship in 1819, removed to Georgia, where from that time until 1833 he was engaged in the manufacture of cotton gins [bridges, and houses.] In the latter year he came to Alabama and settled in Autauga county, where he commenced the manufacture of gins on an extensive scale, having had the benefit of the experience of Mr. [Samuel] Griswold, the oldest and most extensive gin maker in the world. His success in the business is well known in this region, and the celebrity of his machines is almost co-extensive with the cotton culture of this State, Florida, Mississippi, Louisiana and Texas. In a short time he amassed a handsome fortune. He commenced in 1839 a sawmill, then a planing mill, a flour and grist mill and a gin factory. Possessing more capital than was necessary to carry on these establishments, he determined to employ it in such a manner as would contribute the greatest amount of good to the community. The poorer classes in particular he had in view, and to such he has been a great benefactor. It was this spirit that prompted the erection of his cotton factory in 1846, now in complete and successful operation, and consuming 1200 to 1500 bales of cotton annually. He has since built an iron factory, a new brick planing mill, and a door, sash and blind factory. The village built up by these various enterprises possesses an interest but little short of the founder.[48]

DeBow's Review was in the vanguard of those journals which joined the happy and admiring throng which paraded Pratt's virtues to the reading public. On one occasion the cotton gin manufacturer's portrait was carried as the *frontispiece* of the *Review,* and at another time the journal printed an article containing some illus-

---

[48]Mobile *Tribune,* quoted in Montgomery *Weekly Alabama Journal,* March 1, 1851. According to one account, Pratt's "earliest business in Alabama, was the construction, on a limited scale of cotton gins. This was about 1833 or 1834. His first limited purchase was the privilege of water power. The present site of Prattville was bought for $20,000 from Joseph May, and contains 2,000 acres." Pratt believed, in 1848, that he controlled enough water power to operate 30,000 spindles. He said, too, that investments of $1,000,000 in Prattville would create a town of 3,500 people, "and give employment to them." Tuscumbia *North Alabamian,* March 24, 1848.

trations of the town of Prattville, of houses of the factory workers, and of Pratt's residence.[49] The *Review* offered a glowing description of Pratt's accomplishments. The Pratt cotton factory, DeBow reported, was a building of "about 250 feet long, 80 feet of which is 36 feet wide, with a brick basement and two stories of wood," to which were attached one building of four stories and another of three stories. The gin factory, of two stories, was "immediately on a line with the cotton factory, ..." The gin factory was "under the charge of S. Griswold & Co., ..." DeBow added, "Besides the buildings mentioned above, there are three churches, two school houses, four stores, a carriage shop, two smith shops, and about thirty-five dwelling houses. The population is about 800." But this was not all that was of interest to DeBow, and he concluded, "Whatever has had a tendency to improve the community, morally and socially, has not been left undone. Intemperance has been strictly guarded against. In selling building lots, the sale of ardent spirits has been prohibited, by a forfeiture of the lot in any event of the kind. The legislature has also prohibited the retailing of it within two miles of the place."[50]

A few years later the editor of the Cahaba *Dallas Gazette* was so carried away with his admiration of Prattville that he termed it "'the loveliest village of the plain.'" On behalf of Pratt the editor wrote:

He has not only contributed very largely, by his enterprising investments, to the increase of our taxes, but by the successful management of these investments, he has attracted to his village capital, which likewise goes to replenish our treasury. He has opened a graded road leading to his village, he has built a plank road with his own private means four miles in length which the public use without hindrance, he has established Sunday Schools and built churches, has constructed bridges and aided in building up schools for the poor, has opened a market for the products of the county, and has given and does give employment to the needy and industrious, and finally he has been the means of building up a village, which for the refinement of its society, the enterprise of its citizens, the diversity of its industrial pursuits, the conveniences of its location, the neatness of its buildings, and all the advantages of Newspapers, Schools and Churches, has no superior in middle Alabama. Who has done more? Who the hundreth part so much?[51]

---

[49]*DeBow's Review*, X, Frontispiece (February, 1851), XI, 102-103 (1851).

[50]*Ibid.*, X, 225-228 (1851). See also Greensboro *Alabama Beacon*, March 15, 1851.

[51]Cahaba *Dallas Gazette*, September 28, 1855.

In April, 1857, Noah B. Cloud, a long-time friend of Pratt, spent a day examining the various factories in Prattville and came away convinced, if he needed convincing, that Pratt was something of a business genius. As Cloud described it, the first floor of the Pratt cotton gin factory contained seventy drums "for driving the various machines used in the manufacture of gins." The second floor was used, he said, "for breasting and finishing gins," the third floor was where the gins were "painted, varnished, and put in order for boxing and shipping," and an elevator moved the gins from floor to floor. Connected with the gin factory was a lumber house, where lumber was stacked and seasoned for two years before it was used in making the gins. Nearby was an iron foundry, which worked up about 100 tons of iron each year.[52] Fifty hands, "many of whom are slaves" according to Cloud, worked in the gin factory and foundry, turning out about $100,000 worth of gins annually. Cloud said, "There is also quite an extensive and flourishing Cotton Factory here, a large share of the stock of which is owned by Mr. Pratt. It contains twenty-eight hundred spindles, one hundred looms, and is worked by one hundred and fifty hands, several of them slaves. It works up twelve hundred bales of cotton and turns out two thousand bales of osnaburgs annually."[53] Under construction was another building, where Pratt would soon card and spin wool for the manufacture of kerseys.[54] At another time Cloud had the following to say about the intrepid Prattville entrepreneur: "Mr. Pratt's enterprise and public spirit united with his personal industry, has inseparably linked his name with this great leading industrial and commercial pursuit of the civilized world—*the Cotton manufacturing interest*. Mr. Pratt is not only supplying all sections of the Cotton growing States of our country with his unsurpassed Gin Stands, but he is filling orders from Prussia, South America, and for the French in Africa."[55]

---

[52]In 1848, the steel plates for the saws of Pratt's saw gins were "imported from the north, ..." The other parts of his gins were "manufactured upon the place." Tuscumbia *North Alabamian*, March 24, 1848.

[53]*American Cotton Planter and Soil of the South*, I, 156 (1857.)

[54]By 1848, Pratt had already spent $40,000 for the machinery in his cotton factory. Tuscumbia *North Alabamian*, March 24, 1848.

[55]*American Cotton Planter and Soil of the South*, II, 62 (1858).

Pratt's accomplishments, without doubt, were his best advertisements, and he did not hesitate to let the world know of the amount of his cotton gin and other businesses. After all, advertising was good business. A favorite journal where he placed many advertisements was Cloud's *American Cotton Planter,* with its circulation of about 10,000. In the June, 1861, issue of that journal, for example, Pratt stated that he had sold more than 14,000 cotton gins during his "experience of Twenty-nine years in the Gin business." Agents for selling his machines, he reminded his readers, were conveniently located in Montgomery, Mobile, Memphis, New Orleans, Galveston, Vicksburg, in Columbus, Georgia, and in Columbus, Mississippi. Under the heading of "Business of Prattville," he informed the public of the amounts of business conducted by each of his establishments during the preceding four years. Having an average annual gross income of $632,652 during the years 1857 to 1860 made him one of the most active businessmen in the South:[56]

	1857	1858	1859	1860
Cotton Gin Manufactory	$144,000.00	$170,251.50	$253,117.00	$303,062.12
Prattville Manufacturing Company	151,724.00	187,220.42	166,787.00	163,908.02
Foundry	11,432.00	16,747.00	18,443.00	25,958.02
Machine and Blacksmith Shops	3,694.00	7,479.00	12,775.64	15,281.62
Sash, Door and Blind Manufactory	13,360.00	12,642.71	10,865.44	9,064.13
Horse Mills (Corn Mill)	17,160.00	16,720.00	21,500.00	20,252.97
Wagon Manufactory	6,500.00	8,962.00	15,797.00	13,330.00
Tin Manufactory	3,050.00	3,500.00	3,925.00	6,000.00
Printing Business	8,000.00	8,250.00	8,400.00	10,000.00
Mercantile Business	155,249.00	155,519.00	170,027.47	175,657.74
	$519,169.00	$587,291.63	$681,637.55	$742,514.35

Pratt also participated significantly in the industrial gospel of his state and region. Nearly always, when he wrote to editors of

---

[56]*Ibid.,* V, Appendix (June, 1861).

newspapers and other publications, he spoke out in favor of the economic betterment of Alabama and the South; persistently he stated that he favored manufacturing as the most effective way to bring about self-sufficiency; in view of his own outstanding accomplishments, what he had to say usually attracted attention and was received with respect.[57] A letter dated "1847" which he addressed "to the People of Alabama" is a case in point. He was of the opinion that "permanent wealth" was brought to Alabama when a man invested, say $50,000, "in manufacturing" rather than in a plantation. This was so, he said, because a planter might wear out his land and move to another state in order to obtain fresh land. A manufacturer, on the other hand, was not as likely to move as a planter, because "the greater portion [of his $50,000] will be [invested] in heavy machinery that will never be moved from the state." Pratt believed, "If the first owners make a failure, others will take it [purchase the factory], and the business will go on; the capital will increase annually; consequently the State is annually increasing in permanent wealth. . . ." He argued, moreover, that a person who abandoned a worn-out plantation actually caused the state to be "impoverished as much as the plantation thus abandoned has been sunk in value." He posed an important suggestion: "And if such are the facts, ought not the citizens of this State commence a change in their policy immediately? Let them set about it forthwith. Let it be gradual, but sure and permanent. Let every planter invest the surplus of his crop in manufacturing, and no more—not go in debt one dollar; . . . I regard capital invested in manufacturing as almost the only permanent capital." He had no intention of belittling agriculture. Far from it, for as he put it, "I consider agriculturists the bone and sinew of our country." Reiterating his position, he said, "The principal object I have in view is to induce planters to invest in manufacturing." If they did so, he insisted, "They would then become permanent citizens of our State; not only what they invest in manufacturing, but their whole planting interest would be permanent capital. Alabama would soon become a wealthy State."[58]

---

[57]See, for example, Wetumpka *Daily State Guard*, March 29, October 29, 1849.

[58]Montgomery *Flag and Advertiser*, quoted in Tuscaloosa *Independent Monitor*, June 15, 1847.

Furthermore, Pratt believed that the Southern states should encourage industry by granting liberal charters to manufacturers and bankers. He had no sympathy with those persons who opposed banks. "Show me the states that are most prosperous," he said, "and I will show you the states that have the largest banking privileges. Banks may be an evil, but at present they are necessary evils; and no manufacturing state can prosper without them." Alabama businessmen were being retarded because of "the narrow, contracted and short-sighted policy of our legislators," whereas New York, Georgia, North Carolina, and other states were prospering because their legislatures had "granted liberal charters and banking privileges, without which railroads and manufacturers cannot prosper, ..." Alabama possessed the raw materials, labor and businessmen needed to increase its manufacturing, but her legislature had not enacted the proper legislation to encourage industry. The Southern merchant or manufacturer chose to sell his goods in the New York market because "so soon as the goods are disposed of he can draw [on a New York bank] for at least three fourths of their value." New Yorkers could afford this privilege to businessmen of other states "simply because of the monied facilities they possess," and this was the reason that "southern manufacturers ship[ped] their goods to New York." Pratt was positive that "The greater the money facilities the better the market." He wanted to know, "Why is it that we cannot for once lay politics aside and both parties look strictly and akin to the interest of the state?" With proper encouragement, he concluded, manufacturers would furnish jobs to large numbers of people and pay additional taxes into the state treasury. However, Alabama would prosper to the fullest only after creating "a few good stock banks, well managed. . . . My word for it," Pratt said, "such improvements would go on gradually until our state would command as high a position as any in the south."[59]

During the ten years preceding the Civil War, Pratt showed himself to be typical of the successful businessman class of the South. He was active as an industrial propagandist. He followed a consistent political pattern during the decade since he was first

---

[59]Ibid., March 28, 1849, quoting Mobile Tribune.

a Whig, second a Know-Nothing, and finally, in 1860, a supporter of John Bell's party.[60] All of these parties, at the time of their greatest popularity, were the most comfortable parties to which a Southern manufacturer could belong. But it should be said that Pratt was not an abolitionist. Far from it, because on numerous occasions he aired in public his pro-slavery sentiments.[61] However, he was, above all, a man who hoped that the South would turn to manufacturing and become self-sufficient. In a letter entitled "Alabama Improvements and the True Interests of her People," which he wrote for public consumption in 1859, he showed that he had quite fully become a Southern nationalist. In his letter he spoke in a manner which he considered to be moderate and practical and marked by common sense:

I profess to be a Southern-rights man, and strongly contend that the South ought to maintain her rights at all hazards. I would, however, pursue a somewhat different course from that of the politicians. I would not make any flaming fiery speeches and threats, but on the other hand, I would go quietly and peaceably to work, and make ourselves less dependent on those who abuse and would gladly ruin us. I would use our own iron, our own coal, our own lime, our own marble, our own make of axes, hoes, spades, firearms, powder, wagons, carriages, saddles, bridles, and harness, clothing for our negroes, plows, doors, sash and blinds, shoes and boots, and last, but not least, our own cotton gins.

. . . Give us proper encouragement, and you will be furnished with mechanics and manufacturers. I know this will require time. I also know, that hitherto we have at the South pursued a wrong course. Let us attend strictly to our business, and if others interfere we will defend ourselves, and eventually bring them to our terms. I have no patience to listen to a class of persons, who speak of fencing in or penning up slavery. It is all talk. Slavery will eventually go where it can be made profitable, and no where else is it wanted. The New England States to-day would have a greater proportion of their population slaves than Alabama, could they have made them as profitable. . . .

I say, then, let us go on and build such bulwarks, as will not only defend ourselves, but conquer our enemies. I am trying to reverse things a little; I get all my shafting from Etowah, Ga., say 40 tons per annum. I find it a better article than I get from the North, and as cheap. I use about 150 tons of Pig Iron, mostly from Shelby county, Alabama. I think it equal to any iron made. I get all my lime from Alabama, the best I ever used. The Prattville Manufacturing Company, work up about 1,200 bales of Alabama Cotton, and 120,000

[60]Cahaba *Dallas Gazette*, September 28, 1855; Montgomery *Weekly Post*, August 8, 1860.

[61]See, for example, Montgomery *Weekly Alabama Journal*, October 21, November 13, 1850.

lbs. Southern wool annually. For the past twelve years I have been patronizing Southern schools. I have carried it so far as to bring out eight children from the Northern States, and educated them in Alabama. Some pretend to show their works by their faith, I hope to show my faith by my works, so long as God blesses me with health and strength.[62]

Speaking in the same manner, as if he were summarizing the inner-most thoughts of a majority of the Southern advocates of manufacturing, another Alabamian asserted in 1855, "It should be the aim of every political community to become self-sustaining."[63] As far as he and his contemporaries were concerned, Alabama was entitled to a solution of her own problems. She already had her agriculture, and it was improving all the time; if she could balance this with a thriving factory system, she would not be forced to depend entirely on "King Cotton" in time of peace or in case of secession; if she remained in the Union, she would benefit immeasurably if her people had both agriculture and manufacturing. However, Alabama and the South did not develop much of a factory system in the ante-bellum period. Most Southerners of the period were country people; they would not become town people until the twentieth century. Nevertheless, the industrial propagandists did make one great contribution: they helped lay the foundations of a later, eager acceptance of manufacturing and the city as parts of the way of life in the South. In the years before 1860, they were far-sighted; this meant that they were also ahead of their time.

---

[62]*American Cotton Planter and Soil of the South,* III, 114-115 (1859); Montgomery *Daily Mail,* February 25, 1859.
[63]*DeBow's Review,* XVIII, 25 (1855).

BIBLIOGRAPHY

MANUSCRIPTS

This book could not have been written without the use of the following manuscript collections belonging to several Marion and Perry County, Alabama, families: William P. Holman Diary, Mrs. William P. Holman Papers, Edwin W. King Papers, Elisha F. King Papers, and Rhoda B. King Papers, all in possession of Miss Clara Barker; Hugh Davis Papers, held by Mrs. L. I. Davis; Samuel H. Fowlkes Papers, owned by Edward Lee; William A. Jones Papers, held by Miss Emma Jones and Mrs. Mary J. Lowrey; Edwin W. King Diary and Rhoda B. King Family Bible, in possession of Mrs. Leta B. Hart and Mrs. Thad Davis, Sr., respectively; and Martin Marshall Book, which was placed in my hands by the late Alexander J. Marshall.

GOVERNMENT DOCUMENTS

Unpublished government records examined included the Unpublished Census Returns of the United States, Schedules One and Two for Alabama, on deposit in the Department of Archives and History, Montgomery, Alabama; Deed Record, Monroe County, Alabama, located in the Monroe County Court House, Monroeville; and certain materials on file in the Perry County Court House, Marion, Alabama: Commissioners' Court Minutes, Deed Record, Inventory of Estates, Orphan's Court Minutes, Orphan's Court Register, Record Book, Tract Book, Unpublished Census Returns of Perry County for 1855, and Will Book.

Printed government records used were *Eighth Census of the United States, 1860, Agriculture* (Washington, 1864); *Eighth Census of the United States, 1860, Population* (Washington, 1864); *Fifteenth Census of the United States, Population* (Washington, 1931); *Manufactures of the United States in 1860; . . .* (Washington, 1865); *United States Census, 1860, Mortality and Miscellaneous Statistics* (Washington, 1866); and *A Compendium of the Ninth Census* (Washington, 1872). Citations have been made from several *Reports of the Commissioner of Patents, . . . Agriculture,* namely, *Report for 1849* (Washington, 1850), *Report of 1850* (Washington, 1851), *Report of 1858* (Washington, 1859), and *Report of 1859* (Washington, 1860). Also utilized was *Acts, General Assembly of Alabama* (Montgomery, 1856).

___ CONTEMPORARY WRITINGS AND PRINTED SOURCES

Travel books which supplied information were Vicomte de Florimond Jacques Basterot, *De Quebec a Lima; journal d'un voyage dans le deux Ameriques en 1858 et en 1859* (Paris, 1860); Karl Bernhard, *Travels Through North America, during the Years 1825 and 1826,* 2 vols. (Philadelphia, 1828); James Silk Buckingham, *The Slave States in America,* 2 vols. (London, 1841); Louis Xavier Emya [Adolphe Ricard], *Les Deux Ameriques: histoires, moeurs et voyages* (Paris, 1853); Hiram Fuller, *Belle Britain on Tour, at Newport and Here and There* (New York, 1858); Philip Henry Gosse, *Letters from Alabama* (London, 1859); Basil Hall, *Travels through North America in the Years 1827 and 1828,* 3 vols. (Edinburgh, 1829); Thomas Hamilton, *Men and Manners in America,* 2 vols. (Edinburgh, 1833); Reverend G. Lewis, *Impressions of America and the American Churches; from Journal of the Reverend G. Lewis*

(Edinburgh, 1845); Alexander Mackay, *The Western World; or, Travels in the United States in 1846-47*, 2 vols. (Philadelphia, 1849); S. Augustus Mitchell, *A General View of the United States . . .* (Philadelphia, 1846); Charles Olliffe, *Scenes Americaines: Dix-huit Mois dans le Noveau Monde* (Paris, 1853); Frederick Law Olmstead, *Journey in the Seaboard Slave States, With Remarks on Their Economy* (New York, 1859); John Pope, *A Tour through the Southern and Western Territories of the United States of North-America* (New York, 1888 reprint of 1792 edition); Louis Fitzgerald Tasistro, *Random Shots and Southern Breezes*, 2 vols. (New York, 1842); and Lady Emmeline Stuart Wortley, *Travels in the United States, etc. during 1849 and 1850* (New York, 1851).

Of varying interest were the following items published during the period covered in my study: J. & R. Bronson, *The Domestic Manufacturer's Assistant, and Family Directory, in the Arts of Weaving and Dyeing* (Utica, 1817); *Catalogue of the Trustees, Instructors and Students of the Judson Female Institute* (Marion, 1855), and a *Catalogue* of the same Institute (Marion, 1857); *Daughrill's & Walker's General Directory for the City and County of Mobile for 1856* (Mobile, 1856); *Directory of the City of Mobile, 1858-1859* (Mobile, n. d.); Hosea Holcombe, *History of the Rise and Progress of the Baptists in Alabama* (Philadelphia, 1840); *Mobile Directory and Commercial Supplement, for 1855-1856* (Mobile, 1855); John W. Monette, *History of the Discovery and Settlement of the Valley of the Mississippi*, 2 vols. (New York, 1846); Josiah C. Nott, *Two Lectures on the Natural History of the Caucasian and Negro Races* (Mobile, 1844); S. A. Townes, *The History of Marion, . . .* (Marion, 1844); and John Stainbach Wilson, *The Southern Soldier's Health Guide* (Richmond, 1863).

Edited printed sources found to be useful included Weymouth T. Jordan's series of excerpts from "Martin Marshall's Book, . . ." in the *Alabama Historical Quarterly*, II, 158-168, 318-330, 443-459 (1940), III, 117-129, 248-261 (1941); Walter Brownlow Posey, ed., "Alabama in the 1830's As Recorded by British Travellers," *Birmingham-Southern College Bulletin*, XXXI (Birmingham, 1938); A. Elizabeth Taylor, ed., "Regulations Governing Life at the Judson Female Institute during the Decade Preceding the Civil War," *Alabama Historical Quarterly*, III, 23-29 (1941); and William H. Willis, ed., "A Southern Traveler's Diary in 1840," *Publications of the Southern History Association*, VIII, 129-138 (1904).

NEWSPAPERS

The following Alabama newspapers, most of them published in the years 1840-1860, on deposit at the Alabama Department of Archives and History, have been examined: Cahaba *Dallas Gazette*; Carrollton *West Alabamian*; Eufaula *Express*; Florence *Gazette*; Gainesville *Independent*; Greensboro *Alabama Beacon*; Grove Hill *Clarke County Democrat*; the Huntsville newspapers, *Democrat* and *Southern Advocate*; Jacksonville *Republican*; Livingston *Sumter County Whig*; the Mobile newspapers, *Commercial Register and Patriot, Daily Advertiser*, and *Register*; the Montgomery newspapers, *Advertiser and State Gazette, Alabama Journal, Daily Alabama Journal, Daily Advertiser, Daily Confederation, Daily Mail, Daily Messenger, Daily Post, Daily State Sentinel, Southwestern Baptist, State Journal, Tri-Weekly Journal, Tri-Weekly Mail, Weekly Advertiser, Weekly Advertiser and State Gazette, Weekly Alabama Journal, Weekly Journal, Weekly Mail*, and *Weekly Post*; Selma *Southern*

Argus; the Talladega newspapers, *Democratic Watchtower* and *Our Mountain Home;* Troy *Independent American;* the Tuscaloosa newspapers, *Chronicle* and *Independent Monitor;* Tuscumbia *North Alabamian;* the Tuskegee newspapers, *Macon Republican* and *Republican;* the Wetumpka newspapers, *Daily State Guard, Dispatch,* and *Spectator.* Also of importance in my research were the Macon *Daily Telegraph* and Macon *Georgia Journal and Messenger,* in the Public Library, Macon, Georgia; the Marion *Standard,* found in the County Court House, Marion; the Prattville *Autauga Citizen,* in the County Court House, Prattville; the Savannah *Daily Republican,* in the Library of Congress; and the Tallahassee *Florida Sentinel,* in the Florida State University Library, Tallahassee. Numerous issues of the following *Prices-Current,* published by the Mobile newspapers, were discovered in the Hugh Davis Papers, Edwin W. King Papers, and William A. Jones Papers: *Commercial Report & Mobile Price-Current, Mobile Journal of Commerce Letter-Sheet Price-Current, Mobile Shipping and Commercial List,* and *Mobile Register Shipping List and Prices-Current.*

PERIODICALS

Ten years ago I discovered that agricultural magazines for the period 1820 to 1860 were truly amazing sources of information for the study of economic and social history, and I am convinced that the information which they contained will, someday, result in important revisions of Southern and American history. Thus, the entire files of the following Southern agricultural journals of the Pre-Civil War era have been examined and citations made from them: *Alabama Planter* (Mobile), *American Cotton Planter* (Montgomery), *American Cotton Planter and Soil of the South* (Montgomery), *American Farmer* (Baltimore and Washington), *Arator* (Raleigh), *Farmer and Planter* (Pendleton, South Carolina), *Farmer's Journal* (Bath and Raleigh); *Farmer's Register* (Shellbanks and Petersburg), *North Carolina Planter* (Raleigh), *Soil of the South* (Columbus), *Southern Agriculturist* (Charleston), and *Southern Cultivator* (Augusta, Athens, and Atlanta). The files of several Northern agricultural magazines have also been perused in order to compare their contents with Southern magazines, and they were *American Agriculturist* (New York), *Cultivator* (Albany), *Genesee Farmer* (Rochester), *Homestead* (Hartford), *New England Farmer* (Boston), and *Prairie Farmer* (Chicago). *Harper's Weekly* (New York) has also furnished several key bits of information in my study. *Hunt's Merchants' Magazine* (New York) contains a wealth of information about the ante-bellum South. Also of value were the much-used journals, *DeBow's Review* (New Orleans, Washington, Charleston, and Columbia), *Niles' Weekly Register* (Baltimore and Washington), *Southern Quarterly Review* (Charleston), and *Southern Literary Messenger* (Richmond).

SECONDARY MATERIALS

Book-length and monographic studies of Alabama history have proved useful: Thomas P. Abernethy, *The Formative Period in Alabama* (Montgomery, 1922); Safford Berney, *Handbook of Alabama* (Mobile, 1878); William H. Brantley, *A Book About the First Three Capitals of Alabama . . .* (Boston, 1947); John B. Clark, *Populism in Alabama* (Auburn, 1927); Mary Powell Crane, *The Life of James R. Powell . . .* (Brooklyn, 1930); Charles S. Davis, *The Cotton Kingdom in Alabama* (Auburn, 1939); Anna M. Gayle Fry,

Memories of Old Cahaba (Nashville, 1905); Allen J. Going, *Bourbon Democracy in Alabama, 1874-1890* (Tuscaloosa, 1951); Peter J. Hamilton, *Colonial Mobile* (Boston, 1897); *Howard College Bulletin,* XCVIII (Birmingham, 1940); Weymouth T. Jordan, *Hugh Davis and His Alabama Plantation* (Tuscaloosa, 1948); Louise Manly, *History of Judson College* (Atlanta, 1899); Albert B. Moore, *History of Alabama* (Tuscaloosa, 1934); Thomas M. Owen, *History of Alabama and Dictionary of Alabama Biography,* 4 vols. (Chicago, 1921); Albert James Pickett, *The History of Alabama* (Sheffield, Alabama, 1896); B. F. Riley, *Makers and Romance of Alabama History* (n. p., n. d.); James B. Sellars, *Slavery in Alabama* (Tuscaloosa, 1950); Sub Rosa [Paul Ravesies], *Scenes and Settlers of Alabama* (Mobile, 1885); and Charles G. Summersell, *Mobile: History of a Seaport Town* (Tuscaloosa, 1949).

This study contains citations to certain articles on Alabama published in periodicals and monographic publications, namely, Elizabeth McTyeire Essler, "The Agricultural Reform Movement in Alabama, 1850-1860," *Alabama Review,* I, 243-260 (1948); Mell A. Frazer, "Early History of Steamboats in Alabama," *Alabama Polytechnic Institute Historical Studies* (1907); Richard W. Griffin, "Cotton Manufacture in Alabama to 1865," *Alabama Historical Quarterly,* XVIII, 289-307 (1956); Weymouth T. Jordan, "Agricultural Societies in Ante-Bellum Alabama," *Alabama Review,* IV, 241-253 (1951), his "Ante-Bellum Mobile; Alabama's Agricultural Emporium," *ibid.,* I, 180-202 (1948), his "Early Ante-Bellum Marion, Alabama: A Black Belt Town," *Alabama Historical Quarterly,* V, 12-31 (1943), and his "The Elisha F. King Family, Planters of the Alabama Black Belt," *Agricultural History,* XIX, 152-162 (1945); Malcolm Cook McMillan, "The Selection of Montgomery as Alabama's Capital," *Alabama Review,* I, 79-90 (1948); William E. Martin, "Internal Improvements in Alabama," Johns Hopkins University *Studies in Historical and Political Science,* XX, 127-205 (Baltimore, 1902); Thomas McAdory Owen, "Alabama Archives," *Annual Report of the American Historical Association for the Year 1904* (Washington, 1905); Clanton W. Williams, "Early Ante-Bellum Montgomery: A Black Belt Constituency," *Journal of Southern History,* VII, 495-525 (1941); and Gaius Whitfield, Jr., "The French Grant in Alabama, A History of the Founding of Demopolis," and Justus Wyman, "A Geographical Sketch of the Alabama Territory," *Transactions of the Alabama Historical Society,* IV, 321-355 (1904), and III, 107-127 (1899), respectively.

Other biographical and special studies which furnished information were Robert Greenhalgh Albion, *The Rise of New York Port, 1815-1860* (New York, 1939); Solon J. Buck, *The Agrarian Crusade* . . . (New Haven, 1920); Avery O. Craven, *The Growth of Southern Nationalism, 1848-1861* (Baton Rouge, 1953), and his *Soil Exhaustion as a Factor in the Agricultural History of Virginia and Maryland, 1606-1860* (Urbana, 1926); Albert Lowther Demaree, *The American Agricultural Press, 1819-1860* (New York, 1941); Clement Eaton, *Freedom of Thought in the Old South* (Durham, 1940); Lewis C. Gray, *History of Agriculture in the Southern United States to 1860,* 2 vols. (Washington, 1933); William Sumner Jenkins, *Pro-Slavery Thought in the Old South* (Chapel Hill, 1935); Allen Johnson, Dumas Malone, and Harris E. Starr, eds., *Dictionary of American Biography,* 21 vols. and index (New York, 1928-1944); Thomas Cary Johnson, Jr., *Scientific Interests in the Old South* (New York, 1936); Arthur Young Lloyd, *The Slavery Controversy* (Chapel Hill, 1939); John Massey, *Reminiscences* (Nashville, 1916); Wayne C. Neely, *The Agricultural Fair* (New York, 1935); Stuart Noblin, *Leonidas La Fayette Polk: Agrarian Crusader* (Chapel Hill, 1949); H. V. Poor, *Poor's Manual of the Railroads of the United States* (New York, 1868-1924); Williard Range, *A Century of Georgia Agriculture, 1850-1950* (Athens, 1954); Alfred C. True, *A History of Agricultural Education in the United States, 1785-1925* (Washington, 1929); Harvey Wish, *George Fitzhugh, Propagandist of the Old South* (Baton Rouge, 1943); and C. Vann Woodward, *Origins of the New South, 1877-1913* (Baton Rouge, 1951).

Several periodicals contain articles of a general nature which have been utilized in various ways. In the *Journal of Southern History* were James C. Bonner, "Genesis of Agricultural Reform in the Cotton Belt," IX, 475-500 (1943); Herbert Collins, "The Southern Industrial Gospel before 1860," XII, 386-402 (1946); Thomas P. Govan, "Was Plantation Slavery Profitable?" VIII, 513-535 (1942); Philip M. Hamer, "The Records of Southern History," V, 3-17 (1939); C. N. Howard, "Some Economic Aspects of British West Florida, 1763-1768," VI, 201-221 (1940); Weymouth T. Jordan, "Cotton Planters' Conventions in the Old South," XIX, 321-345 (1953); Martha Carolyn Mitchell, "Health and the Medical Profession in the Lower South, 1845-1860," X, 424-446 (1944); John F. Stover, "Southern Ambitions of the Illinois Central Railroad," XX, 499-510 (1954); and Herbert Weaver, "Foreigners in Ante-Bellum Towns of the Lower South," XIII, 62-73 (1947). Cited from the *American Historical Review* were James C. Bonner, "Profile of a Late Ante-Bellum Community," XLIX, 663-680 (1944), and Avery O. Craven, "The Agricultural Reformers of the Ante-Bellum South," XXXIII, 302-315 (1928). Material has been obtained from the following articles in *Agricultural History:* Weymouth T. Jordan, "Noah B. Cloud's Activities on Behalf of Southern Agriculture," XXV, 53-58 (1951); Wendell H. Stephenson, "Ante-Bellum New Orleans as an Agricultural Focus," XV, 161-174 (1941); and Charles W. Turner, "Virginia Agricultural Reform, 1815-1860," XXVI, 80-88 (1952). Other articles of value were Phillip Davidson, "Industrialism in the Ante-Bellum South," *South Atlantic Quarterly*, XXVII, 405-425 (1928); Thomas P. Govan, "An Ante-Bellum Attempt to Regulate the Price and Supply of Cotton," *North Carolina Historical Review*, XVII, 302-312 (1940); John C. Greene, "The American Debate on the Negro's Place in Nature, 1780-1815," *Journal of the History of Ideas*, XV, 384-396 (1954); Weymouth T. Jordan, "Plantation Medicine in the Old South," *Alabama Review*, III, 83-107 (1950), and his " 'The Florida Plan': An Ante-Bellum Effort to Control Cotton Sales," *Florida Historical Quarterly*, XXXV, 205-218 (1957); Grace Lewis Miller, "The Mobile and Ohio Railroad in Ante-Bellum Times," *Alabama Historical Quarterly*, VII, 37-59 (1945); Louis B. Schmidt, "The Agricultural Revolution in the United States, 1860-1930," *Science*, LXII, 585-594 (1930); and R. H. Thompson, "Suffrage in Mississippi," *Publications of the Mississippi Historical Society*, I, 25-49 (1898).

A. and M. College, founded at Auburn, Ala., 108
Affleck, Thomas, 112, 113
Agricultural and Horticultural Society of Western Alabama, 128
Agricultural Association of the Slave-holding States, 120-121
Agriculture, significance of, 1, 21, 60, 107, 136-139, 140, 157; diversification of, 13, 55, 107, 115, 121, 122, 130, 132, 137; magazines, 37, 55, 112, 123, 136-137; scientific farming, 55, 106, 109, 122, 126, 128, 129, 137; crusade in behalf of, 106-139; contour plowing, 107, 115; fertilizers, 107, 110-111, 115, 123, 124, 130, 136, 138; crop rotation, 107, 115; stock breeding, 107, 115, 124, 129, 130, 131, 136; hillside ditching, 107, 115, 130; farm machinery, 107, 124, 132; education, 108, 115, 130; leaders, 109, 111, 113, 119, 129; government aid to, 115, 130, 131, 138, 139; societies, 121-137; fairs, 123-136; accomplishments in the South, 136-139
Agriculturist, 112
Ailments and diseases, 77-81
Alabama, leading cities and towns, 1; river system, 1; population, 1, 6, 9, 15, 17, 22, 23, 32; as a cotton state, 1, 21, 32, 65; Territory of, 4, 22, 25, 64; attains statehood, 4, 23, 64; State Legislature, 4, 25, 31, 131, 132; black belt, 9, 30, 34-36, 40, 41, 51, 60; taxable property, 18-19; as a frontier state, 62, 66; Commission of Industrial Resources, 108; Commissioner of Immigration, 108; State Agricultural Society, 121, 129-136; agricultural accomplishments, 136; University of, 143; unionism and disunionism in, 144
Alabama and Tennessee River Railroad, 53
"Alabama Improvements and the True Interests of her People," 159
Alabama Planter, 13, 93, 96, 114, 115, 123, 142, 145
Alabama River, 2, 6, 7, 16-17, 20, 28, 37, 49, 53, 64, 130, 149
Albany, N. Y., 111
Alleghany Copper Mining Company, 120
American Cotton Planter, 99, 113-119, 120, 129, 156; appraisals and significance of, 113-119
American Cotton Planter and Soil of the South, 102, 103, 105, 113-119; appraisals and significance of, 113-

114, 116-119; circulation of, 114, 116, 156
American Farmer, 85, 92
Amsterdam, The Netherlands, 18
"Ant trap, An," 68
Antwerp, Belgium, 18
"Apostate," 132
Arator, 119
Auburn, Ala., 116, 126
Auburn Gazette, 116
Autaugaville, Ala., 147, 148; description of, 149-150; Manufacturing Company, 149, 150
Autauga County, Ala., 123, 150, 152, 153
Autauga Creek, 152
Baldness, cure of, 81
Baldwin County, Ala., 23
Baltimore, Md., 4, 18, 85
Barbour County Agricultural Society, 123
Barcelona, Spain, 18
Barnett, Gilmer and Company, 151
Bassett, John Y., 93
Bell, John, 159
Benton, Ala., 123
Benton County, Ala., 142
Bibb County, Ala., 55, 128, 142, 148
Birmingham, Ala., 38
Bitters, recipe for, 76
Black belt, 9, 42, 51, 60, 147; bored wells of, 9, 30; as cotton land, 34-36; land entries, 35; significance of, 40
"Black Race in North America, The," 93
Blakely, Ala., 3
Blanchard, Mary, 63
Boards of Agriculture, 137
"Book farmers," 106
Books, care of, 68
Booth, John Wilkes, 132
Bored wells, 9, 30
Boston, Mass., 18
Bourbon politicians, 138
Bremen, Germany, 18
"Burrough's Ferry," 30
"Business of Prattville," 156
Cahaba, Ala., 28, 30, 31, 37, 49, 53, 64, 154
Cahaba Alabama Republican, 37
Cahaba Dallas Gazette, 154
Cahaba Old Town, Ala., 23, 24, 25, 27, 30
Cahaba River, 13, 23, 24, 26, 148
"Calcareous manure," 111
California, 135
Cartwright, Samuel A., 98, 99, 100, 102
Catoma, Ala., 123
Cement, preparation of, 67

Centerville, Ala., 30, 44, 148
Chambers County, Ala., 123
Chambers, James M., 113
Chapped hands, ointment for, 71
Charleston, S. C., 7, 10
Chattahoochee River, 6
"Check system," 112
Chinquepin Ridge, S. C., 94
Choctaw County, Ala., 123, 128
Chunnenuggee Horticultural Society, 123, 124; its fairs, 125-127
Chunnenuggee Ridge, Ala., 124, 126, 127
Cincinnati, Ohio, 112
Clarke County, Ala., 23, 128, 147; Agricultural Society, 123
Clay, Clement C., 19, 126
Clothing, cleaning of, 70-71
Cloud, Noah B., 102, 127, 136, 138, 155, 156; birth, 107; education, 107; moves to Alabama, 107; appraisals and significance of, 107, 108, 109, 110, 112, 113, 115, 119, 120, 121, 129, 152; his politics and public career, 108; death, 108; his system of farming, 109-113; edits *American Cotton Planter*, 113-119; and the *Montgomery Advertiser*, 114; attends conventions, 119-121; and cotton planters' conventions, 120-121; and the Alabama State Agricultural Society, 121, 129-136
Columbia, S. C., 62, 63, 121
Columbiana, Ala., 145
Columbus, Ga., 114, 126, 128, 150, 156
Columbus, Miss., 156
Commercial conventions, 119
Commission merchants, 15, 20, 55-56, 58
Contour plowing, 107, 115, 136
Cooking recipes, 72
Coosa River, 2, 13
Cotton, 55, 110, 111, 113, 122, 123, 124, 126, 132, 144; production, 1, 7, 9, 13-15, 18, 20, 32, 42-43, 109; significance of, 1, 21, 24, 34, 36, 39, 60; exports, 2, 4, 5, 7, 9, 14, 18, 19, 43, 143; blightproof variety, 9, 34; prices, 10, 11, 13, 18, 49-50, 58, 128; factors and factorage system, 12, 15, 20, 45-49, 57-59; attains importance in black belt, 34-36, 42, 107; profits, 60; cotton belt, 106; factories, 140, 142, 148-156; cotton gins, 152-156
Cotton planters' conventions, 120-121
Cotton Planter's Manual, 113
Cotton-seed oil, 14
Credit system, 1, 15, 20, 43-48, 55-57, 58, 59
Croom, Isaac, 129

Cuba, 5
Cultivator, 111
Curtis, Moses Ashley, 89, 90, 91
Dallas County, Ala., 30, 64, 123
Darwin, Charles, 88, 91
Dauphin Island, Ala., 20
Davy, Sir Humphrey, 109
Daybooks, their contents, sources, and significance, 62, 65-67
DeBow's Review, 91, 92, 93, 99, 114, 119, 144, 149, 153, 154
Decatur, Ala., 128, 129
Decatur and Montgomery Railroad, 120
Demopolis, Ala., 5, 128
DeYampart, L. Q. C., 51
"Diseases and Peculiarities of the Negro Race," 99
"Diversity of the Human Race," 91
"Double head girl," 133
Douglas, Stephen A., 133
"Drapetomania," 100
"Dum Vivimus, Vivimus," 28
Durden, John, 24
Dyeing, methods of, 70
"Dysaesthesia, Aethiopia," 100, 101
Edgefield District, S. C., 107
Education, "articles" and "rules," 29; curriculum and textbooks, 29, 38, 39; colleges and universities, 38, 39, 91, 97, 108, 143
Edwards, Miss., 112
Elyton, Ala., 146
Elyton *Alabamian*, 146
Etowah, Ga., 159
Eufaula, Ala., 123
Evans, Joseph, 27
Fairfield District, S. C., 112
Farmer and Planter, 119
Farmers' Alliance, 138, 139
Farmer's Journal, 119
Farmer's Register, 85, 114
Fayette County, Ala., 6, 145
Featherstonhaugh, George W., 36
Fenner, E. D., 94
Fertilizers, 107, 110-111, 115, 123, 124, 130, 136, 138
Fishing Creek Agricultural Society, 112
Flatboats, 5
Flat-irons, care of, 68
Florence, Ala., 144
Florence *Gazette*, 144
Florida, 43, 120, 153
Foods, how to preserve, 73-74
Ford, William, and family, 23, 24, 27
Forsyth, John, 126
Fort Claiborne, Ala., 64, 66, 77
"Fort Jefferson Davis," 131
Fort Mitchell, Ala., 112, 122

Fort Sumter, S. C., 144
Fowlkes, Samuel H., 47
France, 18, 155
"Franklin," 85, 86 , 92, 102
Furniture, care of, 67
Galveston, Tex., 156
Genoa, Italy, 18
Georgia, 15, 106, 113, 116, 120, 121, 122, 125, 140, 153, 158
Georgia and Alabama Agricultural Society, 127-128
Ghent, Belgium, 18
Gibraltar, 5, 18
Glenville, Ala., 123
Gliddon, George R., 91
Godey's Lady's Book, 102
Goree, John R., 46
Grady, Henry, 141
Great Britain, 18
Greenback movement, 138
Greene County, Ala., 128
Greensboro, Ala., 32, 53, 118, 122, 123, 129; Agricultural Society, 122
Greensboro *Alabama Beacon*, 118
Griswold, Samuel, 153; a cotton gin manufacturer, 154
"Hair ointment," 71
Hale County, Ala., 53
Hall, Basil, 8
Hallett, T. L., 3
Hamburg, Ala., 44
Hamburg, Germany, 18
Hamilton, Thomas, 11
Harmon, Garland D., 113
Havana, Cuba, 18
Henry County, Ala., 6
Herb medicines, preparations of, 78-80
"Here We Rest," 134
"Hints to Farmers," 83
Holman, William P., 58, 59
Holt, H. G., 45
Hooper, J. J., 117
Housewarming, a, 30
Howard College, 38
Hunt's Merchants' Magazine, 19-20
Huntsville, Ala., 1, 25, 93, 115, 118, 128, 141
Huntsville *Democrat*, 118
Illinois, 6
Indian Old Town, Ala., 23, 24, 25, 27, 30
Indians, 2, 6, 9, 23, 36, 109
Indigenous Races of the Earth, 91
"Industrial Palace," 130
"Industrial Resources of Alabama, The," 108
Industry, See Manufacturing
Intoxicating drinks, recipes for, 74-76
"Item for housewives," 67

"J. A. C.," 92
Jackson County, Ala., 22, 128
"J. A. W.," 150
Jefferson County, Ala., 146
Jefferson Medical College, 107
Johnson, H. V., 126
Jones, Thomas T., 52
Jones, William Albert, 38
Jones' Valley, Ala., 13
"J. T.," 95, 96
Judson College, The, 38
Judson Female Institute, The, 38; curriculum of, 38-39
Kentucky, 31, 137
Ketchum, George A., 94
King, Edwin D., 52, 61
King, Edwin W., 44, 45; as a landholder, 50, 51; and his slaves, 50, 51, 53, 54-55; his wealth, 50, 58, 61; as a businessman, 50-51, 58; his credit system, 51, 55-57; as a railroad builder, 52-53; and his overseers, 53-54; and his commission merchants, 55-56, 58; purchases plantation supplies, 55-57; his death, 58; appraisal of, 58, 60, 61
King, Elisha F., 26, 52; arrival in Alabama, 41; his wealth, 41, 42, 43, 44, 45, 49, 50, 61; and his slaves, 41, 44-45; appraisal of, 41, 50, 60, 61; as a landholder, 41-42, 43-44; his death, 43, 50; his credit system, 43-48; as a businessman, 44, 47; and his cotton factors, 45-49; purchases plantation supplies, 47
King, Margaret Clarissa, 50
King, Rhoda B., 59
King, Sarah Elizabeth, 50, 55
"King Cotton," 160
King House, 52
King, Upson and Company, 44-45
LaFayette, Ala., 123
Langdon, C. C., 143
"La Place," 110
Lauderdale County, Ala., 22, 123, 128, 145
Lawrence County, Ala., 128
Lea and Langdon Company, 45
Lee, Daniel, 119, 134
Limestone County, Ala., 22, 123, 128
Linden, Ala., 123
"Liquid Japan," 71
Liverpool, England, 4, 48
Livingston *Sumter County Whig*, 118
Lockett, Reuben, 27
London, England, 91
Louisiana, 16, 19, 99, 120, 153; University of, 91; Medical Convention, 99
Louisville, Ky., 10

Lowell, Mass., 145, 150
Lowndes County, Ala., 123, 124
Lynchburg, Ala., 123
McCall, John, 51
McDowell, Doctor, 96, 97
McDowell and Withers Company, 46, 57, 58
McQuire, W. W., 93, 123
Macon County, Ala., 107, 110, 116, 123, 127
Madison, James, 3
Madison County, Ala., 22, 123
"Manufactures," 13
Manufacturing, 13-14, 136; eulogies and promotion of, 13, 126, 133, 135, 140-160; cotton, 140, 142, 148-156; reasons for interest in, 140-160; iron, 142, 143, 145-146; lack of, 147; women laborers, 148, 149; typical towns, 148-156; slave laborers, 149, 152, 155
Marengo County, Ala., 128
Marks and Barnett Company, 150
Marion, Ala., 22-40, 44, 46, 47, 52, 61; its significance, 22, 34, 38, 40; first settlement of, 24-25; naming of, 25; growth of, 25, 27-28, 30-37, 39-40; courthouses, 25, 28, 33; descriptions of, 25, 31, 36, 39; churches and ministers, 26, 27, 31, 33, 40; health conditions, 27; hotels, 28, 52; jail-house, 28; as a trade center, 28, 30, 31, 32, 36-37, 46-47; entertainments, 28, 37-39; cultural developments, 28-30; schools and colleges, 29, 38-39; a housewarming, 30
Marion, Cahaba and Greensboro Railroad, 36, 52
Marion Female Seminary, 38
Marion, Francis "Swamp-fox," 27
Marshall, John, 63
Marshall, Martin, 62-83; birth, 62; his significance, 62; early life, 62-63; and his daybook, 62-83; his training, occupations, and interests, 63-66, 83; moves to Alabama, 63-64; death, 64, 65
Marshall, William, 63
Maryland, 137
Mason, Wylie W., 126
Massachusetts, 15, 152
Medicine, domestic, 76-77; herb, 78-80; veterinary, 81-82; for Negroes, 84-105
Memphis Medical Recorder, 94
Memphis, Tenn., 94, 156
"Miasma," 35
Michigan, 6
Mississippi, 43, 112, 120, 139, 153; Territorial Legislature, 3; Territory

of, 3, 26
Mississippi River, 6, 66
Missouri, 137
Mobile, Ala., 1-21, 42, 45, 46, 47, 48, 49, 64, 88, 89, 91, 92, 94, 96, 115, 123, 124, 130, 134, 142, 143, 146, 147, 148, 150, 153, 156; population, 1, 2, 3, 4, 5, 9, 15, 17, 33, 42, 140; founding of, 1-3; descriptions and growth of, 2, 3, 4, 5-6, 7-9, 11, 14, 15-17, 19-20, 21, 42, 43; exports of, 2, 4, 5, 7, 9, 12, 14, 18, 19, 43, 143; incorporated, 3, 4; real estate values, 3, 11, 19; imports, 4; harbor and warehouse facilities, 4, 5, 11, 12, 16, 18, 19-20, 21; gambling houses, 8; entertainments, 8, 10, 11; fires and fire companies, 8, 10, 12; gas lights, 10; theater, 10; streets, 10, 16; bank deposits and facilities, 10, 20; health conditions, 14, 16; as a trade center, 17, 18, 20-21, 28, 32-33, 37, 40, 42, 46, 64; insurance companies, 20; lighthouses, 20; pilot boats, 20; fluctuating prices in, 46; Horticultural Society, 124
Mobile and Ohio Railroad, 20
Mobile and Ohio Telegraph Company, 20-21
Mobile City Mills, 14
Mobile County, Ala., 23, 128
Mobile *Directory*, 5
Mobile *Mercantile Advertiser*, 12
Mobile *Price-Current*, 47
Mobile *Register*, 5, 9, 143
Mobile River, 2, 22
Mobile *Transcript*, 11
Mobile *Tribune*, 96, 153
"Money are power, and I are got it," 61
"Monkey shows," 133
Monroe County, Ala., 64, 122; Agricultural Society, 122
Monroe and Conecuh Agricultural Society, 122
Montgomery *Advertiser and State Gazette*, 114, 151
Montgomery, Ala., 1, 5, 17, 36, 40, 64, 97, 98, 99, 102, 113, 114, 115, 116, 117, 119, 120, 124, 129, 130, 132, 134, 144, 146, 147, 148, 151, 152, 156; City Council, 130
Montgomery County, Ala., 107, 123
Montgomery *Daily Mail*, 97, 98, 99, 117
Monticello Planters' Society, 112
Moore, Andrew Barry, 38
Moore, John M., 142
Morgan County, Ala., 128
Morrill Act, 108
Morton, Samuel George, 88

Moses, 97
Mt. Meigs, Ala., 36
Muckle, Mickle, 24 ,25
"Muckle's Ridge," 25, 26, 27
Mulattoes, appraisals of , 88, 90, 91, 94, 104
Muscogee and Russell County Agricultural Society, 127
Nashville, Tenn., 10
"Natural History of Man in Connection with Negro Slavery," 91
Negro, the, "peculiarities" and ethnological appraisals of, 84-105
"Negro-Mania — Race," 95
"Negro Races, The," 97
Negroes and Negro Slavery, 98
Nelson, Robert, 113
"New Deal," 139
New Orleans, La., 2, 6, 7, 10, 11, 16, 18, 19, 46, 91, 94, 96, 97, 98, 119, 156
"New Soap," 70
New York, 5, 7, 15, 18, 19, 39, 46-47, 111, 158
Niles' Weekly Register, 4, 7, 150
Norfolk, Va., 7
North Alabama, 6, 41; Agricultural and Mechanical Association, 128
North Carolina, 89, 122, 140, 158
North Carolina Planter, 114, 119
Nott, Josiah C., 88-92, 95, 97, 98, 99, 102
Oil paintings, cleaning of, 68
Old Town Creek, Ala., 23
Oliver, Thomas M., 24
Olmstead, Frederick Law, 20
Origin of Species, The, 88, 91
Packet ships, 7
Panic of 1837, influences, 10, 11-12, 37
Parmentier, Nicholas, 4
Paste, preparation of, 67
Patrons of Husbandry, 138
Peabody, Charles A., 113, 117, 118, 128, 131, 134
"Peculiarities and Diseases of Negroes, The," 102
Pensacola, Fla., 2, 7
Perfumes, making of, 71
Perry County, Ala., 22, 32, 41, 46, 51, 52, 53, 128; first settlement of, 23; frontier characteristics of, 23, 29-30, 33-34, 37; early settlers of, 23-25; growth of, 25-28, 33-37; Orphan's Court, functions of, 26; seat of government, selection of, 26-27, 31; drinking habits, 27, 28, 40; health conditions, 35
Perry Ridge, Ala., 23, 25, 26
Peruvian guano, 111
Pests, control of, 68-69
Petersburg Intelligencer, 97
Petersburg, Va., 97

Phelan, John D., 38
Philadelphia, Pa., 88, 91, 107
Philips, Martin W., 93, 112, 113
"Physical History of the Jewish Race," 91
Physicians, trained, scarcity of, 76-77
Pickens County, Ala., 123, 128
Pictures, cleaning of, 68
Pike County, Ala., 6
Pittsburgh, Pa., 7
Plantation, 113
"Plantation and Family Physician, The," 105
"Planter's Retreat," 110
Pollard, Charles T., 129
Pool, J. K. C., 27
Pope, Alexander, and Sons, 45, 48
Populist party, 138
Powell, Norbonne B., 113, 125
Prattville, Ala., 116, 148, 149; descriptions of, 152-155
Pratt, Daniel, 132; appraisals and significance of, 152-160; his cotton gin factory, 155; his businesses, 156; as a spokesman for manufacturing, 156-160; his politics, 158-159
Prattville Manufacturing Company, 152, 155, 156, 159
Predatory animals and worms, control of, 82-83
Providence, R. I., 18
Prussia, 155
Ramsay, W. G., 86, 87, 92, 102
Raymond, Miss., 112
"Recipe to cure a sore leg," 79
Reid, Nathan, 24
Richland County, S. C., 62, 63
Richmond, Va., 93
Robinson Springs, Ala., 123
Rotterdam, The Netherlands, 18
Ruffin, Edmund, 111, 113
Russell County, Ala., 109, 118, 122
Sanders, W. L., 51
Savannah, Ga., 7, 46, 102, 119
Savannah Journal of Medicine, 102
Saxe-Weimar Eisenach, Duke of, 7
Scientific farming, 55, 106, 109, 122, 126, 128, 129, 137
Scott, Daniel, 149
Scottsville, Ala., descriptions of, 148-150
"Scraps," 96, 97
Second United States Bank, 10
"Secret worth knowing, A," 68
Selma, Ala., 1, 37, 53, 117, 123, 130, 147, 149
Selma Free Press, 37
Selma Reporter, 117
Selma Sentinel, 149
Shackelford, James, 27

Shelby County, Ala., 6, 143, 159
Shoe-blacking, preparation of, 71
Skinner, John Stuart, 119
Slaves and slavery, 34, 41, 44-45, 50, 51, 52, 53, 54-55, 87, 91, 92, 94, 96, 97, 98, 100, 115, 123; number of, 32, 36; care and treatment of, 35, 53, 84-105; patrol system, 54; typical work, 54-55; ethnological justification of, 84-105; clothing, 85
Smith, Mrs. Ann, 27
"Sneak stage kisses," 10
Soap, preparation of, 70
Soil of the South, 114, 116, 117, 134, 149-150
South Alabama, 6, 7, 9, 14, 18, 20, 22, 23, 32, 41, 42, 144
South Carolina, 15, 23, 62, 63, 64, 69, 85, 89, 107, 112, 119, 120, 122
Southern Agriculturist, 85, 86, 92, 114
Southern Cultivator, 102, 114, 116, 119, 134
Southern Literary Messenger, 93
Southern Planter, 114
Southern Quarterly Review, 89, 90, 91, 92, 93, 95
Southern Soldier's Health Guide, The, 105
Southwestern Farmer, 112
Southwestern Industrial Convention, 119
Steamboats, 5, 7, 11, 17, 20
Stock breeding, 107, 115, 124, 129, 130, 131, 136
Stockholm, Sweden, 18
Stoves, care of, 67
St. Petersburg, Russia, 18
Stringfellow and Hanna Company, 46
Sumter County, Ala., 128
"Swamp gas," 35
Swift Creek, 149
Talbot County, Ga., 125
Talladega, Ala., 13, 147; Agricultural and Mechanical Association, 122
Tallapoosa River, 2
Tallassee, Ala., 148; descriptions of, 149-152
Tallassee Falls, 150, 151, 152
"Tariff of abominations," 122
Taylor, James, 45
Temperance movement, 7, 40, 133, 150, 154
Temple, N. H., 153
Tensas River, 3
Tennessee, 6, 23, 25, 120
Tennessee River, 6, 22, 41
Tennessee Valley Agricultural and Mechanical Association, 129
Texas, 106, 137, 153

Tombigbee River, 2, 7, 20, 22
Treaty of Fort Jackson, 22, 23
Trieste, 18
Tuomey, Michael, 143
Turner, J. A., 113
Tuscaloosa, Ala., 1, 30, 37, 123, 142, 146; Manufacturing Company, 148
Tuscaloosa County, Ala., 6, 128
Tuscaloosa *Spirit of the Age*, 37
Tuscaloosa *States Rights Exposition*, 37
Tuscumbia, Ala., 129
Tuskegee *Macon Republican*, 118, 127
Twenty-seven Mile Bluff, 2
"Two Lectures on the Connection between the Biblical and Physical History of Man," 91
Types of Mankind, 91
Uchee Creek, 109
Unionists and unionism, in Ala., 108, 109
Union Springs, Ala., 123, 124
United States, Commissioner of Agriculture, 108; Commissioner of Patents, 136
"Useful Information," 66
"Valuable Recipes," 66
Van Evrie, J. H., 98
Vernon, Ala., 149
Vicksburg, Miss., 156
Vine and Olive Colony, Ala., 4
Virginia, 7, 13, 15, 85, 111, 121, 122, 140
Von Liebig, Baron Justus, 109
War of 1812, influences settlement of Ala., 22, 23
Warrior River, 5, 20, 24, 144
Washington County, Ala., 23, 128
Washington, Henry A., 97
Weaving practices, 69-70
"We despise the Union," 143
Weissenger, George, 27
Weissenger, Leonard A., 38
Welch, John, 27
West, Anderson, 23, 25, 27, 36
West, William, 26
West Florida, 2; becomes United States territory, 3
Western Farmer and Gardner, 112
Wetumpka, Ala., 142, 145
Whigs, Southern, 108, 109, 120, 159
White supremacy, 84-105
William and Mary College, 97
Wilmington, N. C., 7
Wilson, John Stainbach, 102-105, 113
Withers, Robert W., 122
Woman's Book of Health, 102
Wyatt, Mark A., 38
Yancey, William L., 114
Young, Warner, 24